W9-BXX-471

MITCH WEISS & PERRI GAFFNEY

MANAGING ARTISTS IN POP MUSIC

WHAT EVERY ARTIST AND MANAGER MUST KNOW TO SUCCEED

Allworth Press
New York

Allworth Press books may be purchased in bulk at special discounts for sales promotion, corporate gifts, fund-raising, or educational purposes. Special editions can also be created to specifications. For details, contact the Special Sales Department, Allworth Press, 307 West 36th Street, 11th Floor, New York, NY 10018 or info@skyhorsepublishing.com.

15 14 13 12 11   5 4 3 2 1

Published by Allworth Press, an imprint of Skyhorse Publishing, Inc.
307 West 36th Street, 11th Floor, New York, NY 10018.

Allworth Press® is a registered trademark of Skyhorse Publishing, Inc.®, a Delaware corporation.

Visit our website at www.allworth.com

Cover design by Adam Bozarth

Library of Congress Cataloging-in-Publication Data is available on file.
ISBN: 978-1-58115-882-3

Printed in the United States of America

Contents

PART II:
CONTRACTS ANALYSIS FOR MANAGERS AND ARTISTS

Preface: The Buck Starts Here

A good manager's mantra: I don't know but I'll find out.

Attention: The Occupational Safety and Health Administration (OSHA) has determined that the maximum safe load on my butt is two persons at one time unless I install handrails or safety straps. As you have arrived sixth in line to ride my ass today, please take a number and wait your turn.

A good manager spends a ton of time on his and his client's finances and banking, paperwork, bill-paying, next-year's projections, fact-checking, resource-gathering, promotion materials, insurance, budget-cutting concepts—all the boring stuff of business. A good manager must also be prepared to deal with payola demands, homophobia in the radio business, sexism and racism (which are still alive and well in the music industry), massive numbers of charity requests, an airline industry determined to make the cost of touring impossible, paparazzi and demanding press people, and all those family members who think they know everything about the music biz.

That said, there is nothing more important than being an expert at communication with people, and I don't mean social-networking. I mean taking massive amounts of time to communicate every decision and logistical detail that might affect a staff person, artist, promoter, booking agent, accountant, lawyer, insurance broker, sound engineer, songwriter, or family member—everything they might need to know in order for them to excel in their individual work on behalf of your artist and yourself. It's a lot of time and work because it involves editing the information and repeating the information over and over again . . . tactfully!

Unfortunately most young managers and artists think a manager's primary job is to develop an artist's career and find work. If you didn't know it before, money talks when it comes to development. Lots and lots of money. So let's explore the myths and discuss reality in this new world of instant global notoriety courtesy of *American Idol* and *X Factor*.

The music industry is somewhere between chaos and flux. Technology and the Internet continue to affect every rule of artist development, music creation, promotion, sales and distribution, and the source of an artist's and manager's income. The public has new expectations and the industry is still struggling to catch up to its consumer base. The revised edition of this book combines the new digital age with the ageless principles that dictate success or failure in the music industry.

The new options and obstacles faced by managers and artists today are explored in detail from the manager's perspective. To the extent that every artist should learn to be his/her own manager, then this book is just as much for both the established and the hopeful artist as it is for the professional manager.

To make this book more accessible, we tell the story of one manager over a three-day period, providing important lessons in negotiating, artist handholding, and crisis resolution. Through a fictitious client list, we are able to describe in detail real things that have happened, based on firsthand and secondhand experiences known to the authors.

Along with this storyline, we offer cold facts through data boxes, on subjects ranging from choosing a pension plan, selecting a road manager, creating an effective press release, and analyzing a sample recording deal, paragraph by paragraph, in plain English.

The bottom line is to find success and happiness in what we do. Our business is to help singers, musicians, and songwriters do the same. In this regard, the buck starts here.

PART

1

Three Days in
the Life . . .

The Day Begins

Wanted: A job that will allow me to be creative, unrestricted, inspired, happy, productive . . . and FILTHY RICH!!
Happiness is not a state to arrive at, but rather a manner of traveling.

I'm an independent manager—no golden parachute plan in case of early termination by some ranting acid-rock diva and no large staff racing down the hall to copy contracts and get my lunch. I do have a wonderfully motivated intern, Robert O., who gives me twenty hours a week. The rest of the time I have my invaluable assistants, the computer and the cell phone.

Walking down the street on the way to my office . . . reflecting on the music groups and solo artists I have managed and the many others that remain out there to be tapped, it amazes me that some people still think that a recording contract will make them happy. Getting a recording deal rarely means that you'll be making money. People should be actively pursuing the things that will make them happy—and most people have never even thought in those terms. Not just music people, but people in general. Being a music performer is a job, like other jobs, but it's been glamorized and romanticized so much. And many performers, even famous ones, still believe the hype.

Today, I'll try to resolve a booking problem with BoyBand, a well-known pop rock group that continues to pack stadiums, but hasn't been able to get a new record deal after a decade in the business. When I walk in the door, I expect to find Max X., lead guitarist for the reggae-rock recording group RRU, who wants to speak with me confidentially about what he suspects is mismanagement from his group's current representation. I've agreed to talk to my friend's nephew John about his expected career in hip-hop. No doubt he has a clothing line ready to go. There will be calls to promoters, booking agents, attorneys, accountants, and other managers interrupting anything I may be doing. And an agent has asked me to accept a call from Jeremy R., a successful young Aussie horn player who recently immigrated to the U.S. I've got to make an appointment with the lead singer of Goodness, a Marvelettes-style four-girl oldies group, who is trying to revive her dormant career. And hopefully Pollyanne Heart, that Grammy-winning country singer, will call back. She wants me to translate her manager's explanation about why she has no money. I guess I should have her talk with other bankruptcy victims like Toni Braxton, Billy Joel, MC Hammer, TLC, and a whole slew of record labels.

I stop for coffee and my cell phone rings. It's Robert O.

"Hey boss, George at CAA just called and needs a quick answer. Also, Max X., your 10:00 AM, has already been here fifteen minutes." It is 9:55 AM.

Let the day begin.

On the way to the elevator, I call George at CAA. He's the booking agent for BoyBand, responsible for bringing in concert dates and negotiating contract deals, based on my parameters. This is an exciting profession for some. For others it is a prison sentence. George sometimes talks like he's behind bars. I heard he used to perform with a group, and I suspect he's frustrated being behind a desk. I, on the other hand, get a kick out of the creative challenges of the profession.

It seems that the promoter for next week's BoyBand concert in Seattle is having trouble selling tickets and has asked if we would agree to reduce the band's guaranteed fee. Of course, the promoter is the one who takes all the risks, but has the greatest potential if the show is a sellout. I suggest that he call me with additional press interviews and that we wait a few more days before we consider cutting fees. I make sure that George knows that, to date, the promoter has not even called us for one blog interview—and this was after I spoke with his marketing director three times offering our help. This band also has a track record of high volume walk-up sales at its concerts. This is not a new situation for George either; less experienced promoters show their stripes at times like this. We agree to wait a few more days.

Upstairs, Max X. is smiling, impeccably dressed, tall, well-built, about thirty-five years old, and seems quite humble as we shake hands. RRU's funky reggae-rock recordings conjure a picture of a different Max, perhaps a Bob Marley-type. Nobody ever fits my preconceived images, and I now tend to suppress any mental pictures of musicians until I meet them.

First thing I need to know from anybody is what he wants. Of course, most artists don't know what they want beyond some vague notions of fame and fortune. If he says he wants a record deal, I'll need to keep a straight face. I also want to know as much as possible about RRU's current career and advisors.

Max is comfortable, he says. Like all the other members of his group, he's got a home, a car, a happy girlfriend, and an established career. He also eats and dresses well. So what seems to be his problem?

"Our manager has much more than we do. And that doesn't seem right to me. We are his only clients. He may work hard, but he doesn't work harder than us."

"How do the other guys feel?"

"They don't think there's a problem. That's why I'm talking with you alone. They haven't analyzed the books like I have. They don't want to rock the boat. Me, I hate being ripped off."

"But your manager has done good things for you so far, right?"

"Yeah, but that ain't the point. It doesn't make sense that he makes more money than any of us. There are four of us and one of him. If he takes 20 percent, then we should each make 20 percent, too. But we don't. How does that happen if he ain't stealing?"

"Well, he may not be stealing, but he may be using some standard management tricks for his own benefit. I would have to see your management agreement to advise you further—unless you know the basics in that agreement. Do you know if he makes 20 percent, 15 percent or 10 percent? And does he take it from the gross or the net?"

"I think he makes 20 percent."

"Of everything? Concerts, merchandise, recordings, publishing?"

"I know he takes 20 percent from concerts and merchandise, but I'm not sure of the rest."

"That's your first problem."

"What should the manager be making?"

I tell him there are no rules in the music industry. Laws govern agents in New York and California, restricting commissions to 10 percent. But that could be 10 percent of the gross or the net—a difference that could translate into thousands of dollars.

GROSS VS. NET

As a manager, your clients pay you a percentage of their *income*. But unless you define what you mean by income, you can be cheating yourself or your client. Most artists would prefer to hear that you are taking only 10 percent of their money. But believe it or not, a manager making 20 percent of *net* income can earn less than a manager earning 10 percent of *gross* income.

Example: Assume the artist has just earned $10,000 for one concert.

Gross income is all money received from all sources without any deductions for commissions, taxes, union benefits, or expenses of any kind. A manager making "10 percent of gross" will earn $1,000 (10 percent of $10,000).

Net income is the amount of money remaining after you deduct certain agreed-upon expenses such as hotel rooms, travel costs, taxes, the cost of personnel, equipment rentals, etc. If these deductions equal $6,000, then the net income in this example will equal $4,000. A manager making "20 percent of net" will therefore earn $800 (20 percent of $4,000).

Always ask for the definition being used in *your* contract. It may be different in every contract.

THE MANAGER'S COMMISSION

Here is a good example of how Gross vs. Net directly affects the artist's income. In this example, the artist receives a flat guaranteed fee.

1. Some promoters will pay the artist a fee in addition to providing airfare and hotel rooms. The face (front page) of the contract will state that compensation is $8,000 plus air and hotel. In this case, a manager taking 15 percent of gross income earns $1,200 (15 percent of $8,000). If band salaries and other concert expenses equal $5,000, then the artist is left with $1,800 ($8,000 gross less $1,200 manager's commission, less $5,000 expenses = $1,800).

2. Another promoter may want nothing to do with the artist's travel arrangements and pays a fee of $10,000 from which the artist must provide her own air travel and rooms. In this second case, where air and hotel costs the artist $2,500, the same manager, again taking 15 percent of gross income, earns $1,500 (15 percent of $10,000). Assuming the same band salaries and concert expenses of $5,000, the artist is left with $1,000 ($10,000 gross less $2,500 travel expenses, less $1,500 manager's commission, less $5,000 expenses = $1,000). Obviously, if the manager is concerned about the artist's income, the actual cost of travel and hotel should have been checked before agreeing to this all-inclusive fee.

3. In the examples above, if the manager's commission had been on net income (defined as income after deducting travel and expenses), then the two cases end up as follows:

	CASE #1	CASE #2
Manager	$1,200	$1,125
Artist	$1,800	$1,375

Regardless of the percentage a manager receives, it is infinitely more fair to base a commission on some form of net income.

BOX OFFICE RECEIPTS

Sometimes the artist receives a percentage of ticket sales. It then becomes essential to define any deductions that the box office may take before calculating the artist's share. It may make sense to deduct a special entertainment tax imposed by the local government (such as a sales tax). Obviously, neither the promoter nor the concert hall will be enriched by this money that must be immediately forwarded to the government, so why should the artist take a percentage? Sometimes group sales agents send large groups to the concert and are entitled to a commission. Some box offices will deduct the group sales commissions before calculating the artist's share. Credit card (CC) companies charge up to 5 percent of each sale for administrative costs and for their own corporate profits. Again, this is the cost of doing business and is not considered income because it is immediately paid out to the CC companies. The list may be long or short, but the manager should know what is a permissible deduction.

Here's an example of how the fee based on box office receipts might be calculated.

1. A stadium concert sells $250,000 in tickets. The artist is entitled to 15 percent of net. If net income is defined as "after credit cards and 6 percent local tax," then the artist's share is calculated on $225,000 ($250,000 less 4 percent MasterCard/Visa/AmEx and 6 percent tax). The artist earns $33,750.

2. If you add $15,000 in group sales commissions to the above deductions, then the artist's share will be calculated on $210,000 ($250,000 less 4 percent CC, 6 percent tax, and $15,000 commissions). The artist earns $31,500.

This simple difference reduced your artist's income by $2,250 ($33,750 – $31,500). It matters how you negotiate the details of net income.

CREDIT CARDS

A special trick used by concert halls and venues everywhere is "generic credit card deduction." When defining deductions from box office income, a contract may read that the box office may deduct 5 percent for the cost of credit cards. In actuality some credit cards charge 2.75 percent, some 3.2 percent, some 4.75 percent, etc. If you insist on deducting the "actual credit card deduction," they are required to pass along only the actual monies paid to the credit card companies. In some cases, the difference can be tens of thousands of dollars. Always insist on the *actual* credit card cost.

Once again I ask: "How can I help you?"

"I need to know whether we're being ripped off and, if so, whether we can get out of our agreement with our manager. If he did anything illegal, I want to sue the bum. Either way, we may need new management."

"But the rest of the group doesn't agree with you, do they?"

"Not yet."

"So at this point, you need a consultant to help you analyze your situation."

"That sounds right."

Max needs to come back with his management agreement. I also ask for copies of concert gig contracts, their published songs, and other paperwork pertinent to RRU's income. I need to know who produced their merchandise and if the cost of production was subtracted before profits were divvied up.

"Hey, what's all this going to cost me?"

I don't hesitate a second. "Nothing for now. Let's see how involved this gets." I don't like managers who take advantage of their artists. "If you didn't know what you were signing, you need to be educated—assuming you want to learn."

"Absolutely."

In my head, I'm thinking, *yeah, right*. Most artists are quick to agree and submit to anything that sounds good without a true knowledge of what they're agreeing to. As far as the money goes, I have found that I get more substantial income from worthwhile artists by being up front and affordable (free) than by worrying about consultancy fees. I'm not a fool. But I'm not going to make a living off of helping artists already in trouble. Management, as I see it, serves a purpose by keeping artists out of trouble before they get into it.

That means we must be educated. Most music managers I've met have little or no training. There are no standards for managers in the popular music industry, and they often make it up as they go along. While much of management is really "crisis control"—preventing and putting out fires—longevity in this business (the carrot on the stick) requires that the manager, the artist, or both have knowledge of more than twenty topics. They include:

- Medical plans
- Pension plans
- Insurance (life, travel, disability, liability, loss)
- Money management and investment strategies
- Taxes
- Contract law
- Publishing
- Recording contract pitfalls
- Royalties
- Translating legalese into English
- Basic accounting
- Copyrights
- Trademarks
- Booking agreements

- Recording studios
- Musical personnel
- Merchandising
- Publicity, marketing, press, and promotion
- The Internet
- Staffing (accountants, lawyers, engineers, road managers, etc.)
- Music and songwriting
- Image (costumes, makeup, and hair)
- Playing instruments (especially keyboards, because they're not just pianos anymore—a synthesizer or computer keyboard allows you to play almost every instrument)
- Stage presence and performing talent

Do you, the manager or the artist, know anything about these items? Together, artist and manager should complement each other and know something about all of them.

THE WHOLE CIRCLE: HOW AN ARTIST SHOULD CHOOSE A MANAGER

No one knows everything about everything. The best that artists can hope for is to find a manager that complements their talents and experiential education, filling the voids in their knowledge and having the abilities that they lack.

When asked, artists say they want someone personable but aggressive, honest but with great selling abilities. What they ought to be looking for is a manager who is well trained and knowledgeable in business, finances, and artistic arenas (see above list).

Everyone in life is going to be ripped off sometime. Having a knowledgeable partner on your side will help decrease the number and severity of the rip-offs. If both manager and artist are strong in one area, it reinforces that particular area against rip-offs. If either one is weak in an area where the other is strong, then the one should be able to compensate for and strengthen the other's area of weakness. If you're both weak in an area, read a book, seek out an advisor, enroll in a class, ask somebody who might know. Ignorance is expensive. Then find someone you will listen to, at least in those areas that you are not strong. Be willing to accept the blame if things go wrong and you didn't listen. The manager must be willing to listen to you too. No manager is as wise as he wants to believe he is.

It's not absolutely necessary, but there are definitely advantages to finding the manager who likes your music. His passion for your talents can work wonders.

A note to artists just starting out: Your nephew who loves your band may want to help you carry your luggage and get you water, but he's essentially worthless when it comes to tasks beyond a gofer (go for this, go for that). Your uncle may have run his own business for twenty years and be a hard negotiator on the phone, but he'll let you down when a club owner is robbing you blind and the press is misspelling your name. Let your friends and relatives be helpful and love them dearly, but don't sign with them as your manager. When it comes time to replace them, they will be insulted and they will hate you and spread nasty gossip around the neighborhood, or around the world via YouTube, Twitter, Facebook, Tagged, LinkedIn, and whatever else pops up.

The most successful marriage of artist and manager occurs when they each add pieces to the career pie and together complete the circle. It appears that Beyoncé Knowles's parents were special and helped shape the career of their talented child. Perhaps this family together covered the whole pie. But this is definitely a rare exception.

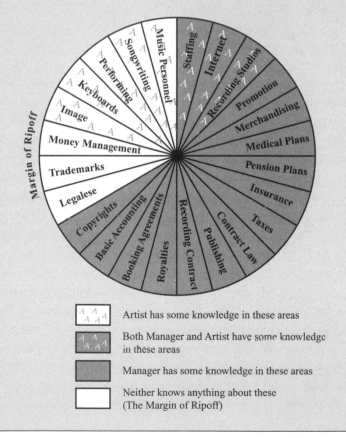

Max stays another fifteen minutes telling me about the band members' various personalities. No druggies (thank God) but RRU's version of the Dwarfs: Lazy, Wimpy, and Crazy (as in certifiably schizophrenic). It's a pleasant hour, but a full hour nonetheless. This has been either charity or a great intro into a new managerial relationship.

Max X. from the reggae band RRU

2

Six Rules of Management

Keep all the tools in mind. Sooner or later you'll need every one.
The courage to speak must be matched by the wisdom to listen.

Robert O. witnesses my meeting with Max, as he does most of my business dealings, because as an intern he is here to learn. I found him five months ago through a university. He is a graduate student in entertainment management. He started out eager to donate his services in exchange for hands-on experience, but things have worked out so well that he has been lightly salaried for the past two months. Graduation is four months away and he is not interested in staying on with me (he needs to make a *real* living). We discussed it. I think it is an excellent practice to apprentice under managers with varying styles. I've introduced him to some possibilities and he has made many good contacts on his own.

Robert O. is ambitious, able, and personable, and he completes every task on or before schedule. In a word, he's overqualified. When I interview assistants, I always look for the overqualified because 1) they often don't get hired (they intimidate their potential bosses); 2) they do good work; 3) they think on their feet. Robert O. is everything my last intern Ned was not. The best assistant I ever had was Gloria. But she was paid. And after three years, I discovered that I couldn't afford the salary she deserved. In this business, change is good and necessary for growth, experience, and sanity. Even the big agencies are often fluid in their employment practices.

I usually learn something from each person I work with. Gloria taught me to hire the overqualified. She asked all the right questions and made no assumptions, even though she was very bright. She laughed and complained, but she cared about all the little important things—spelling, deadlines, phone etiquette, organization, filing, scheduling, keeping cool in crises, money, and the clients. I don't keep secrets from my assistants. I expect complete discretion, and make them sign a statement to that effect for my protection and, more importantly, the protection of my clients.

Many managers don't operate that way, thinking that holding on to knowledge is power. I believe that your staff will do a better job if they know what *the hellest goest on*. It shows you trust them and they usually return it tenfold.

Robert has taken five phone messages during my session with Max X. As a rule, I return all phone calls within seventy-two hours. I consider it rude not to return even the most unwanted call or email, although Robert is certainly capable of relaying answers on my behalf. In business, there are many rude people who must be contacted multiple times before you'll get a response. I teach my assistants good business manners.

When I was apprenticing under General Manager Robert Kamlot for the country's largest nonprofit theatrical producing organization (at that time), every assistant was made to memorize his Six Rules of Management. To this day, I pass them on to young manager-types whenever I can.

KAMLOT'S SIX RULES OF MANAGEMENT

1. Never assume anything.
2. Never give out gratuitous information.
3. When in doubt, do nothing. Sometimes no action is an action.
4. Never play around in your own backyard.
5. Never speak to the press.
6. Diplomacy is at least as important as being right.

I'd come in to the office and at arbitrary points during the day, the general manager would conduct a "call and response," similar to religious services. He'd call out "Rule #4!" and expect us to respond with the appropriate rule. It was an effective education, and has turned out to be applicable to almost every crisis I've encountered.

Let's talk about Ned, who didn't understand a single rule. Ned was enthusiastic, very smart, and very spoiled. His parents made sure he didn't want for anything, so the unpaid internship was a breeze for him. I liked him right off the bat—a real charmer. But crises and deadlines were not in his vocabulary, even though he insisted that they were. Asked to finish filing some new contracts, he spent an entire day rearranging my personal files instead, thinking that I would appreciate his initiative. He assumed wrong (Rule #1). All he had to do was ask me. During contract negotiations, making this kind of an assumption can be deadly.

Ned would ask many questions about contracts. However, I caught him one day on the phone, telling his mother about the size of the fee that one of my clients was making on a show. Sharing this information did nothing to help the client, me, or Ned's mom. And it can destroy trust in a second. Rule #2 broken.

One day while I was at the gym, Ned received a crisis call from a promoter saying he had to book the artist's plane flight within one hour or the reservation would be lost. Ned couldn't reach me on my cell phone, so he authorized the flight. He didn't know that the artist had just called me directly to say he was leaving out of a different state. Rule #3 broken. This is why I prefer refundable tickets for all my clients.

Ned dated one of my clients, unbeknownst to me. But it didn't last. Ned didn't take rejection well. My client, subsequently, felt uncomfortable calling or coming to see me, because Ned would be there. The client didn't show up to a press interview because I had assigned Ned to accompany her. Rule #4, the most dangerous one, broken. And this was only dating. Screwing can get you and your business screwed. All that results from an affair is potential distrust and massive complications. Getting married doesn't make it better. Either manage the artist or marry him/her, never both. There are no doubt exceptions to this rule, but my observations tell me that it's not worth the risk. You can be your spouse's best friend and provide career advice without being the hired manager. You should define your relationship clearly as personal or business. Never both. There are no ifs, ands, or buts. Sorry.

To add insult to injury, when the client didn't show up for the interview, Ned felt free to step in and "protect" the client by inventing an illness. He assumed he was being helpful. He gave out gratuitous information and he took an unwarranted action. The next day, a column item appeared on the gossip page (rather than the desired feature article in the entertainment section), stating that a reliable source had said that the client was seriously ill and depressed over a recent breakup (causing ticket sales for the next day's concert to drop off and a panic call to me from the promoter). In his defense, there is almost no way he could have answered the press' questions safely. Therefore, let the artist make her own mistakes. Managers should keep quiet. Rule #5 broken.

For the record, I let Ned go the next day, promising him a good recommendation should he need it. Rule #6 upheld. Even someone as incompetent as Ned may end up the CEO of a record label. So be careful, the toes you step on today could be connected to the ass you kiss tomorrow.

So I am thrilled to be working with Robert O. Since John, my friend's hip-hop nephew, is already twenty minutes late, Robert takes the opportunity to ask a question or two.

"Why would Max's manager take 20 percent commission and you only take 10 percent? Is that because his manager also acts as his agent?"

I answered. "It's possible. But to be an agent, he needs to be licensed. That's the law in New York and California. Those are the only two U.S. states with any significant entertainment laws. Anybody can be a manager—no laws, no restrictions, no standards, and no education. Pitiful, ain't it?"

"So a licensed agent can also be someone's manager, but a manager can't easily be someone's agent."

"Correct. A good example is the 1982 case of manager Bob Raison, who bragged that he helped get longtime client Jane Wyman a regular role on the CBS television series *Falcon Crest*. He was handcuffed, locked up, and faced a year in jail and a $10,000 fine. He broke the law by getting her a job without being a licensed agent. He was forgiven because he was once a licensed agent and he agreed to renew his expired license. The National Conference of Personal Managers took up the cause and has been fighting for managerial rights ever since."

"What's the difference between an agent and a manager?"

"An agent books work. A manager advises and consults on all aspects of a career."

"And what does a promoter do?"

"Promoters have or can find enough money to produce a concert."

"So what's a producer?"

"Producers are different animals in different fields. Concert producers are called promoters. A record producer does not need to have money invested. Producers are often hired by a record label to oversee production, song selection, and creative presentation. Executive producers in the music industry usually mean the people with the money behind the project. A theatrical producer raises the money from investors but doesn't necessarily have any input in the production. A nonprofit theatrical producer oversees the fundraising and use of tax-exempt contributions to finance a show or a theatre. There are many kinds of producing job titles in film and television—they all mean different things, and are not the same as the above."

"Sounds stupid."

"Well, the automobile industry puts bumpers on cars to protect them, but installs them at all different heights so that they don't meet. I guess 'stupid' is pretty universal in business. Titles are far from standardized. If you want to thank your cousin for giving you free food while you rehearse, you can call him an executive producer. Unfortunately, that happens a lot and some people who get credit don't deserve it. So always look past the titles on someone's résumé and ask what they actually know how to do."

"So what do I call this job on my résumé? Do I need to say intern?"

"Assistant is fine."

The phone rings. Robert answers. I think about how well Robert is working out. But Gloria was still the best.

Robert O., my assistant

3

Commissions and Advances

The Lord didn't do it all in one day. What makes you think you can?
Experience often shows that success is due less to ability than to attitude.

There's a knock at the door. Robert yells, "Come in." It's an informal office.

An energetic young man bounds in, baggy pants hanging off his skinny hips. His face is serious in contrast to his colorful, near comical, urban uniform. Will.i.am would be proud. This is John. And with him is Kathy, his girlfriend and, I find out later, his cheerleader.

John sits down and at first it's like pulling teeth to get him to talk. And when he does, he says the inevitable: "I want a record deal." I change the subject quickly as I always do and try to find the "real" John underneath the façade. This will help me decide if I want to work with him and, more importantly, if I can do anything for him. There's nothing more pitiful than wasting your time trying to help someone when you have no appropriate tools. Inevitably the fights begin and everyone feels like a failure. I want to work with people who can succeed and who will ultimately thank me for at least a portion of their success. Let's be real—most managers are just looking for a commission. And most artists would be wise to avoid those managers.

But that takes business savvy—and business savvy can make the difference between a rapper with a long career and one with no career. So, how much savvy does John have at the age of eighteen? I can see he has a popular look, a handsome face, and a tall and skinny body. He has brought a DVD, very rough-cut, and a CD of four of his original raps produced by his cousin Rafael, who has a home digital studio. From the CD, I can tell he has talent. From the video, I can only tell he knows how to move—otherwise it's worthless. I am glad he's brought anything at all. Now that I am assured that John, who performs under the moniker Phat J, has some talent, I need to find out his goals and priorities in life outside music. How will he deal with a time-consuming but barely lucrative profession? What kind of attitude/baggage does he carry? Is he responsible? What about family, children, siblings, prison, drugs, alcohol, gangs, financial support, hobbies, education, work, etc.? I've never had trouble asking these kinds of questions. People realize I'm interested in them and I have no intention of abusing the knowledge. And Phat J is no different. I feed his ego by showing some sincere interest.

Kathy, who was not officially invited to this party, jumps in with stories about how wonderful John is and how he's going to be as big a star as Tupac. It seems that she wants to be an active part of this discussion, and at this point her comments might be valuable in discovering some hidden truths.

I ask him if he has an agreement with Rafael, either as the producer or engineer or co-writer? He says no.

"I assume that there are almost no costs to producing the CD, since the studio was your cousin's. But what does Rafael want from your career?"

"We haven't talked about it yet."

"That would be one of the first things I could help you with. I'm good at writing agreements between friends, so that they remain friends. Most managers don't know how to do it themselves. They send you to a lawyer."

"My friend wrote his own contract between him and the band he's managing."

"Did a lawyer take a look at it?"

"No, they trust each other."

"Bad idea. If you and I ever sign an agreement, I would tell you to find a lawyer to review it for you. Otherwise, it's really easy for me to rip you off."

"This guy would never rip off the band."

"First, unless your friend is trained in writing good contracts, the band might be ripped off without anyone trying. You want someone who knows all the topics that need to be covered and negotiated in a contract. Second, unless the band is trained in reading contracts, how would they know? If we work together, I require that you learn how to protect yourself in this business. That means going over contracts together, discussing business propositions in detail."

THE ART OF NEGOTIATION

The art of negotiation is the subject of dozens of best-selling books. Before negotiating an agreement—even before an informal discussion of the basic terms of a contract—you should organize your needs carefully. Divide the artist's needs and desires into four categories: basics, options, throwaways, and giveaways. (Many of the topics below are discussed in great detail elsewhere in this book. Check the index.)

BASICS

- Legal Names. The contract must be between those people who are legally allowed to make the deal, usually the artist and whoever the deal is being made with.
- Compensation. Money. Percentage. Benefits.
- Beginning and ending dates.
- Responsibilities.
- Out clauses.
- Warranties and representations.
- Control and ownership. Who owns the performance, the videotape, the product, etc.?
- Arbitration.
- Accounting/Payment methods.
- Checks and balances. (Do you get to check their work and do they get to check yours?)

OPTIONS

(Things worth fighting for)
- Ego-related items. Dressing rooms, costumes, cars, hotels, billing, etc.
- "What ifs." If the sky falls, then . . . If the artist's family shows up, then . . . If the stage is unsafe, then . . . If someone gets sick . . . etc.
- Future changes (How to amend the agreement if it becomes necessary).
- Length of the term of the contract, including possible extensions and early termination.

THROWAWAYS

(Luxury items that you would be willing to give up)
- Limo vs. town car
- Champagne backstage vs. Diet Coke
- Twenty complimentary tickets for friends vs. ten tickets

GIVEAWAYS

(Items you would be willing to give to the other party so that you can get items important to you)
- Photo signing session
- Meet 'n' greet for the executives of the company and their families
- Free second concert for the company employees
- Participation in an auction

CONTRACTUAL CLAUSES TO KNOW

Authors: If you want to make sure that your artist is not paid less than anyone else on the bill, you add this clause.

FAVORED NATIONS

All conditions of employment hereunder shall be considered on a Favored Nations basis. No other artist shall receive compensation greater than that afforded the Artist hereunder, and, in the event any other Artist shall receive greater compensation, Artist hereunder shall immediately receive the same and equal compensation.

Authors: If you want to make sure that your artist is making more money than anyone else on the bill, you add this clause.

MORE FAVORED NATIONS

All conditions of employment hereunder shall be considered on a More Favored Nations basis. No other Artist shall receive compensation equal to or greater than that afforded the Artist hereunder; and, in the event that any other Artist shall receive equal or greater compensation, Artist hereunder shall immediately receive greater compensation to be negotiated immediately and in good faith.

Authors: If you don't have as much money for legal representation in court as the people you're doing business with, or you just want to avoid long, drawn-out court cases, you will want to insist upon this method of resolution: Arbitration.

DISPUTES AND GRIEVANCES

All disputes, differences, or controversies which may arise between the parties under the terms of this agreement shall be resolved in the following manner: Either party may submit the matter to arbitration before a mutually agreeable third party. In the event the parties are unable to agree upon a third party, the demand for arbitration shall be submitted to the American Arbitration Association in New York City (or other major city) and conducted pursuant to the Voluntary Labor Arbitration rules of the Association. The decision of the Arbitrator shall be final and binding upon the parties and their members, and shall not be subject to Court review except that either party may petition an appropriate Court for the enforcement of an award, if necessary. The costs of any arbitration shall be borne equally by the parties [alternative: by the losing party in the arbitration].

●

> **Authors:** If the artist is receiving a percentage of the box office income, there are still monies that are excluded from the "Gross." Demand a clause like the one below that defines the monies that are considered "Gross."
>
> ## GROSS WEEKLY BOX OFFICE RECEIPTS
>
> Gross Weekly Box Office Receipts shall be defined as the gross box office receipts evidenced by statements prepared and signed by the theater/stadium/concert hall and the Artist's management after the following deductions: 1) any federal, state, local and other admission taxes, 2) commissions paid in connection with theater parties, benefits, automated ticket distribution or remote box offices and credit cards and brokers' fees, 3) sums paid to the pension and welfare funds of unions [only certain theaters do this], 4) subscription fees, 5) other deductions and payments similar to those aforesaid.

"I also require you to sign all your own checks and contracts."

"Then why would I need you as a manager after that?"

"You are the artist. You concentrate on your music. I'll concentrate on the business of your career. But you still need at least a basic understanding of what I'm doing for you so that it will be difficult for me to rip you off like so many managers do. And I'm not going to try to rip you off, but I don't want my clients to ever doubt me. Trust is the most essential part of any relationship."

Kathy chimes in, "You listening to this?" then hits his shoulder.

I explain to him the "Circle" concept of teamwork (see chapter 1).

His reaction? "I just want to be a star. That's why I want a manager, so he can do all that other stuff."

"Then we can't work together."

"Well you can explain it to me and I'll watch his back." Kathy suggests.

"That's very sweet, but you may not always be around. In fact, his producer may not always be around—and contracts exist to handle the bad times. In good times, no one needs a contract. Everyone is friendly. But in the music business, good can turn bad and ugly in a matter of seconds. My clients watch their own backs, and I do everything I can to prevent the problems from existing in the first place."

Silence. Then John decides to challenge me. "Well, I've got interest from two big agencies. So we just dialoguing."

"And what happens when you sign a contract giving your booking agency 10 percent of everything you do?"

"What's wrong with that? They all get that."

"It's not the percentage. It's how they calculate it. Do you think it's right for them to take 10 percent of the cost of the airline tickets and hotel rooms for you and your crew?"

"No, of course not."

"Well, the standard agreement lets them do that."

"A lawyer would catch that for me."

"At $350 and up an hour. And he probably wouldn't change it, because it's standard. None of my clients pay commission on their expenses. They pay commission on their *net* income, which means "after expenses." So if you earn $10,000 for a personal appearance, but it costs you $2500 for travel and hotel, your agent should make 10 percent of $7500. However, 90 percent of all acts pay the commission on the entire $10,000. And as your manager, unlike most other managers, I only take a commission on the net. This is not a sales job I'm doing on you, just showing you why you need an honest manager to help you. But if you don't know the difference between an ethical and an unethical manager, you deserve what you get. And that means you need to educate yourself in business."

Kathy says, "I'm going for a business degree but I'd like to work for a record company. Is there any special major I should take?"

"What is it you want to do for a record company? It's a good thing to have a business degree, but it's about what you know how to do. Basic accounting, reading and writing contracts, business law and taxes, marketing, banking, investing—all this makes you valuable to any business, music or otherwise. And it doesn't hurt to know something about music or recording.

"And to answer your earlier question, John, why do you need a manager? It's because your career seems to be at the right stage. Early on you need to concentrate on getting your act together artistically. You need to create your music and an audience who appreciates it. If your friends won't buy your stuff, why would a record label? There are plenty of talented people. No one in business tries to sell talent. You've got to have more. And you've got to show you can make money from your talent. At that point, a manager can help you. Up until that point, you don't need a manager, just a lot of well-intentioned friends. And you wouldn't be able to pay him anyway.

"MC Hammer is a great example. I'm going to paraphrase here, but VH-1 reported that he sold 60,000 of his self-produced CDs out of the trunk of his car. He went from club to club, talked DJs into playing one of his songs, and then cleared the floor when he danced. The audience couldn't get enough of him, and he sold himself. That kind of success gets around and soon Sony approached him. He had no manager; he had no agent, no lawyer, and no accountant, none of the usual suspects. He was a marketable commodity all by himself. After Sony offered him a deal, he figured out that he made more money per CD selling them out of his trunk than he could with Sony. So he turned them down.

"They were impressed with the math he showed them, so Sony returned with an unprecedented offer, which he couldn't refuse. He was soon on top of the industry. The equivalent of selling CDs out of the trunk of your car today is getting a million hits on your YouTube video or thousands of digital sales on iTunes. If you can do this, the record labels will take note. The Internet doesn't make it any easier for you than it was for Hammer, just different.

"There's a lot more to planning a career than the first couple of months or years. And Hammer, like most artists, didn't plan for longevity. I don't know much about his management, but a good manager worries about longevity from the very first day."

Phat J doesn't know too much about Hammer and thinks that was a long time ago. So I mention a recent rap group who have had three top five videos on MTV over the past two years. Their well-known manager had them showcased on major television networks during primetime. The original record deal had involved a low advance of $36,000 that they split four ways, less their manager's commission. Normally the advance would go toward completion of their CD, but they had completed it before they ever got an offer. Of course, I don't know how much was spent completing the CD on their own, but we need to subtract that cost to appreciate their net income.

Videos are not cheap. And the video expenses were to be charged against their royalties, along with travel expenses to Los Angeles to be on some of these network television shows. The videos were costly and the artists were treated to first-class treatment while traveling. These four naïve souls were unaware that everything they spent was coming out of their own pockets. Common problem, I assure Phat J.

Bottom line is these nineteen year olds still live with their parents and made less than $9,000 each over the past two years. The record company made a small profit and the manager made commissions off the group's gross income. "So not only do you have to worry about the industry, you have to worry about who you hire to help you worry about the industry."

Silence.

"Why don't you think about this? You can call me anytime if you've got a question."

"Well, I really want someone else to do all the business stuff. I'm just not into it. But I'll make sure that I watch all the checks that someone else signs."

"Even if we don't work together, you need to make sure that you never sign a Power of Attorney clause."

"What's that?"

"That's where you let someone else sign checks in any amount from your bank account. That's how people steal."

Kathy asks, "But wouldn't you find out about it the next month when you get the bank statement?"

"Not necessarily. First, you have to be looking. If John doesn't know how to check a statement, how will he know? I have a client who, before working with me, hired a separate business manager and gave him Power of Attorney. The manager had all tax and bank statements mailed to himself and not directly to the artist. Five years later, my client owed

$20,000 in back taxes and penalties. The business manager bought himself a car and never paid the tax bill. The client had been told that the taxes were covered."

"Is he in jail?"

"No. The client had given him Power of Attorney and all the evidence was in files in the manager's computer and therefore not available to the client. The IRS finally contacted my client directly after the manager died and his office closed."

John says, "That's deep, man."

I stand up to imply that the meeting is over.

"Give my best to your uncle. He's great."

We all shake hands and smile. I think I came on too strong, but that's my style. I wonder what Robert O. is going to ask me now.

Phat J and Kathy

Becoming an Entertainment Manager

Unless you try to do something beyond what you have already mastered, you will never grow.

You will find as you look back upon your life that the moments that stand out are the moments when you have done things for others.

I don't even turn around before Robert O. asks me about how I started in management. Actually, I started on Broadway. Robert O. is interested in the music industry, but I assure him that my theatrical training is what gave me an edge in my career. Broadway is organized; fourteen unions with small-print rulebooks governing everything from health issues and benefits to lunch hours. Rulebooks tell you how much to pay someone with a hammer compared to someone with a paintbrush.

In order to be a Broadway show manager, I had to apprentice for three years under another union manager, take eighteen required seminars in topics like Box Office Embezzlement, Marketing, Advertising and Press, Payroll and Budgets, Contracts, Touring, and Taxes, and finally pass a six-hour written and two-hour oral examination. It felt like I was passing my bar exam to practice law. After completing that, as a member of ATPAM (Association of Theatrical Press Agents and Managers), I was qualified to apply for a job as a Broadway company or house manager.

I worked almost steadily as a union manager for six years, suffering the divas, negotiating with angry lawyers and agents, avoiding the press, staying one step ahead of Union bosses to prevent work stoppages and salary penalties, and keeping on budget even when the director decided overnight that he needed a live elephant on stage. In short, I maintained organization under the threat of chaos. Which was one of the benefits of Broadway rules—structure. The music industry has no structure and no rules—it is chaotic by nature.

Unlike jazz improvisations or contemporary atonal classical pieces, which may sound chaotic but are built on firm structural musical forms, the music *business* is the opposite, seemingly structured to the outside eye, but built on anarchy with no discernable foundation of any kind. My background provided me with a logical way to approach the music industry.

My friend, a rock 'n' roller who'd approached me to help him with a contractual problem, understood the advantage my experience in ATPAM gave me. He asked if I would review their manager's contract before they signed it. I was shocked. I wouldn't let my worst enemy sign this document. Yet it was a standard Conference of Personal Managers agreement (See chapter 22).

Under the gun from his new management team, my friend claimed that the band would lose its South American tour if they didn't sign the management-artist contract within four days. I suggested that he call an emergency meeting to let me explain what was in the contract. I was sure that once his band knew the details, they would decide on their own not to sign. My friend made the calls and met with great resistance. After all, who was I to advise them?

Nevertheless, we met at 7:30 PM for a two-hour session at my friend's apartment. I put large sheets of paper on a big wall to use as a blackboard. We went point-by-point until 2:00 AM. Not once did I have to point out the obvious—they would be signing a slavery contract. Before they left, they decided to meet the next day, without me, to rewrite this agreement in their own terms. The happy ending is that the management company signed the band's rewritten contract and the South American tour went on as scheduled. The unhappy news is that the band fired this management team four months later when they discovered a "financial discrepancy." Under the terms of the original agreement, there was no "out" clause stating that the band could get out of the agreement for certain reasons. Under the band's revision, there were numerous termination possibilities. A clear understanding in their contract saved them years of problems.

My friend, with the band's OK, asked me to watch over their business finances during the interim period of finding new management. I worked with them for five years as their official manager. This was my introduction to the music world. It was an education by fire.

I no longer represent them for many of the same reasons that couples get divorced. There was no anger or hostility between us, just a lack of appreciation. They no longer trusted my career advice; they turned on each other; they thought they knew more than they did; and in summary, they weren't happy with themselves. They wanted to "control more of the day-to-day operations," without a clue as to what that would entail. Some of them had lost their hunger and ambition. One band member was scared. Fear and lethargy keep people from taking chances. One became cynical and complacent that they were not going to get any bigger or richer than they were. It was my job to work them through this phase, but I guess I wasn't up to being mommy. The music industry does not encourage lifelong business relationships. The band eventually broke up. Some are still working as studio players. One teaches and one works in the post office. It's a hard life.

But Robert O. doesn't need to know all this, so I just tell him, "Oh, it's a long story."

I have to admit, I liked the creativity and the challenges of managing in the music field. The time requirements were just as demanding as Broadway's, but the hours were extremely flexible. Broadway demands long hours six days a week. As company manager, you supervise up to two hundred actors, crew, and staff, and oversee an initial budget of $3–$20 million (which will be spent in a two-month window) plus a weekly operating budget of hundreds of thousands. And every penny must be meticulously accounted for. While there is a show accountant, he depends on your knowledge of every expense and every box office dollar. While there is a show attorney, she depends on your negotiations and often will only *review* the contracts you write. The payroll company produces the checks based on *your* weekly interpretation of the union rules and the hours worked. And on and on.

In spite of everything, music was easier. So there I was, a music manager without an artist. I shopped my talents and was wooed by a big management firm.

I enumerate to Robert O. the pluses and minuses.

First the benefits: regular paycheck, good health benefits, possible pension, my own cubicle, the prestige of the firm's name, potential for significant income growth, development of important business and artist contacts, camaraderie with other managers in the firm.

The drawbacks: less flexible hours, a cubicle for an office, lots of corporate red tape and procedures, serious office politics, significant distance between manager and artist, too many lawyers, too many accountants, little personal participation in concert and celebrity soirees, corporate loyalty may be more important than artist loyalty, loss of individual control.

I chose to turn them down. I know some wonderful people who have been with corporations for decades. For them, the paycheck security alone overcomes the negatives.

I like the autonomy and creative freedom. I like advising a client to be bold and daring. I like to solve problems in my own special way. I also solved the paycheck problem by devising some unorthodox methods of payment. Traditionally, managers and agents are paid on commission. However, I noticed that some of my novice clients needed the kind of early advice that doesn't return commissions immediately.

One artist in particular presented a unique situation. I couldn't be sure at this early stage that the artist's career would develop the way I hoped. So I devised a fee structure aside from commissions and created a clearly defined list of activities that I would do for the fee, such as creating a promotional package suitable for attracting a booking agency and overseeing recording sessions. In at least one other case, I agreed to a weekly paycheck instead of any commissions. Some years, my income is better because of the weekly paycheck; in others I would have been better off on commission, but I enjoyed the security.

Artist/Management Relationship: Business, Ethics, and Music

Expect nothing, blame no one, and keep active.
Be careful. The toes you step on today could be connected to the ass you kiss tomorrow.

If it's tough to break into this business, it's even tougher to stay on top. Artists suffer enough problems developing their art and their careers; a manager should do everything he can to be part of the solution, not part of the problem. If an artist questions the manager's motives, intent, and trustworthiness, the artist will eventually fight the manager's ideas and he won't be able to do the best job.

Which is why I decided to leave my first group, my friend's band. There is a time to leave your client—and the best time is usually before she decides you ought to leave. Unfortunately, most management agreements are based on greed, not good business relationships. These contracts keep artists and managers bonded long after the trust has eroded. The excuse most often heard is that managers need to make money too and they've invested so much time and energy in the artist that they deserve to receive payments from the artist's career as long as they can (although all artist–management agreements guarantee continued income for continuing projects). People need to grow in their careers, and that often means working with new people who inspire that growth. But managers understandably fight dissolving associations that are not working because it means loss of future income. No one ever said that a manager-artist relationship must be lifelong.

On another level, switching management may be a terrible thing. If the artist is stuck in a rut but points the finger at the manager as the problem, then switching managers may be like throwing the baby out with the bathwater. Some artists jump agencies and managers every few years. Perhaps a breakdown in communications is the real problem. I'm in favor of healthy change if it's necessary, but change shouldn't be impulsive. There's a lot to be gained from a loyal and trusted manager who cares.

On yet a third level, there is a unique manager-artist relationship created when a producer (the guy with the money) hires individuals to record and perform as a group. Examples include the Village People, 'NSync, Menudo, Spice Girls, the Ritchie Family, and the Backstreet Boys. A reality television show entitled *Making the Band* followed the creation of the five young male pop singers of O-Town from auditions through first performances. The rigid training process the boys were made to endure particularly disturbed me. Of course, all the professional mentors, artistic staff, costumes, housing, rehearsal halls, and songs were selected and paid for by the producer/manager. Obviously he wanted and deserved something back for his investment. However, paying substandard royalties and denying the singers a voice in their own career development makes for an agreement that is tantamount to slavery. I was fascinated to watch the change in the boys' reaction from when they were selected (elation) to after they received their contracts (distrust, confusion).

The combination of inexperience and youth, lack of business acumen, the prospects of fame and fortune, and the fear of missing this once-in-a-lifetime offer is enough to get a signature from almost anyone on the bottom of this bad contract. So I was especially pleased to see one of the "winners" turn down the offer—however, I am almost sure he is regretting not having his moment in the sun. On the other hand, where is O-Town now?

This contract was created with a take-it-or-leave-it attitude from management to trivialize the artist's contribution to the success of the group. True, sometimes negotiations are not appropriate (the best reason is budget constraints; the worst is pure greed). On the other hand, it is ethically imperative for management to make sure such agreements are fair, that they provide for the mental and physical health of the performers, and that they allow everyone space to breathe and a fair share of prosperity. Good management must prepare for negotiations from the standpoint of what is fair, not just "what can I get away with?"

THE BEST AGREEMENTS ARE THOSE IN WHICH BOTH SIDES THINK THEY'VE WON

There's a reason why we must negotiate instead of one side dictating the terms of a contract for the other. First of all, it's called an "agreement." That implies that all of the people involved have agreed to the terms in the contract. Of course, there are "take it or leave it" deals.

Some organizations operate under strict regulations that are not negotiable. For example, a state university cannot pay deposits on a performance, nor can it pay in cash. The state government has passed a law saying so. A manager can stand on his head but if he wants to make a deal with that university, he must accept these terms.

Some organizations, especially not-for-profit charities, have very limited budgets. Their boards of directors may have enacted rules that ensure the organization stays strictly within its means, such as limiting the amount of money that can be paid to any one artist. A manager should attempt to get to know the organization and its operations. Sometimes research can teach you that there are possible special benefits that can be negotiated. Just don't expect the not-for-profit to offer something you don't ask for.

Good relationships are based on fairness. In the best of all possible worlds, everyone involved gets everything he wants. In reality, a negotiator must give up something important to the other side in order to get something important from him. If there's nothing you have that the other side wants, you are at a disadvantage.

"To be negotiated in good faith" is a legal phrase often added to contracts when there is an issue that can't be resolved at that moment and when it is possible that the issue may never come up at all in the future. The phrase commits both sides of a negotiation to be reasonable, even if only one side will want something. When a negotiator abandons fairness on a postponed contractual issue, the courts can step in and decide if he was or wasn't fair.

At that point, there is animosity between the parties and perhaps significant court expenses. The unfair side can gain a reputation for being untrustworthy. Yet, many lawyers and managers will tell you that they exist to fight for their clients—at all costs. That is a tricky ethical choice. Each negotiator must develop his personal business ethic.

I suggest that in the long run, being obsessively competitive in negotiations will cost you and your client. You may need something from the other side someday and they will remember that you were not completely fair.

The original Backstreet Boys were put together by a producer/manager. They turned into an overnight sensation. They explained on *MTV News* why they decided to take action against the management that created them. It was reported that the group earned $188 million in merchandise, CDs, and related items. Group members then looked at their own more modest bank accounts. Where did all that money go? The CEO-type producers owned a piece of limo companies, catering companies, merchandise companies, etc., and were making incomes from each of these in addition to their commission as management. So, when the band needed limo companies, caterers, and merchandisers, management hired the companies that the producers partly owned. Remember, the managers and producers are the *same* people. Some might see this as a conflict of interest. Some see this as shrewd business maneuvering. It is not illegal. The Backstreet Boys saw it as a "rape."

They were smart enough to ask a court of law for a divorce from their management. They legally couldn't divorce their producers who invested all the capital in their careers and would always be entitled to a financial return. But management is responsible for guiding the course of an artist's career, and they wanted management to represent their interests, not the producers' interests. These producers were the parents that birthed them. The court, however, agreed with the children and their independent rights to protect their own interests.

Think of how much money in legal costs might have been saved if management had shared the wealth just a little more fairly. The producers could have salvaged their management ties. For all the money to be made in this business, there is still no greater joy than working with talented artists you respect and enjoy.

Having chosen to leave my friend's band, I put out the word and opened my own office. The number of artists looking for management is enormous. I had no trouble getting people who wanted my help. But as I said before, not everyone is ready for management. A manager should look for an artist who has already found a distinctive voice. By distinctive voice, I don't mean a singing voice, but an inner voice used to guide the art of the individual. As an instrumentalist or a songwriter or a performer, you need to know yourself well enough to articulate your vision, ambition, and artistry. A manager can only take you where you are able to go and where you want to go. Wanting a record deal is not your inner voice. A good manager should be able to tell if you are ready to be marketed and managed.

QUALITIES TO LOOK FOR IN AN ARTIST

- Marketable talent (you've got it, but who wants it?)
- Good working attitude (arrogance sells, but do you want to work with it?)
- Ambition and drive (laziness kills)
- Clean from drugs and alcohol (destructive behavior costs more than you will ever make)
- Financial support and industry connections (a lot of divas are doing dishes during the day)
- Marketable musical material (who's going to buy it after your record it?)
- Stage presence and charisma on stage (great concerts sell music)

- Public persona and image (bad ain't necessarily bad)
- An angle for marketing (you gotta have a gimmick)
- A realistic sense of your abilities and limitations (writing songs doesn't mean you should sing along)

This is not to say that talent or self-awareness is required to be successful in this business. But they are key ingredients to the longevity of a career. A good song and luck can get you started, but unless you've got a strategic plan and a strong self-marketing instinct, you will fade quickly, and usually go broke. The public and the media are fickle.

So how do rich, famous, enduring talents wind up bankrupt? Sammy Davis Jr., Toni Braxton, TLC, Billy Joel, and Wayne Newton have all made the news with their financial woes. Talent on stage has nothing to do with talent in personal finance. I know plenty of performers who cannot balance their checkbooks; no one ever taught them.

Let's say you are a young star, and you earn $20 million dollars for a leading role in a movie. After commissions for manager and agent, union dues, deductible expenses, and taxes, you may earn less than $4 million dollars. Now that's not peanuts, but thinking that you have $20 million to spend, your accountant suggests that you buy a nine-bedroom mansion in the richest part of Beverly Hills (for tax purposes) and you buy your mom a new home and yourself a new Lexus. Still, all is fine for the moment. But your career slows down and the next year, you don't make a movie. There's an expensive mortgage to pay and your friends still have expensive taste and you're used to first-class airfare, etc. Eventually, the bills pile up. You get a Broadway show with a good salary paying $10,000 a week for three months work. You're already in debt and even $10,000 a week means you're still broke.

One of the saddest stories told is MC Hammer, the miracle man of rap. Remember, he's the guy who sold 60,000 CDs out of the trunk of his car and engineered a great recording deal with Sony. He's one of those good hearts who wanted to share a piece of his enormous success with family, friends, and his neighborhood. He put seventy people on stage. Some were phenomenal dancers like he was, but many seemed to do nothing more than watch the stage and audience. But they were in costume, and they were part of the show. Of course, there was a large backstage crew as well. He paid everyone a living annual wage and took them with him on tour. The cost was astronomical, but at the time, Hammer was making huge sums.

His accountant may have told him he could afford to build his dream house, an $11 million mansion in the Hollywood Hills. Hammer continued to make lots of money, but not as much as he originally made. Therefore his expenses were more than his income. And it's hard to fire all those "friends" on stage. Eventually he lost it all. And a brilliant career was in shambles. Nothing sabotages a creative spirit more than self-doubt, depression, and the feeling that you let people down. Money problems destroy marriages, careers, and friendships. An artist who doesn't know how to be an overnight millionaire needs professional advice. Managers are ethically responsible for not only advising clients, but for protecting them from greedy leeches of all kinds, including themselves.

Robert O. asks, "What if the artist just won't consider your opinions?"

"Most manager–artist agreements are written as if the manager is the boss and the artist is the employee. That is a catastrophe waiting to happen. You need to work as equals and try really hard to reach your clients any way you can. If you can't listen to each other, both of you will suffer financially."

"But after you try everything you can and they still won't listen, then what?"

"Then it's time to move on. 'Moving on' is an important lesson for managers to learn."

"The most important clause in a manager–artist agreement is the 'out' clause," I tell Robert.

You and the artist must be able to end your association without bloodshed. Think of this as a pre-nuptial agreement. Its purpose is to protect all parties in the event that things go terribly wrong. You must think through the ugliest situation imaginable and decide how you want it handled:

How do I continue to get paid *fairly* for work that I've already done?

How will I protect my image with the public and the professional community?

How quickly can I end this working arrangement without kicking myself in the butt?

What duties will I need to continue during the transition?

Take a look at chapter 22, three Artist–Management Agreements (samples 1 and 2). Try to figure out how the artist can get out of these agreements with you. Not in *these* contracts! You, of course, can leave the artist at anytime. Sounds good, huh? This kind of contract gives the industry a bad reputation. The unfortunate message: If the manager can get away with it, he should.

Often contracts run for a year, after which the artist may leave—subject to thirty days' advance written notice, via certified mail, to everyone's attorneys, assuming all commissions are paid in full, etc.; miss one detail and the artist is screwed. Of course, the contract is automatically extended for another year, and another year under the same terms, until the artist notices that something is wrong and wants to make a change. Then, the manager pulls out the agreement and shows the artist what he signed. If it's April, and the contract was signed in February, the artist must send the thirty day notice no later than the following January for the contract to end in February (the one year anniversary of the contract). In the meanwhile, the artist is stuck and unhappy and risks the forward movement of his career because the manager knows that he wants to leave and therefore will not be concerned about his future. The manager will want to make as much money before February as possible. And if the contract says that the artist *must* listen to certain directions from the manager, and the artist refuses, the manager can sue on the basis of his income being negatively affected.

This may sound like an exaggeration, but there are abundant cases of abuse.

"One group was in Singapore for a concert," I tell Robert. "The manager told them to be on a plane to New York for a talk show right after the concert. They then had to take the first flight back (twenty-eight hours nonstop) to Singapore to make the next concert. Of course, they didn't want to do this. Who would? But contractually, the manager had them by the gonads."

I sometimes think I may sound cynical about the music management profession; there are, of course, many good-hearted, well-intentioned managers. Unfortunately, they are not trained. There are numerous training courses and degrees for specialized business fields (i.e., business administration, economics, accounting, marketing, etc.) but there are almost no courses in the specialized field of managing artists. The industry has no standards. Artist managers can be *anyone* with no ethical code or specific experience. If artists are willing to hire them, managers can be their uncle or aunt, accountant or lawyer, hairdresser or mechanic.

I know a Scrooge-like lawyer, who yells before you say hello. I've never met a more unhappy person. I've seen booking agents, managers, and artists who are miserable; some of them remind me of used car salesmen. I also know some very happy professionals who sincerely like what they do. Their happiness seems to be related to their business ethics. They have standards they live by and work by. It's not only about money. Who do you want to be? Answer that question *before* you enter the management business. You'll be too busy to think about it after.

OK—reality. If you are making commissions on the success of a megastar like Whitney Houston, and she is having trouble, do you leave when she refuses help, or do you stay with her because of the money? What is the right decision? Obviously, it's not an easy answer. I don't want to make this sound simple. Many managerial decisions are this complicated. You need to begin with a strong ethical base.

In an interview with Barbara Walters, Wayne Newton revealed the positive influence his manager had on him, early in his career. Newton was in his early twenties and already a millionaire, when his manager asked him, "What do you want to be when you grow up?" Newton was confused and asked what his manager meant by that question. The manager told him, "Every night Johnny Carson, the most powerful talk show host on TV [at that time], makes a Wayne Newton joke. Do you know him? Did you do something to him? If not, you need to tell him to stop. I hear you have a three-octave range. Why are you always singing in the upper register? I hear you play more than two-dozen instruments but we only ever see you with a ukulele. Against your size, it makes you look ridiculous. And speaking of size, when are you going to lose your baby fat?"

The first thing Newton did was call Johnny Carson and tell him to stop with the jokes, which he did. Wayne dropped out of sight for two years to create a new image. He lost his baby fat, dyed his blond hair black and grew a moustache. He changed his singing style to a lower register and showcased his ability to play multiple instruments. He turned down movie and TV deals that wouldn't showcase his instrumental talents. He became "Mr. Las Vegas," breaking records at the Frontier Casino for years. His career was given new life by the straight-shooting words from his manager. Of course, it helped that Newton was receptive to criticism.

Robert O. reminds me that he had to leave for his class. I will field calls myself for a couple of hours until he returns. Both lines ring. I check the Caller ID and pick up the one I recognize. It's one of the two booking agents I work with. Helen has a crisis.

6

Performance Contracts

Promise only what you can deliver; then deliver more than you promised.
Travel agent: I'm afraid, sir, first class is the best we can do. We don't have Diva class.

Helen is a booking agent's assistant whom I have never met. I talk to her almost every day on the phone but know little of her personal life except that her sister has just given birth to a boy. Her friendly phone voice and the ability to stay pleasant under stress have influenced how I've reacted to this agency, and the trust I feel toward it. She's only been in the job for nine months, yet she acts like a seasoned professional. I work with one other booking agency that treats everything as a crisis and reprimands its clients when they take too long to return phone calls. So I prefer to talk with Helen and her boss George.

Helen's crisis today involves a decision to accept a new $5,000 gig in Wisconsin for Jude Franklin, a thirty-three-year-old cabaret singer of moderate note with one hit single to her credit in the ten years she's been performing. Jude and I began work together six months ago after a mutual friend introduced her to me at a Christmas brunch. At the party, she was all over me, wanted to know if a manager could help her jump-start her career. After reviewing her music, watching DVDs of her shows, and discussing life in general, I decided she was a pretty together and talented lady. She has only one flaw as far as I can tell: she doesn't return phone calls promptly.

That makes Helen's crisis double trouble. I don't approve gigs without consulting the artist. It should be noted that those managers who treat their artists as employees will often dictate a performing schedule. I find that counterproductive.

The Wisconsin gig is at a major university and pays well. It also fits into the five-year plan that Jude and I have developed for her career. Unfortunately, she is scheduled to be in Sacramento the day before. The airline industry is not performer-friendly. It may not be possible to get from Sacramento to upper Wisconsin in the time available, and Jude doesn't like early flights. Also, the cost of the flight might be prohibitive.

The booking agency needs to know today because universities, just like state fairs, have their own procedures for contracts and paychecks with strict deadlines. For example, few universities pay deposits. Considering that the artist must lay out the airfare, this is risky business. Plus, we are being asked to decide without knowing the university's contractual details. This is less than ideal.

So I call up our travel agent and ask for a quick assessment of the cost and schedule. I ask myself what would I want to know before signing a performance contract and then research the answers. I would normally wait until I had those kinds of answers before calling the client. I call Jude now and leave a message and send an email, knowing that I may not hear from her anytime soon.

IMPORTANT ISSUES FOR PERFORMANCE CONTRACTS

Note: A sample booking agreement with full discussion of each of the following can be found in chapter 23.

- Fee amount; how does the artist get paid (cash, certified check, company or state check, etc.)? When does the artist get paid: 50 percent deposit two months prior to show and 50 percent just before show time?
- Any withholding taxes or deductions from this fee?
- Hotel provided? Or does it come out of artist's fee? Quality of hotel/motel? Is there food available in the hotel or nearby? Late night after the performance?
- Airfare provided? Or does it come out of artist's fee?
- Ground transportation to and from airports provided?
- Is ground transportation between hotel and concert venue provided?
- Length of show required (does the artist have a show at that length?)
- Will there be a sound check? Will the plane get the artist there in time to do a sound check?
- Is there a per diem or food allowance?
- Can merchandise be sold? Who sells it (artist or concessionaires)? How much of the income does the artist get to keep? Does the artist have someone to sell it?
- Does the venue provide liability and property insurance?
- Is there a *mutual* indemnification clause?
- For international gigs, who provides and pays for the visas?
- Is there a dressing room? Does it meet your artist's needs? Are there backstage refreshments?

- If the artist has special medical needs, are they accounted for?
- Does the contract include the entire necessary band and crew?

Before signing the agreement, has your road manager or tech consultant reviewed the technical requirements (sound and lights) with the production supervisor at the venue to be sure that someone has actually read the technical requirements in the agreement and approved them?

The travel agent calls back and describes a hellish itinerary requiring twelve hours of travel and two connecting flights (plus a two hour drive) to get from Sacramento to upper Wisconsin. Wisconsin also has withholding taxes, but that is not a concern for Jude as she is not a big enough act to draw the attention of the state tax officials—at least, not yet (for more about withholding taxes, see the following chapter). If the university tells us that they must withhold taxes, I need to know *before* the gig is accepted.

The travel alone tells me that the gig is probably not worth it. So I call Helen back and tell her to call the university and ask for another date. The idea is to save the gig without sacrificing the artist's sanity. I remind her that all other aspects of Jude's standard technical and travel needs would have to be met before we go any further. Helen isn't happy with the task but agrees to check.

Today we're lucky. The date is movable to the following week. The airline costs are reduced and I can now talk to Jude with some confidence. If she ever calls me back. The crisis is over because unless Jude has a surprise wedding to go to, I can reasonably assure the booking agency that she will accept the date. But I don't accept the date yet. I will wait for Jude's call because of Rules of Management #1 and #3.

I check the messages and emails that have come in while I was on the phone. None of them are from Jude.

I call Helen and beg/insist/whine that she must get me more time. I also tell Helen to get me some details about the payment and conditions or we're spinning wheels. Booking agents hate to lose business and promoters need artists to promote, so somehow the deadline gets extended. It always happens that way. I've rarely lost a gig because of a missed deadline—but it's only because I consider the booking agent to be a partner and we work *together* to find the best compromises and money for the artist.

The promoter is not a partner. Usually the promoter is an obstacle. He sees the artist as a commodity to be sold and the less he needs to spend and the less he needs to do for the artist, the happier he is. Promoters supply the venue for the concert and finance and design the promotion to sell tickets so that they don't lose their shirts each night. There is a lot of his money at stake. While both the risks and the potential profit are high, the promoter must be more concerned with the risks. He will not know until the last minute whether ticket sales are enough to cover the expenses. He must always be prepared for the worst.

So when an artist requires backstage refreshments, or a dressing room painted pink, or free passes for the artist's friends and family, the promoter has little patience. This is why many promoters prefer to pay more money to the artist in exchange for the artist being responsible for his own airfare, hotels, and other amenities. The trick is to make the artist think his every need is being catered to. The reality is that each concert is a major production with a million and one details requiring money to solve each problem. The promoter sees the artist as only one factor in the giant scheme of the promoter's creation. It is about his control and power and money. The "art"—the music—is the artist's "small" contribution to the big picture, so hey, let the artist worry about that.

The booking agreement is therefore the only tool that the manager has available to protect his client from the big bad promoter. I am, of course, being somewhat facetious—a good promoter is a work of art unto himself.

Many promoters believe that they are above certain rules, laws, governing contracts, verbal agreements, financial commitments, deadlines, and other obligations. A manager cannot control a promoter, especially when he won't abide by the contract, and he must be prepared to battle on behalf of an artist with every legal trick known or unknown to entertainment attorneys.

There are many different types of concert promoters. In the case of a major $80 million tour of a superstar band, the band and its management may be co-promoters of their own tour along with a corporate sponsor laying out the big bucks. The corporation wants to see its name in every ad and in each stadium and gets much of the proceeds. Not every major tour is successful. So, the corporate sponsors have their accountants put it in the company's overall promotion budget as a method to write off losses.

Going to court against a promoter is a royal pain. In general, a promoter doesn't want to pay for lawsuits and therefore will stall you and frustrate you as long as possible. Corporations can keep you in court for years because their lawyers are paid year-round whether they are in court or not. Either way, it's a pain. The manager must decide when an artist's rights are worth the trouble and the cost. The artist will often make an emotional decision, but the manager must be objective and realistic.

Everyone in the music industry has a story where the promoter didn't do what the contract said he would do. Limos didn't show up. Hotel rooms were unsatisfactory. There was no food. The required sound equipment was never rented and you were stuck with the junk that came with the house system. The artist's fee wasn't delivered. The list is never-ending.

The only helpful tool is a good, signed contract. God help the artist who has a manager who doesn't know how to write a thorough contract. Having your attorney draw up a sample agreement isn't good enough. Many institutional venues (i.e., state fairs, arenas) will rewrite your agreement and send their own rider, addendum, or complete contract to override yours. If the manager can't read and understand agreements, the client is doomed.

CONTRACT FACES AND RIDERS

Detailed contracts are available in chapters 22, 23, and 25. The basic components of any agreement are the face and the rider.

The cover page of any agreement is called the "face" and it usually includes the key elements of the deal such as where, when, who, compensation, and essential promises.

A "rider" can be any number of pages. This is where important details are spelled out, including legal items that may not affect the concert unless something goes wrong, i.e., insurance, indemnification, travel requirements, dressing rooms, contacts, technical elements, complimentary tickets, backstage refreshments, merchandising, etc.

Booking agent George

7

Taxes

If you think nobody cares, try missing a couple of payments.
Pain is inevitable. Misery is optional.

I turn my attention to Sonny Redd and the Redd Family, an old Gospel troupe, well-known for a quarter of a century, which a few years ago faced a serious state tax audit covering more than ten years of tax neglect. They performed in more than forty U.S. states during these years and never paid a penny in state taxes to any of them. This week, we were about to pay off the last of Sonny's past tax obligations.

Most people logically believe they owe taxes in their home state in addition to federal taxes. I mean, how could our government expect anyone to pay taxes to a state where he doesn't live? The problem is that U.S. states, and many countries, are poor and are always looking for new ways to earn tax dollars. They discovered in the 1980s that entertainers might be taxed as businesses. Other businesses with multi-state operations pay multi-state taxes. Why not performers?

At first, only a few states required promoters to withhold tax from the fees paid to performers. Most states tended to let performers "slide" on taxes. Entertainment brought money into the state anyway. Motto: Let's not discourage performers from working in our state. When politicians went looking for needed dollars during recessions, they rediscovered the withholding laws.

The range of withholding fees start with 2 percent of the fee all the way up to 15 percent. On a $50,000 gig, that means the performer leaves up to $7,500 in that state. That could wipe out the entire profit above salaries and expenses paid to the band.

Other countries want a piece of your performers' income as well. Canada requires 15 percent be withheld and Mexico requires 25 percent. Almost all of Europe wants to keep more than 25 percent of your fee. When possible, it is essential that your fees are paid with "no deductions of any kind, including taxes." However, this may not be doable. All of this must be calculated into your budget *before* you accept a show.

SAMPLE BUDGET BOX WITH OR WITHOUT STATE WITHHOLDING TAXES

The numbers here are totally fictional. The band gets paid a $50,000 guaranteed fee by the promoter for one concert in California.

The band is responsible for its own airfare, hotels, backstage food, ground transportation, rehearsal space, rehearsal salaries, publicity photos, tips, road manager, costume cleaning, stage props, key technicians (there may be other techies hired by the promoter), per diems, support dancers, manager's and booking agent's commissions, amortized* insurance, amortized business taxes, and amortized equipment.

Band salaries	$10,000
Staff salaries	$ 5,000
Commissions	$15,000
Travel & hotels	$12,000
Administrative (insurance, phone, etc.)	$ 1,000
Rehearsal costs & salaries	$ 4,000
Per diems	$ 1,500
Miscellaneous (tips, backstage food, photos)	$ 1,000
	$49,500
Profit	$ 500
Oops, we didn't pay our state taxes**	$ 7,500
Loss	($ 7,000)

*If a microphone costs $2,000 and is expected to be used for two years before it is replaced or breaks . . . and the band usually performs 100 times each year . . . then the cost of the microphone for each concert is $2,000 / 200 shows (100 × 2 years) = $10. This is the amortized cost of the microphone.

**All states allow you to get this money back in the same way that you as an individual might get money back from your federal income taxes. You file a tax return for *each and every state* you worked in. Now you need an accountant. It's more expensive, but pay it. Don't try this by yourself. It is a dangerous activity for a novice.

However, a manager needs to know how to find a good, creative—but law-abiding—professional accountant. The manager must also determine, based on the accountant's advice, whether the cost of filing a return in Wisconsin, for example, is worth the $100 that was withheld in that particular year. Once you file in a particular state, you will always have to file. You may not owe any money if you haven't worked there, but the state will want to know that. When your band is poor, no one cares. When your band makes good money, everyone wants a piece. Including the government.

In Canada, you can go online, find forms to request tax waivers or reductions, and file them with required support documents. Canada Revenue Agency now requires a year-end tax return too. Officials will actually answer the phone and talk to you; it's good to make friends, if you can.

American accountants will probably not help you with most foreign returns, since they are not appropriately trained to do so. In Australia, you must use an Australian accounting firm, another costly expense. Much of South America has large entrance fees, unique health concerns (check U.S. and international warnings online), and inflexible visa procedures.

How does a manager learn to deal with this? Managers must ask questions and do extensive research about travel costs, tariffs for bringing merchandise, possible union regulations, visa costs, and procedures. The concert buyer should be required to help you, but be assured, it is time-consuming, obnoxious, and sometimes expensive.

In 1995, the Redd family had been performing for twenty-five years. Before the mid-1990s, the business tax laws were not interpreted to include low- to mid-income entertainers as businesses. So no state had asked the Redd's for any tax money—until 1995. As their income rose, so did their visibility to tax officials. Sonny was not trying to cheat the system. He never knew about the new tax law interpretation that made their group a multi-state business, but as in all matters of legal concern, ignorance is no excuse.

Now let's talk about Sonny Redd and what he'd done to himself and his family. Sonny is fifty-five years old and he's been performing the gospel professionally since he was twenty as a solo act. He married a gifted gospel vocalist and they had four talented children. At the age of thirty, as he found his popularity and time away from home increasing, he included his family in the tour, paying them allowances from each concert's earnings. However, this arrangement meant that all of the tax liabilities and responsibilities were his. He alone got paid for the gigs. And then he paid his family members as their employer.

This worked out well until his children became adults. His two oldest girls married young and only sang when their busy home schedules allowed. For them, these allowances were still not a problem, since performing wasn't the newlyweds' main source of income.

But when his first son married and became the sole provider for his budding brood, Sonny averaged his son's total expected annual "allowances" and gave him a regular weekly pay-check. However, all concert earnings were still paid directly to Sonny personally, which allowed him to maintain not only financial control over the group, but also the tax responsi-bilities that go with it. Record deals, special television appearances, and additional sources of income were paid directly to Sonny and stayed in Sonny's personal bank account. No one complained because whenever any special hardship arose, he was the generous doting father he'd always been. It wasn't until this tax situation arose that he regretted the financial arrangements he'd created and never altered.

He discovered the group owed over $100,000 in combined back state taxes. He alone would have to pay any business taxes due from performances. He had distributed most of the monies to individual family members. And the rest of the family was in the clear as long as they each filed their individual state and federal taxes. He'd considered bankruptcy, but I reminded him that taxes survive bankruptcy and even death.

I wasn't the one who'd gotten him in this predicament, but if he was going to survive and continue to prosper as a performer, someone was going to have to walk him through this scary and costly mistake. A manager is a trusted advisor in all matters that may affect a career, positively or negatively. My first suggestion was that he should pray really hard, maybe sing one of his more moving gospels (smile) . . . and then we got down to work.

My accountant told us to make a chart of all the Redd Family concerts by state over the last ten years, including dates and fees paid. He should also provide copies of his tax returns and "allowances" paid to his family members. We discussed what we could do to keep the accountant's costs down to a minimum. One of Sonny's sons with a penchant for business volunteered to help. Together we set up a work schedule and completed the task within a month. This took care of the past. We wanted to avoid adding to the problem, so I began calling the tax departments of every state the Redd's would visit in the coming year to determine their liability. Since they might not owe a lot of money and would most likely get the entire amount back upon filing at the end of the year, I was able to get this year's state taxes reduced or waived completely. All I had to do was fax to each state tax department a projected budget (like the one on page 42) showing costs versus income, plus the cover page of the signed performance contract at least one month in advance. This is not always possible because some contracts do not arrive signed until weeks or days before the actual show. Still, in most cases the state tax department contacted the promoter directly (copies to me) to adjust the withholding requirement based on their assessment of our estimated profits.

Sonny was about to make his final installment to five remaining states. He had sac-rificed material things, like a new car and a 3-D television. But his honesty and his on-time payments kept him out of jail and kept him working. His family was supportive but, quite honestly, didn't really understand what trouble he was almost in. His son who helped him provides the best hope for a new financial order in the family. He is both a talented artist and an ethical businessman. A rare breed from a rare breed.

Sonny makes his own contacts, finds his own gigs, and writes his own music—all within the tight world of his religious community. He didn't need me to do the things he does. He needed me to complement his talents with my own. Even though I'm not a gospel music expert, or even a follower of his faith, we have remained strong allies and partners in business.

He and his son will visit me next week to sign tax checks. We're making a celebration of the end of these many long hard years.

The Redd Family at a gospel tent revival

8

Drugs and Rehab

Today I will not imagine what I would do if things were different. They are not different. I will make success with what material I have.
There are no Best Ways. There are only Alternatives.

I'm meeting Suzanne for lunch at the Edison Café, a New York haunt for theatre producers and tourists. It's not a classy joint, but it's notorious for deal-making and quick service. She represents Pamela, Marie, and Sandra—otherwise known as PMS—a female heavy metal group whose reputation is climbing almost as fast as the problems they're creating for themselves trying to play the "hard-boy" card. Pamela is a very responsible single mother of two toddlers. Marie is a substance abuser of any substance she can find to abuse. Sandra is the talented songwriter who threatens daily to go solo. Suzanne, their manager, is a great mediator for PMS, but some of her tactics are ones I'd never employ . . . like carrying a gun.

Suzanne, an energetic go-getter, is a super dealmaker but she doesn't "manage" their success, only their *rise* to stardom. She is responsible for taking the group from obscurity at local pubs to an independent record label, to universities, to opening for groups in the category of Guns N' Roses, Green Day, and KISS. Now she is working out a deal she wants to discuss with me. I have never helped her before, so this intrigues me.

I have a running gag with her. Instead of shaking hands or the friendly kiss on the cheek, I throw my hands in the air like I'm being held up. She only finds this funny from me. You see, Suzanne carries a pistol at every concert. Female staff and crew, a rare breed backstage, usually don't get frisked. Certainly, someone who carries herself like Suzanne, powerfully and confidently, can walk anywhere she wants without question.

To be clear, after the World Trade Center attack on September 11, 2001, security everywhere including backstage has increased. Airlines have not stopped Suzanne from traveling with her gun, which she stows in her checked luggage. Sometimes she borrows weapons from local friends instead.

For bands and their staff, security is still a joke. I guess most concert halls think rock 'n' rollers have been causing damage without bombs for decades. Only a few years after the peaceful love fest at Woodstock in 1968, The Rolling Stones, at an outdoor concert in Altamont, California, hired Hell's Angels as security at the suggestion of locals—the logic being that if they were for you, they couldn't be against you. The result was three people killed after a brawl of questionable origin. Heavy metal, rap, rave, and acid rock groups carry the reputation of drugs, sex, and violence—on-, off-, and backstage. Contracts with concert halls have gotten strict about liability and security. Bands, in return, have put the onus on the concert halls to check the audience for weapons, drugs, and alcohol—and recording devices. Both sides have done a mediocre job.

Boys and Girls High School in Brooklyn has a free summer Monday concert series where violence once broke out. In response, they hired the Fruit of Islam for their security. Women check women and men check men. Everyone gets thoroughly checked. Even nail files are confiscated and returned after the show! Everyone is polite and the process is quick and effective. Security can be done right. A manager can sometimes be ridiculed when insisting on more than ordinary security. And it will probably be at the band's cost, which is why nothing happens. At the time of this printing, security at most venues includes rifling through handbags only. There are no metal detectors and only random frisking of audience members. So this must be why Suzanne carries her gun. Right?

Wrong.

Suzanne wants to make sure that her band gets paid. That's it. She doesn't have experience with box office cheating, contract enforcement, and negotiations. Having been burned once or twice, she knows that we can't trust every promoter. And they usually won't renege on a deal if they're standing at the other end of a gun barrel. However, there are other bands that won't work with her acts because they don't want to be on stage with a "crazy gun-toting broad in the wings" (their words, not mine). It also intimidates the headlining band's crew when PMS's setup is in conflict with theirs.

Suzanne is talented, but it's true—she's crazy.

"It's just me, don't shoot," I tease her.

"Sit down you bozo," she laughs. We make small talk and order.

"Seriously, what's up?"

"I need you to keep this in confidence. I've been working on getting PMS to open with 'The Star-Spangled Banner' for an upcoming WWE match. Everything was going good, too good I guess. I found Marie OD'd in her hotel room. She's OK but she's going to be released from the hospital this afternoon, and I've got to have some plan because the other girls want something done about her. I know you've had some experience with this kind of thing before, haven't you?"

"Well, twice. Once on Broadway and once with the bass player of a now-defunct jazz trio."

"What'd you do?"

"The actor was given two choices: Go to rehab and stay clean for two months—and get your job back. Or, you're fired. [Broadway unions allow termination for verifiable drug or alcohol abuse, but they don't require you to offer options. The popular music industry has no such rules.] He went to rehab and stayed clean. The bass player's tale did not end so happily ever after. With the help of a professional, I organized an 'intervention' with him, his family, and the group led by the professional counselor. On his birthday, we invited him to the drummer's house and surprised him, not with a cake, but with an ultimatum: Get clean or get fired! He called me two days later and quit. His marriage lasted two more months and he's been in and out of jail ever since."

I continue with the most important part: "But every case is different, Suzanne. You need to consult with a professional counselor to find out what's best for Marie. But before you go through all that, do you think Marie should be replaced? Can she be replaced?"

"Yes she can be replaced, Sandra is probably the only one we can't do without. She writes their songs and plays lead guitar. She's wanted Marie out for a year now. But Pamela is a sympathetic mother—I mean the type with kids. She's got a nurturing, never-say-die spirit and wants to be supportive of Marie."

"What do you want?"

"I've lost lots of sleep because of her, but she's great on stage. I think the deeper problem is her fear of success. It's one thing if she sabotages herself, but another thing if she's doing it to the whole group. I don't think rehab will work for her, but I'm not sure the group will stay together if she's gone."

"It seems likely the group won't survive if she stays either."

"Good point. So, what do I do?"

"How fast can you replace her?"

"Not in time to sing 'The Star-Spangled Banner.'"

"So I assume then you want to help her . . . at least long enough to get through the anthem. Or is it possible to stall the anthem opening long enough to get her replacement? That seems like the ideal situation to me."

"I'm already trying to change the date we were offered and this ain't a done deal yet. I don't want to lose this."

"Either way, do you want to help Marie?"

"She's a good kid, but she's done rehab at least three times that I know of."

"So you don't need the name of an intervention counselor then?"

"It's really not my job. I get them gigs."

This is how many managers think—and they're wrong professionally, ethically, and humanely. Suzanne comes from the old school, which is no school. I learned from the theatre world, which has rules and regulations and people who seem to care about each other. Management in the theatre is a catchall. If there's no one assigned to the task, the manager must pick up the slack. "The show must go on" is the cliché, but it's true. And the manager's job is to see that no crisis, large or small, prevents the show from going on (and the money from rolling in).

Compared to the theatre industry, there's much more money in the music business to win and lose, suggesting that there is more reason to cheat, lie, steal, manipulate and, in general, abuse. The music industry can afford to provide cocaine as a fringe benefit; theatre people must buy their own. I don't know how Marie got started on drugs; obviously the other women in PMS didn't fall prey. The fact that there are drugs all around is no excuse for Marie's continued use. But it is an important element in the music professional world and it *must* be dealt with by sane, strong people who care. The question is: should managers care? And how much?

A simple answer is that any ignored crisis will lead back to the manager and wreak havoc on the manager's life, love, health, family, sleep, and finances. It would be nice to say that managers should care because they are good people, but let's be real: managers *must* care because they need to care about themselves.

The airline regulations tell us that when the oxygen masks fall, the parent should "place the mask over her own face *first*, and then assist the child" next to her. The rationale behind this is that you are no good to anyone if you die, so take care of yourself first in order to best help those around you. I think this is the best advice anyone has ever given! And it is a great rule of life—especially for people responsible for managing other people's affairs.

The truth is, I want to lecture Suzanne on her principles, and tell her that she needs to get deeply involved in solving her client's problem. But I know the gunslinger isn't about to listen to a lecture. So, I tell her what I would do under these circumstances.

"Suzanne, after contacting a counselor and meeting with the hospital, I would make some arrangements to get Marie serious help. Then I would tell Pamela and Sandra to start looking for a replacement. Marie's problem will not be solved overnight and she needs to be replaced until you know the outcome of her treatment. That may be months, years, or never. The hell with 'The Star-Spangled Banner'—cancel the gig. It will show up again, and at least you don't risk ruining PMS's future with a bad high-profile performance."

Suzanne thinks for a minute. I ask her what she plans to do.

"Don't know yet. But I'd hate to lose the anthem gig."

In a capitalistic society, priorities sometimes go haywire. Suzanne has great instincts for what moves a career. She's talented that way. Any artist prays for someone with this kind of instinct. But perhaps that's all she has. She misses the big picture. After she "makes" the career, what happens next? Where does it go? How does it last? Will it make you happy?

The most important question when making any decision about any career is, *Will it make you happy*? This refers to the artist as well as the manager. Making money is obvious. Pamela, however, has two children. If she embarks on a national publicity tour for her first album, will her family suffer? Will she be able to travel with them? Or visit them often? Or will she be so tired and moody that her family doesn't enjoy seeing her?

If PMS has great success with its first CD, will Sandra feel trapped? Her daily mantra of "I'm gonna go solo" could become a source of serious depression rather than a realized dream. And if she's not happy and tries to leave, PMS becomes another one-hit wonder. If she's not happy but stays, it might affect her songwriting and kill the second CD. Her friends and family will no doubt notice an unhappy person and Sandra's entire life may fall apart before her eyes. Is this success?

If Marie is afraid of success, as Suzanne suggests she might be, should it be thrust upon her? Will it not send her further over the edge? Someone in her condition is ripe for being ripped off by a variety of advisors and consultants. And when she learns five years later that her taxes haven't been paid because she was depending on an accountant to send in the check (being too high to do it herself), her fleeting moment of success will become a lifetime of regret.

And all three of these ladies are single. Will success make it less possible to find true love? I personally don't know anyone who isn't happier when in love.

I doubt Suzanne has ever thought about any of this for PMS or herself.

Postscript: Well, PMS performed the national anthem as expected—and did fine. Marie is still on drugs and visits a rehab center every year or so. Pamela was the first to leave the group to care for her young children. Sandra is trying to go solo with a different manager. To date, Sandra has not made an impact as a single performer, but she has written a hit for another group. Their manager Suzanne made a good living off of them for about eighteen months. (Not everyone can do well with PMS.) She has other acts and is doing fine.

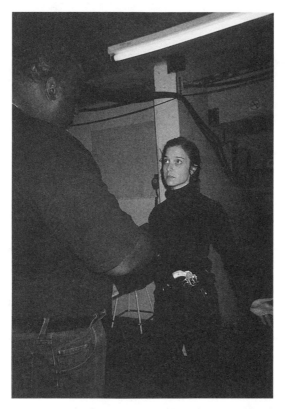

Suzanne, manager of PMS, going through security backstage

L–R: Pamela, Sandra, and Marie of PMS in concert

9

The Media and Manager

What other people think of me is none of my business.
In Billie Holiday and Lenny Bruce's time, marketing was in its infancy. Today it is an artform. Tomorrow it may be a science.

Walking back to the office, I pass a kiosk with every manner of tabloid paper and magazine. So many "news" magazines carry personalities on their covers.

A manager's responsibility, in part, is to create a demand for clients. Since it's the agent's job to get work, the manager's job must be to help make it easier for the agent to get better and more work for the client. Putting the client's name "out there" puts the client in the minds of producers, directors, fans, etc. If you're not in their face, you're out of the picture for new projects. Social networking sites cannot create a star, but they have value as a marketing tool if used correctly.

It is sometimes said that any publicity is good publicity. That's because even scandals create interest. No one wants to read bad things about themselves in the press. However, the careers of movie stars Charlie Sheen, Robert Downey, Jr., and Lindsay Lohan have not suffered from shocking news stories about sex or drugs. The reason is box office draw. Producers want sales and sales are created by converting audience awareness into dollars. But you can't make the dollars unless the awareness is there first. Hence, the value of tweeting and friending on Facebook—awareness.

You can advertise. Hollywood is notorious for large billboards. Of course, movie studios and record companies have large budgets. Rarely does an individual artist have enough money to afford an effective ad campaign. And because advertising space is increasingly expensive, producers and record companies hire press agents to develop news stories, which cost nothing. However, with every manager and company vying for the same limited gossip space, it helps to have a great "angle" for a story, or a good contact at a newspaper. When your client gets picked up for drug possession or with his genitals publicly compromised and it makes the front page, it is a godsend. Pitiful but true. You couldn't buy this kind of exposure.

A good manager must know what to do with this kind of good luck. Of course, I am being facetious, but only to a point. A great manager will create a worthy news story based on something positive about the client.

No one can control the press. However, most of the press can be managed. It's about understanding that a reporter has a job and is trying to sell entertainment in the form of a newspaper, magazine, etc. A boring article won't get printed, even if it contains all the information about your artist's next concert. There needs to be an *angle*—a controversy, a surprise, a tragedy, a piece of gossip, a secret, human-interest disclosure, a funny or ironic story. And it needs to sell product. Name recognition is worth getting good or bad publicity. The image your artist is trying to develop will either be helped or hindered by the kinds of stories that get out to the public. So someone needs to think about this before the press decides what to do on its own. This is about media manipulation—who's doin' who. If you don't give the media the direction you want, the media may give you the kind of presentation you'll regret.

But don't fool yourself into thinking that you can tell the media what to print. Each format has its own audience and age group with unique attitudes and interests. And each reporter has her own agenda. And each blogger has a different agenda and level of sophistication. You need to know who your artist is talking to. Shock jocks on radio are the most extreme case of "watch out!" that I can think of. "Morning zoo" radio programs are very popular. These DJs keep early morning commuters awake by saying and reporting shocking things. One of my artists was awoken at 6:30 AM on his home phone by a DJ who asked: "When's the last time you had sex with a little boy?" Joe, my client, had been in a deep sleep and said something irrelevant and obnoxious to the DJ. Joe was then informed that he was live on the air. You can't take back what's already been transmitted to fifty thousand listeners. Rule: never give out a performer's home phone number to any reporter. They talk to each other and may pass the information around. In Joe's case, the DJ got the number from a promoter.

Clearly, the intention of the reporter was to embarrass the artist. There's no law against that. It's just entertainment for people who like to laugh at other people's expense. And in this world, there is a large audience for this kind of humor. If there were no demand for this kind of entertainment, this type of thing wouldn't happen.

But since we know the most popular newspapers in the world are tabloids like the *National Enquirer, Star*, and *Globe*, we know the demand is high. The only way a young blogger can get fame is to make headlines and often these headlines are mean-spirited. A manager can protect an artist from this kind of journalism to the extent that he limits direct access to the artist by not giving out personal information, and that he helps keep the artist controversy-free in the artist's personal life. If the bad stuff on the artist is revealed, then the manager must do damage control and make the most of the publicity, turning the negative into the positive.

For this reason, it's essential that the manager and artist know each other well. A *bad boy* image is often good for business, but the artist must not be self-destructive. Artists that continually get caught doing drugs or other illegal things may destroy their own careers, no matter what you do for them. And the public has a limited "forgive and forget" policy. There are some things it will eventually overlook, and some it won't. As a manager, you want your artist to stay within the realm of "forgiveness" and to allow enough time for the public to "forget."

Michael Jackson waited years to release a CD after terrible unsubstantiated rumors about his personal life. But he waited, and his next CD sold millions. He was honored with star-studded support and phenomenal Nielson ratings in a 1990s television special. After being tried a second time on similar charges twelve years later, he was found not guilty on all counts. Still, he waited before launching a fifty-city tour in 2009, which (had he lived) might have been the world's most successful tour. Timing is important. Sometimes waiting is important. Sometimes no action is an action (Rule #3 of management).

Not every celebrity has had the same good fortune. Lenny Bruce was a revolutionary comic in the 1950s in his raw social satire, but because of the era and his flagrant use of drugs, his negative public image lost him support when he went up against the now-archaic laws and mores of his time. Billie Holiday was arrested, and her cabaret license was revoked, while in rehab seeking help for her addictions. In her time, both drugs and pharmaceutical treatment for addictions were both legal no-nos. Her management devised a comeback plan and must have thought that with great reviews from her performance at Carnegie Hall, her career would take off. But she was not given her cabaret license back and therefore couldn't work. Laws and mores have changed. Today, addictions and lifestyles gain performers free publicity that is not only tolerated, but celebrated. Timing is important. Today, there is television, film, the Internet, videos—not just cabarets. Today, publicity has developed into an art form to be used and abused.

PROMO PACKAGES

The media seem to enjoy working under unnecessarily tight deadlines. If your artist isn't available for the interview tomorrow, then she may lose the interview altogether. And, they need information and materials immediately. Digital photos that can be emailed instantaneously are essential, although they might only be used if the shot is exciting and appropriate for the publication's readership. Photographer credits and a clear list of names identifying those people in the photo must be noted.

Interviewers don't always know much about your artist and need background material. Biographical data and accomplishments keep the interviewer from asking stupid questions and the artist from getting angry at the stupid questions being asked.

In most cases, you won't know what the publication is going to use, so you send everything. Always be prepared should be your motto.

A collection of information and supplies frequently requested by the media is called a promo package. Luckily, this isn't a case where "more is better." Reporters don't have a lot of time to read. Write short and interesting bios. Help the reporter by providing little-known hobbies, activities, and talents that may lead to worthwhile questions. If you have a talent for writing, write your own article. You'd be surprised how many smaller newspapers with overworked staffs will quote you word for word. Provide two or three photos, horizontal and vertical. If you have the opportunity to ask, find out what format the publication wants.

Notice where you see video being used on television, blogs, and YouTube. I don't mean music videos. I'm referring to concert footage, backstage interviews, clips, and references from movies and television shows. (The *Saturday Night Live* cast performed as the Village People in the late 1970s and the group played themselves on *Married . . . with Children.*) Reviewers use video clips on the local news. Talk show hosts such as Oprah Winfrey and David Letterman introduce an artist with clips. Entertainment and paparazzi news shows like *ET, Access Hollywood,* and *TMZ* use as many clips as they can get. Some acts use video on a screen behind their live stage show. Some promoters will want to make a television commercial from quality video that you supply.

Television still asks for "B-roll footage," an industry phrase for video footage that can be legally used online and in television programming. Make sure you own the rights. (See chapter 13: *The Internet Takeover.*)

Having all your best video and audio (MP3) available on your computer is essential. You can respond immediately and send out promotional materials as quickly as the new media demands. The press and bloggers wait for no one.

I firmly believe that the next revolution in this country, following the Industrial Revolution, the Technological Revolution, and the Information Revolution, will be the Marketing Revolution. We will be able to sell absolutely anything to absolutely anyone, whether it's needed, desired, or not. The techniques are being refined every day by brilliant and perhaps devious minds. Social networking has created new opportunities, but to what result? Almost everyone is excited to learn that they have thousands of hits, tens of thousands of Facebook friends, thousands of Twitter followers—but how does this become valuable in creating or enhancing a career?

Tweeting with fans is a gift to fans. The artist gives them her time, for free—similar to signing free autographs for hours. However, these people are already fans and so no new concert tickets are sold; few, if any, non-fans will purchase songs on iTunes because of a day of tweeting. This is a challenge for the manager because social networking is extremely time consuming and the payback is not guaranteed. Networking specialists are being added to production staffs, even though none of them have extensive experience and few know why they are communicating with the public except to solidify an already fickle fan base.

On the other hand, once the entertainment industry finds a few success stories, it will expand its reach. However, it is predicted that social networking will be very different in just a few years. If your artist enjoys social networking, be happy. Its true power is still unknown, and its current popularity may fade quickly in coming years.

A manager must therefore be a marketing agent, understanding the language and tools of the media, including press representatives and advertising executives. Crisis management requires quick reaction to a fast-moving gossip machine. First, find effective messages to share with the public and then send them out using all methods of publicity— newspapers, blogs, social networking. Keep the public busy with positive stories and the negative ones may have a smaller impact.

As I am unlocking my office door, my cell phone goes off. A tabloid à la the *National Enquirer* is calling about the rumors that Rasta Rican is fighting full-blown AIDS. This is how far behind the times they are. Rasta Rican was one of my first clients to go platinum twice, but he and I parted our ways professionally last year. I react badly to the phone call. The reporter says, "We don't need your confirmation about this information. But we were wondering when you found out and how you felt about the news that Rasta Rican was going on television in two weeks to announce that he was HIV positive. His road manager is suing him for putting him at unnecessary risk of infection from a car accident two years ago involving both of them, where they each sustained open wounds."

Normally I would follow one of the management rules, "Never speak to the press," but I am so outraged (they count on that) that I scream a denial into the phone that I know Rasta well enough that had he been HIV positive, I would know. I threaten that they should check their facts before they print anything. I also tell the reporter that I think he is mean and horrible. The reporter apologizes for bothering me and hangs up.

Two things occur to me: that I should call Rasta, and that they are going to print every word I've just said. Ouch! I tell Rasta what has happened. He confirms their story. Ouch! He explains that he had planned to call me and other good friends just prior to his television interview. He had kept this quiet so that those around him would not have to lie to the press should they call. He was pretty savvy about the press.

"How long have you known you were HIV positive?"

"Five years now. I lost sleep for two years worrying 'bout that car accident, but you know I always roll with my wife. She's a physician, man. She was in the car that night. She the one first dressed our wounds. They were no big deal, but she was real careful that

Lonnie, you know, my road manager, didn't come in contact with me. I don't know why Lonnie wanna start a big stink."

"How are you feeling otherwise?"

"The first five years was rough man, but I got a new program going now with some experimental drugs that're working real good. Thanks for asking."

"How's your wife handling all this?"

"She's a rock, man. A rock."

Now I understand why Rasta turned down so much work when we were together and why he decided to take time off from the business, which eventually dissolved our working relationship.

I ask him why he's going to the press with this story. Turns out, he's advertising a new book. D'oh! As I said, Rasta Rican is a savvy guy. He wants to tell his story his way—before the press can spin its own angle. And he's hoping to create a new, lucrative career of speaking engagements based on his stories and philosophies.

Lonnie, Rasta Rican's road manager

10

Image and the Press

Action may not always bring happiness, but there is no happiness without action.
The art of prophecy is very difficult, especially with respect to the future. (Mark Twain)

Who is your target audience? I am tired of hearing young performers say "everyone." That tells me that they don't yet know who they are. Think of it another way. Who will absolutely not want to be in your audience? Who will loathe you and your music? Who will perhaps tolerate your talents but never buy them? Is there anyone who will eat, drink, sleep, and breathe because of your music?

If you can't answer these questions now, then you need to perform, perform, perform anywhere and everywhere until you figure it out. You don't need a manager until after you've figured it out. Do free gigs, talent shows, street fairs, family reunions, sweet sixteens (remember the age of most music buyers is under eighteen), and political events. You never know where you will end up. While you are in the process of determining your target audience, you will discover you have been creating an image for that audience. Selling that image (in ways other than buying ad space in newspapers, magazines, or on television and radio) is called *marketing* and *promotion*.

Lady Gaga has taken the world by storm as much by her amazing and expensive costumes as by her music. Her career is still developing, but the world is fascinated. Madonna, king and queen of self-image making, has engineered a multitude of successful and challenging impressions of her persona. She has reinvented her look over and over again: going from sexual goddess a la Marilyn Monroe, to anything-goes sex slut, to proper and pristine mother of two. Her shows upset some people and excite others. She is known for changing her public image like some people change shoes or hairstyles. And she does all of it so well and naturally that I suspect she manages herself. In her case, she needs a manager with expert administrative skills to keep up with her financial, legal, and creative needs. The duties of Madonna's administrator may vary from those generally associated with the role of manager. Lady Gaga seems to be vying to be this generation's Madonna but Madonna runs an empire—her own record company, artist development company, touring group, business operations, and more. The manager or CEO for her operations, or whatever she feels like calling her right-hand assistant, most likely has similar duties to a theatrical general manager, who is responsible for putting the theatrical producer's wishes into action and overseeing all business operations. The GM hires the accountant, lawyer, press representative, design team (lights, costumes, set, hair and make-up, choreography, etc.), and company manager (who writes the checks and payroll), and takes a hands-on approach to making a profit for the enterprise and the artist.

Madonna, of course, can afford a marketing director, a press representative, and a publicity department. Most artists can't afford any of them, yet all artists need to get their names out into the minds of their potential audiences if they are going to succeed.

A record label will provide publicity when releasing a new CD. However, there is great value to publicity and media hype even when the artist has nothing new to sell, because that publicity can help keep you in public demand. And as long as there's a demand for your music, your image, and/or your antics, then somebody's always going to find a way to supply "you" to the public with a moneymaking deal. It's basic economics.

Village People's original management in the late 1970s worked with the members themselves to create the group's famous image with the use of costumes and characters that are now icons. The mere mention to the general public of a cop, Native American, construction worker, GI, cowboy, and leatherman results in an exclamation of recognition. The choice of songs, costumes, and album covers can make or break a career. Managers can have great influence on the public's perception of their artists.

Artists' images affect the kinds of jobs they do or do not get. If they are troublemakers, many stadiums will avoid them to prevent lawsuits, damage to their property, and rising liability insurance costs. Some religious groups and conservative corporations will not hire flamboyant acts, even if they perform high-quality and absolutely fun shows. Most promoters love these groups anyway because they deliver great entertainment and sell tickets.

But the buying public is fickle. Styles change. Trends in music, like everything else, come and go. New artists take the spotlight from the old masters. If you're going to stay in the game, without joining the ranks of the oldies but goodies, you've got to keep up with the changes. Everything gets old, so an artist must reinvent, rehash, repackage, redefine, and refine her act and her music—once again, like Madonna has done. Some artists are brilliant that way—and others can learn. A manager can either choose to leave an artist when she's down, or work with her to develop a *new* direction. No one can change who the artist is. Some rappers can't sing and some singers can't rap. But if you know your client is multitalented, why not develop the whole artist so that she can branch out into new careers? The twenty-five-year-old artist may be playing a stadium now, but by the age of thirty-five she may not be able to fill a nightclub. It's always preparing for the future, not just today.

Still, if an artist is lucky enough to have had a hit song, she cannot abandon it. If an artist is lucky enough to have developed a following, she cannot abandon them. She must be true to her old image while growing up with her audience. This takes planning, reinventing and clever marketing strategies. Will Smith could have chosen to produce more rap songs, but instead he moved into television acting and then returned with a new rap CD. He then had an additional audience ready to buy it and a *fresh* image to go with it. His Grammy award for the CD *Big Willie Style* propelled his already zooming film career over the top. Smith often writes songs for the movies he stars in. Each dimension of his career has aided the next.

Images need to be exploited in order to profit from them. The more expensive approach is to buy advertising. Then you can say whatever you want. But it costs lots of money and doesn't guarantee a return on the investment. The best publicity is free. *Free* means any return is 100% profit. Free publicity is the domain of the press representative.

The press representative comes up with column items, newsworthy stories, and pictures that keep an artist or event in the public's eye. These newsworthy stories will hopefully be picked up by the press and bloggers, and don't cost the artist anything (except for the cost of the press agent). It should not be news that not everything you read in newspapers is the truth; press agents can be very creative.

My solo folk artist, a Richie Havens-type named Jake Rosby with a number of hits under his belt, was helping New York City's mayor, Michael Bloomberg, with a charity ceremony at City Hall in 2011. His press agent had made the contact with city officials and talked her way into the ceremony. Now it was up to the press agent to get some much-needed press for his upcoming concert. The agent called up her friend, a big-time columnist for one of the three major New York papers, and offered an exclusive story about what happened on the stage outside city hall between the mayor and Rosby. Let's be clear—nothing actually happened. The agent told the story that Rosby made the mayor bust a gut laughing from a joke he told. The invented joke, told to the columnist by the agent, cleverly included the place and date of Rosby's concert. The story appeared the next day in the paper.

The agent called Rosby later that day and told him what she had said. Since it was not negative, and since it was funny enough for the columnist to use it, the singer had no problems with the story. The mayor was not contacted. The agent told me that politicians always appreciate *any* positive publicity. And they understand the need for hype.

Most press agents I know are ATPAM members, but only certain theatres and institutions require union membership. The music industry has no such requirement. Theatrical press agents are most often hired on a monthly contingency. Even when there is little demand, they are available to answer questions from the media and they must keep publicity files up to date. When there is demand, they are often inundated with requests around the clock. Also when there is no demand, they are trying to create some.

The other thing that makes press agents important is their extensive email lists. New York City itself has many local papers and magazines online and/or at newsstands. However, the entire country is interested in Broadway shows. (Remember that reporters get to see the show free of charge.)

A Broadway press agent has almost a thousand media contacts to invite to see the show and write an article or review about it. Imagine the music industry—worldwide.

As a manager, I stopped keeping tabs on radio station managers and local area reporters years ago. Originally I thought these would be great contacts for the future. In some cases, not only was the reporter replaced, but also the phones were disconnected in less than a year. Do not underestimate the difficulty of keeping an up-to-date email and phone list of media contacts. Considering that many music reporters are part-time or temporarily employed, keeping track of them is an art.

So how do you reach out to the media? You reach out with a press release. The press agent knows how to correctly write one. This is important because most professional news writers will not give the time of day to any announcement presented in a non-professional format. If you want the reporter to notice your release, it better be special. The press agent's job is to make it special and to make it right. The agent also knows the person who should receive the press release.

PRESS RELEASE

The following format is not to be taken lightly. One *New York Times* reporter told me she received more than seventy press announcements daily. The first thing she notices is the format—the contact names on the upper right, the phrase "for immediate release" on the upper left, the three evenly spaced number signs # # # at the end of the release, the short length of the note, the clarity of information (hopefully with some excitement) in the all-caps headline and the most important information listed in the first paragraph. (Sometimes the publication doesn't have room for more than a few sentences and the reporter will merely "lift" the first paragraph of your release. Reporters will rarely try to write their own short blurb based on your release.) This *Times* reporter deletes the ones that aren't correct assuming that they come from non-professionals. She relies on well-written professional releases to help her get the job done quickly. It doesn't have to come from a press representative; it just has to look and read like it does. Here's an example of a press announcement about a concert at Radio City Music Hall.

For immediate release   Contact: [Press Rep Name]

212-555-1234 / fax: 212-555-1235

pressrep@promo.org

AWARD-WINNING JOHN LEGEND WON'T WANT TO BE AROUND WHEN FOLK LEGEND JAKE ROSBY TAKES THE STAGE AT RADIO CITY MUSIC HALL ON JUNE 22 AND 23.

Tickets go on sale Wednesday June 1st for Jake Rosby online and at the Radio City Music Hall box office at 10 AM. Jake Rosby will perform two nights on the world's most famous stage with no fewer than twenty-five musicians, singers, and dancers giving his fans the excitement audiences rarely find in a solo folk singer's performance. His show will include songs from his upcoming release on Jammin' Records, entitled *Folks R Us*.

Jake Rosby has sold fourteen million CDs and is best known for his four top-five hits "One," "Two," "Three," and "Four." Two of his three albums have gone platinum. He has been seen on television recently on *The Tonight Show with Jay Leno* and spent an entire hour with Oprah.

Originally from Georgia, Rosby began singing at the age of eight. He formed his own band at the age of twelve and made his first recording at age thirteen. Jammin' Records executive Johnny Smith saw the teenager performing at a street fair in Brooklyn and signed him to a deal at the age of eighteen.

Jake Rosby performs with an orchestra featuring Jack (bass guitar), Martella (drums), Felipe (keyboards), and his brother Raphael on percussion.

Tickets are $30, $70, and $140 and are available online at www@xxx or 1-888-000-0000.

Press releases are for announcements of all kinds. When a musician in a famous band died, his family wanted to make sure that the media told the life story they wanted him remembered for. If you wait for the media to call you to check facts, you'll wait a long time. Some major magazines like *Variety*, *Billboard*, and *Rolling Stone* actually call before writing obituaries. You can bet that if *Variety*, *Billboard*, and *Rolling Stone* call about you, you were *somebody* before you passed. Most papers don't call and smaller papers may not bother to list lesser-known musical artists at all. And hometown papers are often the last to know.

So the bereaved family of our musician wants an official obit. It's going to cost them the price of a press rep. There is no way to make a universal announcement without a press list of email addresses.

I knew this family didn't have the money to pay for a press agent. Because I had worked as a press rep's assistant for five different Broadway shows, I was familiar with the release format. I wrote the release/obit myself, got the family's OK, and emailed it to six key publications. The phone calls started within hours. Instead of answering a hundred questions, I was able to offer a carefully written press release to everyone who called.

The point is, as a manager, it's good to make this a part of your education. Press reps are invaluable, but in the early stages of a career, there will always be times where your job responsibilities will include press representation.

Artists are often willing to spend money trying to get their name out to the media and the public. Until the artist provides a satisfactory answer to the question *Why should the media care?*, a press agent can do very little and is a waste of money. For a beginner, this is very frustrating.

Even for a seasoned performer, a press agent can only do so much without full co-operation. If the artist is sharp and values the press, he can do miracles for his own career. In the mid-1980s, Linda Ronstadt, Kevin Kline, Rex Smith, and other name performers starred in *The Pirates of Penzance* in Central Park's outdoor Delacorte Theater (the show later moved to Broadway). The opening night audience was star-studded, but the focus of attention was on Oscar-winning film director Mike Nichols, whose date for the evening was the paparazzi's favorite celebrity pic Jackie "O" (Onassis), the former First Lady and wife of assassinated president John F. Kennedy.

When the curtain came down, everyone with an invitation rushed to the backstage party. The press photographers surrounded Jackie O, taking shots nonstop. Linda Ronstadt was the second big name that the press was awaiting. Rex Smith, a talented singer in his own right, seems to have had a plan. While the other actors went to change out of their costumes, Rex threw off his shirt (revealing a chiseled torso) and hustled over to Jackie O. The press went wild. Flash cameras blinded us all. The next day, every paper in the country carried only one photo from the opening night gala: half-nude Rex with Jackie O. I saw at least twenty newspapers and magazines that week and not one of them had a photo of Linda or Kevin. Rex saw an opportunity and seized it. What I wouldn't give to represent artists as publicity-wise as Rex Smith.

11

Artist Interviews and the Press

'Learning' is suddenly understanding something you've understood all your life, but in a new way.
The easiest way for me to grow as a person is to surround myself with people smarter than I am.

I'm surprised at how shy many artists are. It seems that the stage lights give them a license to be someone else. A good manager can provide a solid education in the art of interviewing and working an audience. Sometimes a consultant should be hired to offer training. I've found that most artists resent and resist a "business person" interfering with their personal style, *especially if they don't have one.* The manager must tread lightly. It's not easy to tell a new artist that she isn't star material—yet. It's even harder to tell her that she should spend some money on training—when she's not yet making much money. It's one of the difficult but necessary choices artists must make. This training may be the difference between a career that goes nowhere and one that succeeds. Of course, this same manager would try to use his contacts to get this training for free.

I don't know why some artists think they were born with stardom in their veins. Singers take singing lessons—even those with natural talent. Dancers, acrobats, actors, directors, designers, musicians, and models all need continued training in their primary fields and in the business of "show." The art of giving a good interview is not the same as, for example, that of skillfully playing a guitar; why would an artist expect to excel at it without preparation?

A manager can save an interview. In one case, two former clients time and time again during interviews would forget to mention the release of their new CD. One time, I was able to save the day by passing a note to the radio announcer in the midst of the on-the-air interview asking him to mention the CD after the commercial break. Although not necessarily due to this bad habit alone, these two artists now work at a hometown Hallmark store.

GOOD INTERVIEWS, BAD INTERVIEWS

It's not *all* about the artist. Interviewers have egos too. They want to write about something interesting and they want to be respected. They also have deadlines and don't have time to go fishing for the information they need. They don't see the need to do you a favor. In some towns, interviewers have little experience and sometimes no writing talent. They may distort information and take guesses instead of researching facts. In big city papers, the interviewers usually have experience and talent, and they consider the article to be a work of art in itself. The artist may be the subject matter, but for these interviewers, it's all about the writing. The concert you want to advertise is not a high priority in the writer's mind.

If you can't go with the artist to the interview, send someone responsible who has experience with the media. This person should make sure the artist is on time. Get as much of the information to the interviewer in advance as possible—including a bio with interesting facts—by phone, fax, e-mail, messenger, or carrier pigeon. Get as much information about the interviewer and the kind of newspaper, radio show, etc., as possible, preferably before you accept the interview. Teach your client good habits at interviews.

Artists should learn these good habits:
- Interviews are part of the job of being a celebrity. Take them seriously.
- The artist should have the essential facts of the event you are promoting in writing (i.e., album, concert, etc.). If possible, the artist should take written information to the interview.
- Dress for the occasion, without overdressing. It shows respect, and you never know when someone will be there with a camera.
- Answer questions with more than one word.
- Try to have an interesting story or two in mind before the interview begins.
- Be prepared to answer controversial questions. Remember the interviewer may be trying to get you to overreact.
- Bring signed photos to give to the staff, fans, and interviewers.
- Engage the interviewer in conversation about himself before the interview officially begins. What you learn about the interviewer can be very helpful and a good rapport may affect the tone of the final article or edit. However, a friendly interview does not necessarily mean a positive report.

- Invite the interviewer to the concert but never promise to take care of the tickets. Always tell the interviewer to call the road or tour manager for details. Make sure you have the road manager's business cards with a cell phone number.
- The artist should make arrangements with the management representative to end the interview on schedule, either with a secret sign language or by the clock. A thirty-minute interview should take thirty minutes, unless the artist wants it to go longer.
- Passion. If you have it for your music, the press will spend less time reporting about your personal life.
- Good interviews include wit, insight, attitude, energy, and an appearance that you enjoy being with the interviewer and being interviewed.

Artists should avoid these bad habits:
- For the purposes of advertising, the worst thing you can do is forget to sell your product (concert date, CD, band name). Not knowing your own information (What city are we in?) is just plain ignorant.
- An unflattering appearance will become an unflattering photograph.
- Never display anger toward anyone for any reason. Reporters remember lateness, rudeness, and impatience, and these qualities may be mentioned in articles now and forever.
- The worst thing you can be is boring. If the interviewer asks bad questions, be prepared to segue into your own exciting agenda.
- Bad attitude gets you nowhere and may turn a reporter against you. Everyone in the building will know about it and a bad reputation will be reported for years to come.
- It is hard to disguise dishonesty in your answers. Most reporters are trained to detect it.
- Berating your coworkers or family is more interesting to a reporter than anything positive you may say. Negative comments will end up the lead story and you will hurt the people you care about.
- Never let your guard down. Interviewers are not your friends. If you talk with them the way you talk to your friends, they will write what you say—including comments about drugs, the audience, other people's music, sex. If you don't want it in writing, don't say it.

Now for a story about the worst thing you can do in an interview. Joe Q., a prominent contemporary crooner, with a large female following, did not want anyone to know he was gay. Of course, everyone in the business knew. He was performing in Dallas and had an interview lined up with a major daily newspaper. The reporter was gay and his column had a gay bent. Joe advised the press rep to tell the reporter that he would not discuss his personal life, only his music and his opinions of the world. The reporter agreed but didn't keep his word. He tried valiantly to lure Joe out of the closet. Joe stonewalled him as best he could. The interview was deadly silent. Reporters need to fill space. So Mr. Reporter wrote an entire article about how disgusting it was for Joe to deny his sexuality. It was a boring article and the concert date and Joe's new CD were never mentioned. A total bomb.

The issue is honesty. A reporter can smell someone with something to hide. Joe Q. later officially admitted his sexuality. His career has been unaffected. His interviews are immensely improved.

Press, especially from interviews, is the first and least-expensive promotional tools. It is a great way to promote an artist's image without a performance.

12

Creating a Marketable Image

Start finding solutions.
Fake it till you make it.

Deborah Jones from Indiana entered my life a few months ago. My good friend Bruce had invited me to a cabaret showcase in New York City. Cabarets are styled after old-time speakeasies and nightclubs that used to flourish in many urban centers. Remember Billie Holiday? The cabarets that still exist in New York exhibit singers and comedians who don't require large stages or fancy technical elements. Often this is a place for a performer to invite his friends and relatives, providing the cabaret/restaurant with patrons they wouldn't otherwise get. If the performer has a friend who knows a friend who knows "someone in the industry," then maybe the audience will include an agent or manager or celebrity. I was one such person in Deborah's audience and her voice blew me away.

On the other hand, her selection of songs was only pleasant—not what one would expect from a woman in her mid-twenties—plus her look was plain, unflattering, and uninteresting. She spoke with confidence but didn't have anything to say. ("Are you enjoying yourself tonight? My next song is . . . and it was written by . . . Thank you.")

This was the only time I had been to a cabaret in over three years. It's just not enjoyable watching mediocre talent performing mediocre material. To be fair, there is an elite in the cabaret world—including Barbara Cook, Karen Mason, and Michael Feinstein—that is always worth seeing, but for the most part, the cabaret scene is made up of unemployed theatre artists putting themselves out there for various reasons. For these people, there is no profit to be made in cabaret. Again, *no profit*. The restaurant/bar makes the money off the minimum drink requirement and food. The door admission is shared by artist and bar or goes entirely to the artist. However, the cost of producing and advertising the act is rarely covered. In the case of the elite cabaret singers, there is definitely money to be made because they can charge a significant entrance fee and perform this same act in more than one cabaret over a period of time. Often they are using the cabaret to advertise and sell their CD.

Comedians operate under a different system, often performing at multiple venues in a single night for the purpose of trying out new material. At the larger comedy clubs, comedians can earn a buck if they have a following. It's all about guaranteeing the club or restaurant paying patrons. Doing a cabaret gives you the opportunity to develop your material, get over the jitters, and define your style. I suggest cabaret for solo or duo performers who are looking to get their act together *and* can afford to produce themselves. Don't forget that you have to attract an audience with announcements containing a photo, etc.

I sincerely loved Deborah's voice, but there was lots of work necessary if she was going to have a chance in the music industry. She impressed me as extremely hungry. Since she was going to have to do most of the work, that's essential for any manager to know about his client.

I wouldn't have chosen to work with Deborah except that my friend was enamored with her and he was willing to put up money to help develop her career. The truth is that we're all whores. Money talks. And I don't front money.

I wish that statement was an *absolute* for everyone in the business, but some managers fall in lust or love with their clients now and then and want to make them happy. I call it the "Pygmalion syndrome." If you can feed your client's ego, your client will fall in love or lust with you. Music is one of the most competitive industries. It's cynical and unfortunate, but artists with their own money or rich investors or industry connections have a better chance of getting somewhere than most poor slobs. Managers are good for advice and connections—not money.

DON'T FRONT MONEY . . .

If you've ever lent money to a relative, you know that in 90 percent of the cases, it ends in agony. Imagine if your income depended on it. It's not just about getting paid back; many management agreements allow the manager to take the money out of the artist's income before the artist ever sees it. It just doesn't do any good to spend your brief time together discussing a loan when you could be spending the time discussing the next step in a career.

A variation on this theme is the "advance on salary." The artist or the manager needs some cash today for bills, a car, a family emergency, whatever. This is not always a bad thing but it is a judgment call. If the request is reasonably small, and if it is only a matter of a week or so before the money is legitimately available, then what's the harm—it shows good will.

Wait, you say. If it's the artist's money in the first place, why does the manager have to approve it? Or the reverse: Why should the artist have to approve an advance on commission money that will rightfully soon be paid to the manager? Because the financial affairs of one affect the financial affairs of the other. And money woes destroy relationships.

An alternative is the bank loan. If the artist has a good credit rating, and the manager has good contacts at the bank, set up a revolving credit line. The interest is not low and there is often a substantial annual fee charged by the bank. This should discourage both manager and artist from taking the loan without careful thought. But, let's be honest, every business has cash flow problems now and then. Better to borrow from a bank than from your business partner.

Robert O., who returned early, yells into my inner office: "That corn-fed child from Indiana is waiting for you." He enjoys making fun of her look and she seems to take it in stride. Deborah enters wearing a virginal white cotton blouse and black pedal pushers with heels that made her look at least five foot five. Her bangs covered her entire forehead and her makeup is too much for daytime and not glamorous enough for night. Her face is one shade of pink while her hands and legs are pale white. She has a sweet smile and perfectly white teeth that are almost lost to her maroon lipstick. Her eye shadow, eyeliner, and eyebrows are the same brown as her box cut hair. She looks and smells like manufactured innocence. She'd be an immediate hit in the pornography industry.

Bruce has offered her $10,000 to get a CD together, a new look, a promotional package and plan—and me. It doesn't really cost that much to do these things at the level we are working, but it's good to know it's there if we need it. My deal with her is a flat fee for a period of time after which we will determine if we want to continue working together.

We have already discussed changing her repertoire of songs and she has already agreed to the suggested stage name of "Indiana." We are still looking for the best original hit songs for her first recording. She had written a few but they are not good enough for a single. For the purpose of songwriting royalties, we will try to get one or two of her originals on the CD, but only after we have a few potential hits.

Today's meeting is to discuss an overhaul of her appearance.

Nothing makes me happier than prompt people. It is insulting to keep someone waiting. No excuses (except *true* emergencies). Managers and agents, like doctors, often make clients wait for them for inordinate amounts of time. This is a rude power play and unnecessary for anyone with real power. Fashionably late or unavoidably detained is ten minutes. After that, you're rude.

BE ON TIME . . .

Celebrities can be late. Artists can be excused for lateness due to the proverbial artistic temperament. Sometimes the artist is really bad at time management, never able to anticipate how long it will take to drive from one place to another. No one likes to be kept waiting. It has nothing to do with talent or business. Any way it's rationalized, it's still rude.

Some managers keep a prospective client waiting to look busy and seem important. Sometimes they really are busy. But managers don't have artistic temperament to blame. If they apologize, they might be forgiven—once. After that, they are just rude.

"Hey, Indiana. Right on time as usual."

"Am I a star yet?" she cleverly digs in.

"Let's get to work and make it happen."

"I've been thinking about today's agenda and I've seen quite a few things I like at Saks Fifth Avenue, but it's kind of costly."

"Let's try not to spend money yet. I know a lady with a wonderful eye for fashion—Francine. She's suggested that we first peruse your closet to see if there's anything appropriate. If you don't have a problem with that, I'll call her now and she can meet you at your place."

"Well, you think? You already said you hated my clothes, my hair, and my makeup. What makes you think I have something in my closet you'll like? Do you think I'm hiding something?"

"It's not about me. It's about Francine. She works wonders."

"OK by me."

I call Francine and make an appointment for today at 4:00 PM.

I addressed her music next. "I want you to listen to two new songs I've found. See what you think. But first, let's talk about your audience and how we're going to market you to them. You can potentially sound as good as anything Streisand puts out, but she's got an adult contemporary audience. And we've already got a Streisand—not much demand for a second one. You're still young and can tap the massive teen market with the right material. Your records could compete with Britney or Rihanna and your range can match Mariah or Whitney."

"As long as I don't have to walk around half-naked."

"Sexy doesn't require nudity. We'll leave that to Francine. But can you dance? I never asked you."

"I've got some mean polka moves for you." We both laugh. "Actually I love dancing, but I've never tried any choreography. I'm used to standing at a mic and singing."

"Look at Bette Midler. She uses movement to make her songs dramatic or funny. The right moves also get a crowd excited, even if they don't look choreographed. Your cabaret show was on a tight stage so I didn't expect anything, but it always helps to do more than just stand there."

"Uh huh. I see what you mean. Do you know choreographers?"

"Yes. But first, I think we need to see what you can do naturally. If you like one of these songs, maybe you can show me what you would do to sell it on stage. Then we'll decide if an outside consultant is needed."

We need to match Indiana's look with the new sexy and explosive sounds we've decided are the best showcase for her voice. I am convinced that with her range and control, she can sing just about anything. But she needs the proper packaging to clearly delineate her audience market. Who is she singing to?

Right now, Indiana has that clean-cut, wholesome, fresh-milk-and-eggs appeal that I think could successfully vie for the kiddy birthday party market. One young woman wanted to be a pop singer so badly that she was willing to perform for toddlers. She would make up Seussical-type songs about dinosaurs and eggs and farm animals and the kids went crazy. She is now famous for these songs and rules the kiddy market in celebrity homes. She has released CDs too. Who knew?

Indiana might make loads of money and become a well-known kiddy icon too, but if she limited her instrument to this alone it would be such a loss to the world. That would be as if Streisand or Sinatra were the headline acts for toddlers and pre-schoolers alone.

Indiana wants more and I want more for her. She doesn't always agree with my vision, but it is key to her development that she consider every option.

You don't need a manager until after you've figured all of this out yourself. Deborah is paying for my opinions and for a makeover. She might have spent her money learning to develop her image and presentation on her own. But she opted for my sources and services which I would not normally be inclined to offer to a young incomplete performer. And even with a manager's advice, there are still no guarantees.

When I first explained to Deborah what I expected an artist to know before I felt right working with her, she chimed, "No one can figure that out by the age of twenty-five."

"Wrong. That's what separates the stars from the wannabes."

There are so many talented singers, but not all of them can be superstars in the recording world. Many bands spend decades playing to local crowds for small change. When someone at a record company takes notice, it is because they have developed an image, a sound and a following that work in sync with each other. Some artists' marketing instincts are phenomenal. They are the ones you want to manage because they bring tremendous potential to the table. Managers, contrary to what some managers claim, cannot create careers or stars by themselves. Artists create their own careers. Managers make the most of them.

When I hear friends bad-mouth some recording diva, I always correct them. It takes clarity and self-awareness to be an enduring talent. I bow to a diva's success even when I don't like her music.

Indiana must overcome her desire to be an overnight sensation. She must learn to enjoy the process because for most people, that's all they'll have. Some people become "overnight" successes after thirty years of "enjoying the process." Some never do. But if you truly enjoy what you're doing, then it's not *work*. So if it takes you a lifetime to get a hit, or if you never get a hit, unlike most people, you will have had a happy life without ever *working* at all.

"My plan," she offers, "is to have my first hit single by the age of twenty-seven. Do you think it's possible?"

"Ouch. We've all made the mistake of setting age deadlines for careers. It is possible but it usually doesn't work that way. Why aim for twenty-seven? You could have a hit this year, or maybe in five years. It's all one long process with interruptions. Do you plan to quit at age twenty-eight if you don't have a hit CD by twenty-seven?"

She laughed. "No. Maybe. I don't know."

"Well, I don't know either so let's not dwell on this. I made the same kind of promises to myself at your age, but I never could have guessed that I'd be managing musical groups. It's better to decide on a plan of action and just keep going."

13

The Internet Takeover

It's what you know and who you know.
The music business is a cruel and shallow money trench, a long plastic hallway where thieves and pimps run free and good men die like dogs. There's also a negative side.

By the time you read this, everything in this chapter may be obsolete. But as of 2012, the Internet has changed the face, body, and soul of the music industry (and a lot of other industries).

Today I am being interviewed by a major media blogger known as Big Wayne, who is interested in comparing the music business before and after the creation of the Internet. Normally I won't talk with the Press (management rule #5) but since it's not about my clients, and I think he's serious about the subject matter, I'm making an exception.

Because I'm working on a trip to Brazil today, the first thing that comes to mind is the vast improvement in communicating with international promoters and travel, including passports and personal data shared with foreign bureaus that process working visas. In the past, this required a trip to the closest embassy with the actual passports and many other documents, mailed overnight back and forth between promoter and artist management. But today, passports can be scanned so that they can be emailed directly to the promoter for processing, along with documents and personal data required by the foreign embassies.

But I'm getting ahead of myself. Big Wayne asks first for a little history: Just after the turn of the 21st century, Napster, a noncommercial website, allowed music to be heard and copied free of charge by anyone with an MP3 player. The music industry went into an uproar because no royalties were being paid to songwriters, record labels, or artists. When sued by the major record labels, Napster's defense was that it was no different than inviting friends, say in the 1970s, to your home to listen to your private collection of LPs and allowing them to copy their favorites onto music cassettes to take home. It was technically illegal then too, but no one made a stink.

Variety, a daily entertainment business publication, reported in its February 25, 2002 edition that record-label-sponsored websites (i.e. Pressplay and MusicNet) were trying to compete with Napster, but had more restrictions. The Recording Industry Association of America (RIAA) took other alternative sites like Morpheus, Kazaa, and Grokster to court. None of these websites exist today.

Managers need to realize that today's technology and sales methods may not be available to artists next year. Long-term planning becomes almost impossible, so the basics (good promotion, good music, careful financial planning, and strong contacts) are still the most important part of an artist's career.

Internet access and digital recordings created a significant loss of CD sales, which signaled a revolution in the music business. Perhaps the most significant change in the strategy for making money for your artist and yourself is the emphasis between recordings and performance income. Before, a business plan had the artist go out on tour to promote the sales of CDs, which brought in more income than the concerts. Now, live performances earn more money for artists than royalties from recordings. CDs are now being used to promote concert tours. To be fair, if you have a multi-platinum hit, you can still earn a pretty penny from royalties, but that is not the usual situation for most CDs.

Big Wayne is particularly interested in the industry's new revenue generating entities like Sound Exchange and Alliance of Artists and Recording Companies (AARC) that pay royalties directly to the artists. Royalties paid for radio, television, and jukebox air play are collected by the American Society of Composers, Authors and Publishers (ASCAP), Broadcast Music, Inc. (BMI), or the Society of European Stage Authors and Composers (SESAC) who then pay out royalties to publishers and songwriters. Record companies receive income from album/CD/MP3 sales, and then pay out royalties to producers and artists. Performers' income from record companies rely on the accuracy of their accounting departments, assuming a neo-CPA with a $400/week paycheck can understand and follow the intricate contracts that often baffle accountants, CEOs, and nonindustry attorneys and are usually beyond the artists' comprehension.

To be fair, it's not that the performers don't make money; some make a fortune. But it is almost impossible to know if the calculations are complete and accurate without an audit. Some artists from the 1950s and 1960s actually made no royalty monies from their recordings and went to court decades later. The courts decided these performers were due money and the industry looked for a new way to protect artists.

In 2005, Congress finally enacted a law which created new music royalty collection agencies specifically to channel digital format and air play monies directly to the performers. Every artist whose music is broadcast should sign up with both Sound Exchange (satellite and Internet radio, cable TV music channels, other streaming sound recordings) and AARC (private home taping devices and rentals) to directly tap another previously unavailable source of income from domestic and international royalties. Your royalties will be collected whether you sign up or not, but the money won't be released to you unless you're registered with them and you can prove who you are.

Big Wayne asks how this will affect BoyBand if the unsubstantiated rumors about Preston leaving BoyBand to go solo are true.

Ignoring his blatant attempt to get some client gossip out of me, I answer that these new well-intended royalty organizations are still waiting for the laws to catch up with some questions, i.e. if BoyBand applies to Sound Exchange as five individuals, what is the correct way to split the royalties among them if they disagree? Do lead singers deserve more than the others? Imagine how murky this gets if a song has been recorded more than once by different group members, or replacement members, over time. Sound Exchange is not able to distinguish who performed on a particular version of the work without being told by the artist or their legal representative. Nevertheless, these agencies are a major breakthrough for artists in the digital age.

"So when do you think Preston is going to announce his departure from the group?" Big Wayne sneaks into the conversation. I remind him that we agreed to leave all client discussions out of this interview. And we move on, noting that a successful blog is very different from a successful website.

The Internet is primarily an audio-visual instrument. Website designers need to remember this when developing a format. The truth is that people and the press don't read long passages of information. We need to be entertained by websites in short, perky, provocative presentations. There are so many websites; what will bring me to yours and what will make me take notice once I'm there? Ironically, this is the same basic question for your music: How will I hear about it and why will I want to buy it?

Because of the Internet, an artist doesn't need a record label to produce or distribute music. Music sales websites like iTunes and Rhapsody can list your music, but it doesn't mean anyone will buy it, or even know about it! If you, the artist, independently produce yourself, the promotional costs and more will be paid by you. You will need your own money to move forward, along with much creative aggressiveness.

This is where the word "hits" can mean success or failure. The word "hit" means more than just a successful recording. It is also a documentation of the number of times people visit your work on the Internet. Record labels consider the big "hitters" as having a potentially large fan base which translates into possible sales. But remember your video/song has to appeal to the record label executives whose tastes have often been questionable.

So what about all of the unknowns who were discovered by the Internet? We have a new mechanism, but just because we have it, that doesn't mean it will work for you. Let's start the discussion with the case of Justin Bieber.

His mother was possibly his biggest fan and uploaded a video of Justin singing on YouTube. Care to venture a guess how many enthusiastic mothers have made videos of their children and used YouTube thinking it will launch their nascent careers? Why did Bieber's career blow up, while a million other children's talents remain ignored?

First, an objective someone needs to recognize an extraordinary "X" factor in mommy's little darling. Usher and L.A. Reid decided that Justin Bieber was worth an investment of time and money. They financed his transition from the basement to the concert stage, hiring staff and using their own professional experience to make him a star. The Internet and his mother certainly deserve credit, but the real story of his success began when the professionals took over. The Internet is a wonderful discovery and promotional tool, but in and of itself is no reason to quit your day job . . . prematurely.

Susan Boyle auditioned for *Britain's Got Talent*, a popular TV reality contest in the U.K., and blew the judges and the audience away. YouTube presented her audition and the word spread worldwide, leading to a spectacular recording career. The judges and her new professional staff and financiers remade her, packaged her and promoted her in a way that allowed her amazing and natural talent to shine. Until the professionals got involved, she was living an unremarkable life. The Internet did not make her; it was a terrific marketing vehicle.

Whether you are seeking a record label or not, a lot of hits don't necessarily translate into income. There has to be multiple and easily accessible ways for fans to buy your work. As before the Internet existed, marketing and distribution are the key elements to monetary success. Before, worldwide distribution was only available through major record labels. Now many ex-label and marketing employees have started their own Internet companies to help individual artists market and distribute their music through digital channels—for a fee, of course.

Don't fool yourself; you can't be "in it to win it" without your own cash and without professional connections. Few independent record labels can afford to pay advances to the artist, but they expect artists to cover the label's expenses. The music world has turned upside down.

In the past, the major record labels would lay out the money for touring and backline (musicians, costumes, backup singers, gratuities for sharing the major artists' crew, etc.) so unknown performers could open for major artists and receive exposure. The "unknowns" reimbursed their record labels who deducted those expenses from their future royalties. Today, the reason you won't see "unknowns" opening for major artists is because they have to front their own expenses. And when venues hire a major act to perform, they rarely have any money left over to hire opening acts. So new artists are screwed. New artists must create their own buzz so that they can attract their own audience and build their own fanbase.

It sounds bleak. Keep reading; for the moment it's going to look even bleaker. Google and other search engines can be paid to position your website's listing at the top, but who's looking for you? You can e-blast friends, family, and associates through Facebook, Twitter, and the like to let them know about your newest music, but there's no income from any of this.

So you direct your audience to your website or your YouTube video, with production expenses paid out of your own pocket, in the hope that your "fans" will purchase your music.

Either way, in this digital era the developing artist must have cash in the bank to move ahead without the help of a record label. The professional artwork used in connection with your song costs money, and the shipping and handling charges will also come out of your sales. You want to look professional at all costs, don't you? If you are printing hardcopies of your music on CD or other format for DJ use, mailings, or Amazon sales, you must decide how many you want to pay for so you won't wind up with a pile of CDs stored in your basement; that's wasted money. You can hire a professional promoter whose job is to "sell" your music to radio stations and club DJs, if he likes your music and if you have a few thousand dollars. The DJs will want various mixes of your music, preferably mixed by the best sound engineers/producers you can afford. Each mix could cost you thousands. The money you spend at clubs, concerts, and parties to network with professionals is a key element to success.

If you have no money, you can hope that one of the four big record labels sees you on YouTube, signs you, and does all of this for you. It is hoped that supreme talent will always find success, but we know that it's often one-in-a-million that is signed to a corporate deal. And a record label will deduct all of the above expenses, and more, from your royalties.

As a business strategy, many artists create their own record labels at great legal cost. These labels have no cash and usually can't help anyone with promotions. Running a label effectively is a full-time job. If an artist is not also talented in business, then this is probably a waste of money and time. It is easy to spend money and feel like you've accomplished something, but spending money unwisely assures a longer road.

Computer programs have replaced expensive equipment in recording studios, but expertise is often still missing and a talented engineer is worth a million dollars. This affords the artist and neo-producer the ability to experiment and to develop a song until they think it's ready.

Music videos are essential for introducing a new artist. Nowadays, the artist can experiment with creating his own videos on his home computer. However, he won't get a second chance to make a first impression, so a mediocre amateur video should not be uploaded. There are no shortcuts; new technology is amazing but he's better off saving his ducats and working with professionals who will ensure his work is professional grade.

From the manager's perspective, a good song must be critiqued by its ability to be sold in the marketplace. Selling the song is actually much more difficult than writing and producing the song. Radio stations are not easily accessible to anyone but major labels.

For a famous act, managers trying to protect their artists' work can hire the "Internet police" to prevent the unauthorized use of their clients' artistic property on YouTube, etc. This protects the original songwriters, producers, and artists. You can give permission and the "police" will put a watermark (similar to embossed stationery) under the video image. Big Wayne admits that he has never heard of the "police" but I explain that he can Google "Internet police" for more information.

Big Wayne thanks me and tells me to expect his interview to be online the next day. Preston emails me the next morning "LOL" and the link to the blog which is an intelligent discussion about Internet resources and includes only one quote from me: "The Internet has turned the music world upside down." Big Wayne ends the blog with the line "Preston's manager did not substantiate his BoyBand defection or his rumored sexuality." Despite his "LOL" comment, I know Preston is not really laughing.

Administratively, there is much more to discuss about computers, files, and the web. This is not very interesting to the general public and it is not unique to the music industry. Except that losing music files and press e-kits can be catastrophic for you. Electronic banking and purchases put you and your business at great risk.

There are "virtual" protections from hard-drive crashes, fires, and theft through Quickbooks Online (versus desktop Quickbooks) and Carbonite (computer file storage as low as $50 per year). Be resourceful and never stop researching ways to protect yourself and your artist.

The Internet and computers represent a new danger in the music world as well as an opportunity. Technology created a new world order; it is impossible to predict where it will end.

14

Demos and Material

A day is wasted without laughter.
Never sign anything written by an attorney.

What I've noticed about Indiana is her healthy sense of humor. That's what helped us to find her new stage name. It also guided me toward the kind of songs that may work for her. She has a naturally dramatic flare and her innocence is authentic. Too bad. She might need protection from the big bad wolves of the music world.

As a manager, I consider it my responsibility to teach my clients about business. If nothing else, it helps them to know when management is taking advantage of them. One client of mine, before coming to me, lost her home because of an unscrupulous lawyer who billed her for a monthly retainer of $5,000 and only processed one small legal document in over four years. Her former manager once told me that his responsibility ended when the client got paid. And now we understand Enron. . .

Deborah Jones has the good fortune to have parents who taught her about finances. Her father is a CPA and her mother is a corporate lawyer. Not quite the down-home farm roots I originally thought I was dealing with. Her parents sent her to school for business but supported her private singing lessons and her career decision. It was their $950 that paid for the cabaret show. And now our mutual friend is paying for her career development. We should all be so fortunate.

"Who's your accountant?" I ask.

"My dad. Why?"

"Does he know anything about the arts?"

"I don't think so."

"Well, ask him. You see, there are unique entertainment laws in New York and California as well as special tax benefits and liabilities for being in the entertainment business in each state."

Without disclosing the identity of my other client, Sonny Redd, I tell her about his problems with state taxes. I also explain that entertainers potentially have more deductions than priests do.

"Don't forget to use your financial knowledge and don't rely on your Dad or any other consultant. Always insist on signing every check and reviewing every financial and legal document. If you don't understand something, ask your Dad or your Mom—or me. Let's get your career off on a good footing. Which leads me to your arrangement with our mutual friend, your benefactor. What does he expect in return for his investment in your career?"

"Nothing."

"Are you sure? Do you have anything in writing that says it's a gift?"

"No. But he's told me so."

"I don't mean to pry, but are the two of you in a relationship?"

"If you mean do I spank him—well, I have, but not nightly." She smiles coyly.

"Would you feel comfortable asking him or having me ask him about putting something in writing?"

"Sure. But is it necessary? We're great friends. You know Bruce, he's a great guy."

"Yes he is. But let's make sure that we all remain great friends forever. Contracts are about what happens when good things fall apart, not about what happens when everyone is happy."

"I don't want to insult him. Is this about protecting your fee?"

"I already have a written agreement with you. Our agreement says I get paid by you. Whether the money comes from your parents, your own bank account, or a boyfriend, doesn't affect me. Your happiness will affect the way you work on your career and therefore will affect me. That's what I'd like to protect. If he's on the up-and-up, as honest as I know he is, he will have no problem with a written agreement."

"Well, I'd prefer not to ask him. If you want to, it's OK with me."

"You'll have to be here with us when we discuss it."

"Why?"

"Because your career is *your* career, not mine. If you want to turn a blind eye to the business side of things, then you deserve what you get. I can't protect you if you don't want to even know what's going on in your financial life. What are you willing to give him for $10,000—other than an occasional spanking?"

"I thought you didn't mean to pry . . . "

"You're not as innocent as you act. Neither is Bruce."

"Well, I think it's just a gift."

"That's great. Let's hope so. If not . . . ?"

"What can I give him?"

"A piece of your career . . . for a limited time. Maybe just a return on his 'loan.' We'll have to ask him. Doris Day . . . do you know who she is?"

"Of course. I do her song *Que Sera, Sera* in my act."

Of course. Now how did I forget that?

"Her loving husband disappeared one day with all of her money. She trusted him with almost everything she had. That great guy gave her a spanking to remember. We all learn too late. In the words of Joan Rivers, *grow up*! There are lots of similar stories all over the entertainment biz. My job is to prevent you from becoming a victim. Work with me, not against me."

"Yes, Daddy," she coos.

"Don't make me spank you," I threaten. Then we laugh. "Now that that's out of the way, let's listen to these songs. Both songs were submitted by Karl Milton, a writer-producer out of Minnesota. He's the one singing in the demos. He has a great voice and has had two of his own hits over the past ten years. Ironically, this is a good track record for a pop/R&B composer."

Indiana wasn't moved by either number. She couldn't hear herself singing them.

It is sometimes difficult to get past the gender of a demo voice. The key is oriented to his male voice and the arrangement and interpretation are macho. However I can hear Indiana's voice on it, making it all her own. I ask her to take it home and let it grow on her. Some of her reaction is based on her old way of choosing material—sweet and cheerful. I am looking to bring out the strong "I am woman, hear me roar" side of her personality.

I send her home to muse over the new songs and to prepare for Francine. Robert O. tells her he hopes she will butch up. Walking out the door, she says, "I'll butch up if you will." I am hoping this is a good sign that Deborah is finding her roar.

After she leaves, I admit to myself that Karl Milton's demo is not as good as it could've been. So I understand her hesitation and am reminded of a story that was relayed to me once by a writer friend of mine. She was in a car with a lot of old songwriters who were explaining the songwriting process to her. This is how she related the story:

"One old guy, the driver, asked me in a raspy voice, 'Y'ever hear of Joe Breedlove?'

"I told him no.

"The guy sitting next to him demanded, 'You ain't never heard of Joe Breedlove?'

"I told him, 'I'm sorry, but no.'

"I was sitting in the back sandwiched between two other elder songwriters and the gentleman on my right proceeded to explain. 'The way songwriting used to be done back when we were doing it was you wrote a song and you got someone to sing it, see, and then you put it on a demo and you send it off to the person you hoped would record it. Then if they listened to it and if they liked it, they would put it in their own style and you would have yourself a record.'

"The gentleman on my left chimed in, 'Now back when we was writing, when they was calling Elvis Presley "The King," ever'body in the business wanted t'write a song for him. 'Cause now we knew if he recorded a song, we be set for life. We wouldn' never have t'write 'nother song. So ever'body want t'write for Elvis.'

"Then the driver explained, 'And ever'body in the bi'ness know that if you wanted Elvis t'seriously think 'bout what you done wrote, you got t'git Joe Breedlove t'sing that demo.'

"And the front passenger excitedly interrupted, 'Tha's right, 'cause if Joe Breedlove wasn't singing it, Elvis wasn't even goin' t'listen to it. Elvis didn't take a song by Joe Breedlove and make it his own, that boy was trying t'sing it like Joe Breedlove.'

"Then the driver took back the conversation by adding, 'And he wasn't jus' trying t'sound like him neither, he was always tryin' t'git his moves. That Elvis was really tryin t'*be* Joe Breedlove!'

"In the backseat on my right, the gentleman continued, 'Now the pitiful thing about all this is that everybody recorded him for the demos, but Joe Breedlove couldn't get a recording contract for himself. I believe that's what killed him.'

"The guy on the left said, 'Yeah 'cause that man was a baby when he died. He wasn't sixty I don't think.'

"The driver ended with, 'Ever'body in the bi'ness knowed it at the time. Mos' people in the bi'ness don't know it no mo', and ain't nobody outside the business ever know it. You wanna write you a story? You need to write this . . . leastwise somebody do. If they don't, it's gonna die with us.'

I can't verify the truth behind a word of this, except that these were reputable and successful songwriters and I trust the friend who told this to me.

The big difference in demos these days is twofold. Unless you're personally connected with a famous singer, it's almost impossible to get your demo to him directly. Singers have agents, managers, and personal assistants who intercept unsolicited letters, etc. Their lawyers warn them about listening to anyone's CD because they can be sued later on if a composer thinks that someone plagiarized the song. Also, there's only so much time in a day, and believe it or not, celebrity artists can receive hundreds of demos. Most get their songs from people they know or work with at labels, publishing companies, and agencies. Or they write them themselves.

The second big difference is in the quality. I listened to an early demo of Dionne Warwick singing an early Burt Bacharach song. Piano, bass, and drums with a voice are not acceptable anymore. In early decades of pop and rock 'n' roll, artists chose a song to record. Now, a CD may be more production than melody. Producers win Grammys because the song is really a compilation of sampling, rapping, and rhythm, much like a special effects movie relies heavily on the effects and sublimates character and plot. That is why there are separate Best Song and Best Record categories at the Grammys. One represents melody and words. The other represents what the producer, artist, engineer, and arranger did with the song.

Because of the technical revolution in computer multi-track recording programs and sound equipment, demos *must* be finished products. They must be ready to release to the public and be absolutely finished when presented to a recording label. Labels have no time and often no money to risk on demos that may need more work. The label wants to hear what they are going to sell before they sign an agreement. If it's hot, a label may sign the producer, songwriter, and artist. Otherwise, it may sign only one or two of the people responsible for the recording, possibly leaving the others out of future ventures. This is why it's so important for "friends" working on a demo to have an understanding (written agreement) between them before submitting material to a label. This is another way a good manager can protect his clients' interests.

This doesn't mean that a music publisher or label won't hear your demo and pass it on to another artist to remake. But now you want to create the saleable product, not just the raw idea that used to be known as a demo.

Computer recording programs and additional equipment can cost a pretty penny and few people receive a return on this investment, if you don't count personal enjoyment. At least home recording equipment, which used to cost $30,000 or more, is a thing of the past.

Five young associates bought their home analog studio months before the digital revolution took over. The difference between analog and digital is the scratchiness of a vinyl record versus the perfect clarity of a CD. These five may have just as well thrown their money out of the window. They can still record for their own enjoyment, but no one's going to buy it.

I suggest for the home market any one of a number of self-contained four, eight, or more track digital studio units that let you experiment for less than $1,500. If you end up with a song that everyone loves, spend the money and hire an engineer who works for a professional studio and do it right.

Most A&R people, the ones at the first tier of decision-making for labels, receive massive numbers of CDs each week and admit to listening to five. The rest get thrown away. The process of getting heard is the second biggest hurdle; the first is creating a CD worth listening to. All artists I know think they have a hit. A few months later, after a little time and perspective, and after their friends have shown less than overwhelming enthusiasm, most will put the CD away in their drawer and move on. Some will have spent $1,500 producing a thousand CDs with cover art, copyright registration, and mailings to labels that don't accept unsolicited work.

Case in point: after the World Trade Center attacks in September 2001, six different composers known personally to me each produced their own new patriotic music. They all thought they were the first, the best, and, in one case, the only one to think of the idea. Imagine how many submissions from renowned composers made it to record labels. Why would a label need anything from someone new? Because it's a great song? The business does not revolve around quality or talent . . . but that's another chapter.

I take a cab over to Indiana's because she is on the other side of town. On my way over, I pass a novelty store with long colorful boas and glistening glass and plastic baubles and beads of a wide variety. I make a mental note to discuss with Francine whether any of this would work for the new Indiana.

I get there about 4:30 PM. I didn't need to be there during the elimination process, I just want to see the fruits of their labor.

Everything in her closets, dresser drawers, storage boxes, and bags must have been explored. I am pleasantly surprised to see one or two bright, slinky gowns, some spandex, a long colorful boa and more than a few beaded baubles. Francine has literally "outed" Indiana from her closet.

"Oh boy, can you believe *this*!" Francine rushes over to me with a gold lame gown draped over one arm and a pair of thinly strapped stilettos in her hands. "I mean look at this girl...who'd a thunk it!"

"Indiana, will you never cease to amaze me." I quip.

"So what's the deal?" Francine asks me. "She looks pretty well stocked to me."

"Well I'm no expert, but she looks pretty well set to me, too—if that's the direction we agree to follow. Step one is getting her in these things and seeing what it says to us. I'm serious Indy, do you ever wear this stuff?"

She gives one of her perky-but-shy-blushes and explains, "Once upon a time, I thought this was the type of stuff I'd need on stage. I wore the boa in a high school musical. My friends each gave me a different opinion, but the one thing they all seemed to agree on was that these things were all passé. They said I needed to look extreme, either urban-hip or its opposite. I tried urban-chic because that's so far removed from who I am. The songs I was singing didn't go with that look. Also I don't want to do anything I would feel uncomfortable inviting my parents to see. That's why my cabaret act is like it is."

"Well let's get you into all of this and see what happens."

Francine remarks that nothing is going to work if we don't change her hairdo first. I remind her that we aren't making major decisions today, only exploring. I once saw Cyndi Lauper backstage at a television taping. Her outfit offended me but once she was on stage, it was gorgeous. I was mesmerized not only by her performance but by her costume. And that's what clothes are on stage—costumes. Colors that don't match often look perfectly sane under lights designed to bring out the flash. I'm not a fashion expert nor am I a cultural guru, so I leave these kinds of decisions to someone like Francine during the interim. In the end, my opinion matters, but the artist must feel comfortable. This will not be a five-minute makeover.

She looks good in a few things—enough to introduce her to her public without spending large bankrolls of cash. Today's hot look is still urban-chic and she has the voice to sell to an urban market. She doesn't have a model's thin body or an athlete's tight one, so the Christina Aguilera look is out. The gowns are kicking when worn with boots. Francine suggests slacks with vests and a bowtie or necktie without the shirt. For now Indiana's hair is pushed and pulled into a variety of upsweeps with wisps framing her face and neck. Long strands of pearls or colorful beads adorn two different solid black outfits. Nothing is perfect, but it is a vast improvement over her cabaret look. Francine likes the black outfits. I want more color.

The only thing she'll have to spend real money on is the makeup. I am clueless in this department but Francine says "Trust me," and I do.

Indiana's sense of humor and her body type suggest more the direction of a Cyndi Lauper or Grace Slick than Britney Spears or Janet Jackson. I know Francine's mind is whirling so we adjourn for the day. Francine and I will discuss this privately without Indiana. I need to find the right songs before we solidify the look.

I take the subway to midtown to visit Marjorie, a marketing consultant for Broadway who has helped me with many Broadway shows while I was in the theatre. She comes up with ways to target specific audiences. On Broadway shows, she charges an up-front fee of more than $30,000, plus a weekly fee of $1,000 or more. My clients are not the same as a Broadway show, but someone with her experience and contacts can be immensely helpful in my opinion. Her payment from my client will not be anywhere near that of a Broadway show. Her fee is relative to the product being marketed. Broadway shows can cost millions of dollars to produce with weekly expenses of over half a million dollars.

Since Indiana has some money to spend from Bruce's $10,000, I am exploring the most productive way for her to use it for maximum results. Marjorie is intrigued by the idea of working with a budding recording artist and, because of our friendship, willing to discuss a token fee. The goal, I propose, is to get her noticed by as many recording bureaucrats as possible. In some way I am putting the cart before the horse. We don't have a CD ready and we haven't defined her stage style. Still I think I can develop some ideas with Marjorie for any number of my clients while we are focusing on Indiana. And it always helps to begin the marketing process early. Nothing will be decided today.

Marjorie feels she will be most helpful in designing a unique introductory package for recording executives. When it comes time to present Indiana on stage, she can approach stores or products that might sponsor her because of some tie-in to her show or image. We need an image first. She also thinks that a store appearance might create some hubbub, and a benefit appearance with a high-profile fundraising event would give her some credibility, exposure, and some word-of-mouth promotion.

Marketing people think of everything. Not everything is good. That's where managers come in. Marjorie has just worked a deal with the American Association of Retired People (AARP). In exchange for some volunteer work she gave them, they gave her some free magazine advertising space. The magazine goes to millions of people fifty and older who are not Indiana's key targeted market; it's not a very direct way to get to the industry professionals that we want to attract. I suggest that we use the free ad space for another one of my clients. She says fine as long as she is hired to work on that account.

It's important not to sweat the small stuff when dealing with marketing ideas. Many marketing executives like to look busy in front of their bosses and clients. They create clever ways of getting information out to the public, but some projects take too much energy to produce. Spending twenty-eight man hours to put together a window display at a local department store advertising hip-hop music in some remote location that caters to a Lawrence

Welk buying public is a waste of time. I believe a project must reach large numbers of people or why bother? The marketing project's effectiveness should be measurable. In this day of computer analysis, managers must be computer literate and analysis-minded. Details matter. Time-burning projects that don't produce results are stupid.

Most of my other clients don't believe in marketing consultants. Actually coming up with marketing ideas is another one of the manager's responsibilities. But there are times when a manager needs specialized help. Indiana could use that help.

Also, those artists that have a label know that the label has its own marketing people. The marketing person's loyalty belongs to the label in these cases and I always think the artist gets the short end of the stick. That's why I like private marketing help.

I thank Marjorie for her gratis input and tell her that I will let her know if Indiana is agreeable to hiring her. I go back to the office. It's just after 6:00 PM.

Robert O. has left. I unlock the door and analyze the day. I have not spent a minute on my most important and lucrative performer, Don Juan.

Deborah Jones a.k.a. Indiana

15

Managing a Star

If you're not living on the edge, you're taking up too much space.
If everything seems to be going well, you have obviously overlooked something.

Don Juan, a big star for two years after ten years of fighting his way up from the bottom, has been able to use the Latin crossover craze symbolized by Ricky Martin and Enrique Iglesias to sell over eight million CDs in only four years. Thirty-two years old, he was first noticed in the tough underground Latino clubs for his loose-limbed comedic parodies of the most popular local break-dancers, many of whom were gang members. He was considered fearless and daring for this reason. He made the dancers laugh at themselves in spite of themselves, and so bridged a major gap. The girls loved him too, not only for his apparent bravado, but also for his suave detached treatment of them and his sexy good looks.

When it was discovered that he could also sing, he was often the featured guest artist at these late-night dance clubs. Juan (his given first name) got noticed and had a small recurring role on a television sitcom that opened each week with a version of his comedic break-dancing. Soon he began writing his own music to dance to on the show and that's what launched his recording debut. He was given a spin-off of his own that failed within a season.

Juan, of course, had saved no money. He also had no management. He used a lawyer referred to him by the television show producer's assistant to negotiate his deal and "protect his rights." And so he had nothing.

A major recording label approached him after hearing about his songwriting abilities from a fan of the show who just happened to be the niece of the president of the label. To his credit, he refused to sign the first contract presented to him by the record label before talking with someone knowledgeable. He was given my phone number by one of my clients who met him at a party.

THE MAJOR LABELS

There are only four major recording labels in the world at the time of this writing: Universal Music Group, Warner Music Group, Sony BMG, and EMI. There are many well-known labels owned by these four giant corporations which control more then 80 percent of the music marketplace worldwide. Some independent labels are actually *independent*, but most have little money to spend and little influence with radio stations and distributors. This, I often tell aspiring but frustrated hopefuls, is why you feel like you're hitting a brick wall when you try to get your music heard.

Each label has a limited amount of funds and a quota of acts it can handle. Label XYZ has four R&B artists, five country-western acts, six popular, two adult contemporary, seven heavy metal and four rap. They also handle three jazz acts on a special subsidiary label. This year, XYZ has dropped a country-western act. If you are a heavy metal band, you're out of luck unless you can heehaw. Artist & Repertoire (A&R) personnel find a favorite or two from the performances they see or the CDs they hear, bring these songs to company meetings, and then get voted down by executives above them who have their own favorites or corporate agendas to follow. I've heard those in A&R complain that they fall in love with a performer or a song and can't do anything about it. And remember how little music reaches the ears of A&R people.

I've personally known two A&R men who were tone-deaf but were responsible for two big hits each. There is no special training for this corporate position and the turnover is extremely high. Don't bother memorizing the name and number of most A&R people—they'll be gone before your CD is complete.

A disclaimer: This is not true of all labels. Creative and talented people as well as properly run companies exist. They're just hard to find.

A manager must stay alert and informed. There is rarely a reason to be surprised by changes in the industry if you stay current with news about the industry. For example: In the mid 1990s, the *Los Angeles Times* ran an article about the technological research being conducted by major recording companies. Their research departments were trying to connect the world to one global entertainment system where you could buy or rent visual and audio products for personal use. With your remote, you would choose the music or movie you wanted and be billed via your cable-like company. There would be no Blockbuster Video stores, Tower Records, and like distributors, or CDs themselves for that matter. Nothing would be in tangible form. This prediction has mostly come true; music distribution has changed permanently. We should not have been surprised.

In this same article, it was predicted that the major labels would rely on their already famous artists like Michael Jackson and Madonna to sell product. In this century we would probably name Usher, Mary J. Blige, Alicia Keys, and Lady Gaga. While not abandoning the concept of developing new talent, they would spend a whole lot less on new artist development. Investments in new artists are expensive, especially if they fail. These researchers called the equipment "hardware" and the performers "software." An interesting perspective as you contemplate the direction your new artist should take.

Don Juan had a look, a recording contract being offered to him from a major label, and a good reputation from his work on television. He's a nice guy too. I felt fortunate when he decided to let me represent him on the record deal. I didn't try to lock him into a management agreement right from the start and I think he appreciated that. The fact that I wasn't trying to "own" him helped build a foundation of trust. We did agree on a few financial points and spent a long evening getting to know each other and discovering what was truly important to him.

That was almost four years ago. Tonight I had promised Juan I'd research changes in his new pension plan and his old medical plan, two of the truly important items on a list we created together. He had never thought about either one and considered them to be boring topics. Nevertheless he had the good sense to recognize their value to his future.

Beyond that he had no intention of trying to understand them.

Managers get bored too. However, the welfare of their clients' health and security will affect both client and manager. The most dangerous part of a successful career in entertainment is the descent to the street corner after you've been to the mountaintop. Almost all entertainment careers have ups and downs. If your manager isn't thinking about the downs when you are enjoying the ups, then your manager needs to be replaced.

There are simple ways to learn about pensions, annuities, and health and other insurance plans without cracking a book. Medical and life insurance are sold from two sources: individual companies and brokers that agent for a multitude of companies. I prefer brokers because there's a greater selection of companies and policies to choose from. As with all consultants, if you find a broker you trust, he can be a lifelong resource.

Artists can get medical insurance coverage through entertainment unions like Screen Actors Guild (SAG), Actors' Equity, etc., but the premiums are paid by employers when and if a performer works in a union job. The reason so many employers don't like unions is that they require payments for benefits like health insurance and pensions that can add up to as much as 50 percent above total wages. Promoters pay performers as independent contractors, a title that affects the performer's taxes and government benefits.

INDEPENDENT CONTRACTOR VS. EMPLOYEE STATUS

- If you are not a company or corporation, you are hired as an employee or as an independent contractor.
- Employees have payroll taxes deducted from paychecks and paid on their behalf to the government by a company that hires them for consistent work. This is *your* portion of the tax bill. The company will pay the government additional funds up to 17 percent of your total wages. Most companies must pay out both your portion and their portion of your taxes each and every week. An example: If you make $1,000 a week, and you claim "X" number of dependents that result in a tax deduction of $200, the company is actually paying $800 to you, $200 to the government on your behalf plus an additional $170 (17 percent of $1,000) out of its own pocket to the government as payroll taxes.
- Payroll taxes differ from state to state because they include federal taxes, Social Security, Medicare, state taxes, local/city/county taxes, state disability insurance, and unemployment taxes. The federal tax is the same in each state; the local arrangements vary.
- If you are not being paid as an employee with taxes deducted from your paycheck, you are not entitled to unemployment insurance because no one is paying into the system on your behalf. You cannot pay into the system on your own behalf.
- For performers and groups who incorporate themselves into *Inc*s or *Ltd*s or *LLP*s, etc., one of the major drawbacks can be unemployment. If you are on the board of directors of your company and get paid for performing as an employee, you are paying into the unemployment and disability systems but you may not be covered under the programs. Each state or circumstance may be different. Make sure you check with your accountant and lawyer before deciding your relationship to your company.
- Contractually, a fee is a payment that isn't taxed; salaries or wages are payments that are taxed.
- If no one company regularly employs you, you can be paid by fee. You are considered to be your own employer, your own boss. You may work for many companies, but the decision is always yours. You are not committed to any one company.

- The law is strict about who is and who isn't an independent contractor because the government wants its payroll tax money whenever it can get it. Don't fool yourself, you will have to pay the same taxes as if there were payroll taxes deducted anyway, only you have to pay the company's portion as well. For example: If you earn a $1,000 fee for one night at a local club, you will receive a full $1,000 check from the club. Based on similar tax deductions in the example above, you will later owe the government your $200 plus an additional amount covering what would have been the company's contributions.
- The previous example is much more complicated than I have stated. Being your own boss, you are entitled to year-end tax deductions and benefits you might not otherwise have as an employee. Each case is different. It may cost you more to be an independent contractor. It may cost you less.
- If you are a corporation, you are automatically paid by fee and are treated like an independent contractor.
- Disclaimer: Be smart and discuss your personal situation with a CPA and an attorney. The cost of a consultation, often free, is nothing compared to the cost of making a big mistake. Always put some money aside for these "mundane" issues.

So when an artist gets paid by fee, the artist is giving up unemployment, state disability, and other government benefits that the promoter would have been obligated to pay.

Don Juan has plenty of money right now. I am trying to secure the rates for as many relevant and worthwhile insurance policies as possible to make sure that his financial life will not end if his performing career does. I put together the following report explaining the different types of insurances and pensions so that Juan can understand the options he has:

INSURANCE OVERVIEW FOR DON JUAN

MEDICAL INSURANCE

It may take years to know how the Obama health plan plays out—which features will continue, which will be replaced or cancelled. Everything written here is subject to those changes. Working with an independent insurance broker is the safest bet to keep ahead of changes as they happen. Right now, HMOs are the cheapest type of policy, but they're hardly relevant to an artist who tours. The doctors are restricted and often the policies are regionally based. Each insurance company offers many types of policies. There are many sections to each complete policy: major medical that covers hospitals and operations, prescription drug plans, individual doctor visits and lab tests, psychiatric care, eyeglasses and exams, dental work. Your policy may exclude any number of these categories. Dental is usually the least-offered policy. Sometimes you need to put together different companies and policies to create the kind of plan you want. Some medical plans come with a small amount of life insurance.

Even with more comprehensive health policies, your artist's lifestyle may not be covered. If you end up in a hospital in Zimbabwe, you will have to shell out the entire medical bill yourself and may or may not get reimbursed by your plan. There are a few specialized, more expensive plans available that cover touring, foreign countries, and exotic diseases if you are able to describe your needs accurately. This policy is only worth its price if the artist is consistently traveling out of country.

There is also a special health insurance required by individual countries to cover transportation back to the United States in the event an artist is admitted to the hospital. That's because an airlift of a patient can cost over $20,000 and no country wants you in their hospital for more than a few days. The foreign consulates or online visa instructions will highlight the requirements of any one country with information about where to go online to find American companies that provide this service. Premiums are based on the age of the artist and the length of the artist's tour.

Changing policies is not as easy as you would think. Medical plans and costs are revised all the time and sometimes come with start dates. Premiums are usually lower during the first years of a policy. This is how the company entices you to sign up. Every few years, you should ask your broker to revisit your policy and look for better and less expensive plans. They will be out there. The broker will help you with the paperwork.

You will want to coordinate the end of your old plan with the start of your new plan so that there is no lapse of coverage. Artists will always get sick during the period their policy lapses. New health care laws allow people with "pre-existing medical conditions" like diabetes, HIV, and heart disease to acquire health insurance when they previously would have been denied coverage.

LIABILITY INSURANCE

Audiences sue. Promoters sue. Roadies sue. Everybody sues. Liability insurance to the tune of $1–$5 million is usually required by promoters, stadiums, and larger concert venues to cover accidents and personal injuries related to a gig. Usually everyone involved with the concert, from promoters to artists to management, gets sued. It is left up to the courts to determine who is at fault, if anyone. Still everyone sued has to pay for lawyers and court fees. Some musical styles and performers encourage and/or incite dangerous dance styles, audience interaction, and destruction of equipment. There is a fifty-fifty chance that someone onstage or off will get hurt and sound equipment damaged. No artist alone can afford to pay for court-awarded damages that can reach into the millions. (Luckily Don Juan is not one of these artists, but he has a strong gang following from his early club beginnings and any number of crazy fans could rush the stage and cause damage to themselves and others.)

Your insurance company will probably ask for a calendar of pending concert dates. The cost of the policy will depend on how much risk the insurance company is taking; the more concerts, the more risk. In some cases, the policy may not cover the entire year and you'd have to renew it often. There may not be a giant corporation backing up your policy; often there are individual investors or investment companies who underwrite the policies. Essentially they are betting that they can keep your premium payments without having to pay off a lawsuit during the limited time your policy is in effect.

DISABILITY/SALARY CONTINUANCE/WORKERS' COMPENSATION INSURANCE

A disability can mean the end to a career. Having disability insurance won't save the career but can ease the transition. Most states will pay employees who have been hurt a small stipend for a limited time. Not enough to live on, but better than nothing.

If you have a family to worry about, you may want to be sure you have income even if you're paralyzed. Shit happens. Curtis Mayfield was performing when overhead stage lights fell on him and put him in a wheel chair permanently. Jackie Wilson collapsed on stage and went in and out of a coma for years. People who make lots of money in the arts often like to insure their income from accidents and catastrophe.

Disability policies are not common. In one case, I had to go to Lloyd's of London, an insurer-extraordinaire, because no U.S. insurance company would cover my artist. They put together a team of underwriters to devise a policy to cover the entire band. It was not cheap. Ask your broker about extended disability benefits which can pay, in some states, up to five times the normal rate for very little in additional premiums.

Actors' Equity Association requires producers to pay a weekly salary continuance insurance amount of less than $2 per actor to be sure the union could cover salaries that were unpaid by the producers. Since pop music performers are usually paid by fees that vary from year to year, there's no way to determine a weekly salary; therefore no such insurance exists.

Workers' compensation is a state-required and state-regulated insurance that pays workers who are hurt on the job. Your boss will automatically deduct it from your paycheck and send it to the government on your behalf. If you are a corporation or independent contractor, you cannot participate in the program, but you are still responsible for contributing to it through your taxes.

Maternity leave may be covered under disability.

Until recently, maternity was only considered an undesirable liability. Now many companies cover the cost and time involved in having a child for the mother and even sometimes for the father. Husbands may also want to stay home to be with their wives, or sometimes they end up being the stay-at-home father. Some companies provide daycare in the office. Some artists travel with their infants and children and need a nanny, a tutor, and an extra hotel room.

For pop music artists, taking time out for childbearing and childcare is elective time off from work. There is no coverage unless the artist has put away enough money to live on during her absence from the stage or unless the child's father is a sugar daddy. Performing groups have to decide how they will fill the space—with a permanent or temporary replacement or by waiting it out. Often this is a good time to go into the studio to record rather than perform live.

(None of Juan's small staff is pregnant or plans to be anytime soon, but I will include this in tomorrow's rundown to give him the full scope of his potential obligations.)

LIFE INSURANCE

You pay premiums forever for the right to provide your family or friends with money after you're gone. This can help pay for the funeral you want or provide security for your children. The earlier you begin, the less you pay in premiums each year. The more you want left to your survivors, the higher the premiums. Simple. Beyond the obvious, there's another good reason to start an insurance policy when you're young. Once you develop certain diseases like diabetes, getting life insurance is almost impossible.

There are two kinds of life insurance—whole and term. Whole life insurance lets you borrow against the money you've paid in premiums or cash it in. However, you can only cash in or borrow against the amount you've paid in.

In one way, whole life is like a savings account accruing interest over many years. The difference is that you receive a payout much larger than your investment, especially if you die young. For example, if you begin premiums at the age of thirty on a $100,000 policy and die at age thirty-two, your family receives $100,000 and it cost you only a few hundred dollars. As long as you continue to pay your premiums on time. Listen up: if you think you can pay your premiums six months late like your phone bill, think again. Whole life insurance will stay active to your very last day of life, whenever that is, as long as you continue to pay your premiums.

Term life ends at a specific age. So if your term life says the policy is good through age seventy but you live longer, you will not see a penny. Term life is less expensive than whole life and is therefore very popular. You can't borrow against it and you can't cash it in like whole life. There is only one way you benefit from term life: If you expire *before* your policy expires.

TRAVEL INSURANCE

Different kinds of insurance for people who travel a lot can be purchased to cover theft, trip interruption, accidents, illness, and death.

UMBRELLA COVERAGE

A very few insurance firms offer a combination of property (your sound equipment, costumes, props, computers, lighting, musical instruments, etc.) and liability coverage (see above) that is specialized for the entertainment industry. These cost a little bit less than if you buy separate policies. Some brokers can't offer this because it is not widely known or offered. Companies based in New York City and Los Angeles will be your best bet to research these types of policies. Other firms may offer what is called umbrella coverage, but it is not necessarily unique to entertainment.

ACCIDENT INSURANCE

These policies are very specific in setting the value of a lost eye or arm or leg. Sometimes the accidents must also be very specific, for example, they happen in a car or an airplane. These policy offerings often arrive in your mailbox and are rather inexpensive. That's because the chances of being in an accident of this kind are reasonably low.

SPECIALIZED INSURANCE

For a musician's hands or a lively performer's feet or a pretty singer's face, loss or injury can mean financial catastrophe.

Calling Lloyd's of London made it possible for Liberace to insure his hands for more than $1 million each. Some actresses have insured their faces, some singers their voices.If your artist's career depends on a specific body part, this may be worth it, but it's going to cost a pretty penny.

PENSION

There are many government-endorsed concepts like 401K, IRAs, Roth IRAs, Keogh, and annuity plans. Some are only valid if you have a corporation sponsoring them. Some only work if it's an individual putting money away for himself and his family. Some allow early deductions for your child's education. Some take away the interest you earned if you dare to take money out before retirement age. Some allow you to deduct pension payments from your tax liabilities, but not all. For example, if you have a pension plan through your company or union, your individual IRA may not be fully tax deductible. The mathematical computations used to develop each plan leave the ordinary citizen in tears. Again, there should be plan executives who will answer your questions and report progress on your money.

If you think you can trust a pension plan to take care of itself, just look what happened to the employees of Enron who lost everything when the company went bankrupt. Since many plans are tied into the stock market, the plan can be as volatile as any stock. If you want to retire during a recession, you're going to be upset. There are times to move money out of existing retirement accounts and move them into safer funds. This is called "rollover." If you're not a financial wiz, get a financial advisor. They cost nothing upfront. They get a commission from your plan and every time you change your plan.

Overall, the most important thing to know is that the earlier you begin saving for retirement, the more you will have when you retire. Interest is earned on top of interest on top of interest on top of the original money you put away. The sooner you put down the original money, the more interest will accrue over time. The more you add to the pile along the way, the more interest on top of interest will accrue.

Only unusually forward-thinking performers ponder pension while they're still in their twenties. Don Juan was exceptional in this respect, as he lost his mother and father in a car accident when he was twelve, so he knew old age was not promised to anyone. Yet finding the right pension plan for a single thirty-two-year-old whose career might blow up or blow away at any time, and who likes living in the present, was going to be a challenge. Juan listens as well as he sings and I found it refreshing that I didn't have to pull teeth to convince him that a pension plan was important. Never make the artist feel bad that he doesn't understand the complexities of a pension plan. Even the experts look confused.

Financial advisors are people. They are as smart and as stupid as the rest of us. They, one hopes, have been trained to understand investment better than you. Get their references. Listen to their advice and get a second opinion from your accountant, your uncle, the stockbroker, whomever. You and your client must feel comfortable asking questions and must receive regular updates, even when you don't ask for them. And you must always feel free to leave them and go to someone else. This is that important.

A manager has the obligation to teach artists to plan for tomorrow at the same time as they live for today. One is not exclusive of the other.

When I meet with Juan tomorrow, I'll present the entire package to him with estimated costs. He may have money now, but all of this insurance can cost him as much as $50,000 a year. If his career slumps or he decides to take a year off, he'll still owe $50,000 to maintain this level of insurance Slow and easy is often a good approach to committing finances; there, we will prioritize the possibilities and make choices based on lower-than-current earnings—if he is earning $400,000 this year, we'll work off an annual salary of $100,000 so that he won't feel pressured when he finds himself in a tight year. If his career zooms and we're able to sock away the excess earnings, then we can always add to the pile.

At the end of the report, I included my written assessment of Don Juan's insurance needs, taking into account a conservative financial outlook. Because he is a company unto himself, much of this insurance covers not only him, but also his staff and equipment.

SUGGESTED COVERAGE FOR DON JUAN

$ 9,300	Health Insurance	Top-of-the-line, covering all nations *
$ 6,000	Umbrella Coverage	$2 million liability & $100 thousand property loss or damage
$ 2,500	Disability & Accident	Personalized combination includes travel #
$ 5,200	Workers' Comp	from New York State (required) ~
$ 0	Employee Maternity	Will not be an issue this year
$ 0	Annuity Plan	(maybe in a few years)
$ 1,500	Whole Life	$50,000 paid at death—for now. We'll add more each year.
$25,000	Annual contributions to a combination of pension plans +	
$49,500	Total premiums due each and every year!	

* Comes with $20,000 worth of life insurance.

\# Although Juan's company has two employees, the disability plan is for him alone. It therefore does not have any special maternity plan.

~ Amount depends on the actual salaries and the number of employees and the sex of the employee. It is audited by the state to confirm your numbers and adjusted every year or so.

+ One of these plans requires at least $10,000 contribution each year in exchange for getting a higher interest plan, but other than that, Juan can alter the amount of the contribution he makes each year based on what he can afford. The goal is to pay into the plan as much as he can right now, so that it can blossom over the years into a significant pension fund.

If Don Juan doesn't wish to spend $50,000 this year, we can reduce the amount of life insurance he acquires, reduce or eliminate disability and accident, reduce his umbrella coverage to $1 million liability, reduce workers' comp by reducing the number of employees and using people who are legitimate corporations and independent contractors, or choose a less comprehensive medical plan. I will fight him on any suggestion to reduce his pension contribution; if he doesn't contribute while he's making the bucks, he'll never have a decent retirement.

16

Money Matters

When everything is coming your way, you're in the wrong lane. Keep control.
Be not afraid of growing slowly. Be afraid only of standing still.

It's hard to teach someone who is used to making $30,000 a year how to handle $400,000. Most kids dream of expensive cars or buying their mother a home. LL Cool J, a star rapper/actor, speaks of his naiveté with money in his autobiography. He asked his manager what he should do with his first $50,000 royalty check. His manager told him to buy whatever he wanted and enjoy it. LL gave his mother $8,000 to hold and bought a car with the rest. It was a long time until his next royalty check and he had nothing to live on except the money he gave his mother. He learned an important lesson about large checks and his manager.

Juan and I are having this meeting tomorrow to prevent repeating LL's mistake. To his credit, Juan is coming to the meeting with certain savings and benefits already in mind, not a car. It makes mapping out a five-year career plan a lot easier because I don't have to first convince him of the importance of any of this. I'm going to help him make banking choices, too. He didn't grow up with a lot of money and therefore doesn't have much experience managing his money.

I didn't grow up with a lot of money either, but my father did teach me the basics. I've always been surprised by how many adults don't know how to balance a checkbook. Believe it or not, I've met artists who don't know how to pay a bill. They shouldn't be embarrassed, they should just learn how.

The first step for anyone is to open a checking account. Money orders at the post office may be inexpensive, but for someone without a lot of money, it's a waste. And they will add up. Banks require a valid piece of photo identification. (Actually *everyone* requires a valid photo ID.) Managers cannot underestimate the lack of financial sophistication that runs rampant in this twenty-first century and this is particularly true for people in the arts, where getting ripped off seems to be a way of life. Singers think musicians are stupid, musicians think actors are stupid, and everyone thinks dancers are stupid. I know this isn't true. As a manager, I consider it my responsibility to educate my clients, as I educate myself.

To many managers knowledge is power, so they hoard what they know. To me the dissemination of knowledge is power, that's why I share information even when someone doesn't care to know. It's why I insist all my clients sign their own checks and review financial statements with me. Artists are often bored by this, but they'll never have to worry about me stealing from them and they will always know how much they have and where it is.

Juan has made $400,000 this year, and he's asked whether he should start investing in the stock market. I am not a financial advisor and the stock market is both lucrative and risky, so I gave him the names of two certified financial advisors who came recommended to me by trusted friends. I work with one of the advisors and so far, so good. I would never advise a client in potential investments, except to refer them to specialists in real estate, art, etc. I would and do advise clients in choosing a bank.

Ninety-five percent of my clients don't know the difference between checking, savings, money market, or CD accounts. Once upon a time, Don Juan was one of them. He now has a checking, a money market, and a few CDs.

BANKING ACCOUNTS

Bank Types: Commercial Banks like HSBC, Chase, CitiBank, Bank of America, etc., are primarily for corporations, not people. Their fees are higher and restrictions tighter but they offer specialized services for businesses. Credit unions and savings banks like Dime, Carver, Emigrant, and TD etc., are primarily for people and offer better interest and reduced fees. Because commercial banks usually have more branches and infinitely more ATMs, individuals mistakenly think they are always a better choice. Sometimes they are. You must shop and don't give in until you get what you want and need.

Why Bank?: Because if the bank loses your money, the federal government will return up to $250,000 of your money. To get this, you must make sure your bank account is FDIC insured. And the bank will *pay you* for depositing your money with them. It's called interest. They do this because the bank uses your money as a loan to someone else from which they get even more interest. Try getting that from a piggy bank or a mattress!

Checking: Unlimited free checking without minimum deposits is limited to a few savings banks. Shop around or it will cost you money to pay your bills. Banks charge a lot more to print checks than those check/address label

	printers that advertise in Sunday newspapers. Of course, making deposits and paying bills online are becoming more common and often reduce bank fees or increase interest on your savings. Shop around.
Savings:	This category usually pays a minimal amount of interest and sometimes requires that you have a checking account, too. You cannot write checks against this account.
Money Market:	A savings account that allows you to write a few checks. There are sometimes minimum balances required and the number of checks you can write each month for free is often restricted to three or four. So all you do is write a few big checks or transfer the monies to your checking account and write the checks from there. It pays higher interest than savings accounts and like savings accounts, has no risk.
CD:	Certificate of Deposit, not music discs. Banks pay even more interest than money market accounts if you are willing to leave some money with them for a guaranteed amount of time—usually three months to five years. The longer you lock the money up, the higher the interest they'll pay you. If you know you're going to buy a car next year, but not before, it makes sense to put the money aside in a CD that becomes available for your use in nine or twelve months.

Sometimes it doesn't pay to sweat the small stuff. The difference between 3 percent interest and 3.5 percent interest on $1,000 may not be worth changing accounts or banks.

Once Juan and his financial advisor decide how to invest his money, Juan will probably dissolve his CDs and move the money into stocks, bonds, and mutual funds. Rule of thumb is the more money you stand to make on an investment, the more risk you take. Anyone who has lived through a stock market crash or a real estate decline knows they can lose some or all of their money.

Managers may not want to advise clients about investing money, because they can make just as many bad choices as anyone else. I didn't make much money when I was young and didn't know that I could have started preparing for my senior years with only $25 a month. When you're young, you have better things to do with your cash. I try not to let my clients make the same mistake.

It's so easy to put $25 away if there's someone to help show you how. This ought to be the job of a parent, but reality teaches us that most parents didn't learn this stuff either. Of all the managers I know, only two agree with me. Most think the manager's job is career-oriented only. These managers believe avoiding mistakes in your *personal* life should be the responsibility of the individual. Personal life often affects professional life, as I see it. I point to Jeremy R.

Jeremy R. is an Australian horn player who, like Kenny G., crossed over onto the international pop charts with three platinum-sellers in five years. He had traveled to the U.S. and Europe for major concert tours and, by all standards, was a popular artist. Jeremy R. had a string of R&B hits (latest CD title: *Rhythm and Blues from Down Under*). He probably was due more than $1 million in royalties per year for the first two years of his career. The next three years saw a rapid decline in income, although he seemed to be selling just as many CDs. I say *probably* because his first manager mismanaged his money and it may be legally too late to audit the books.

Management had power of attorney, accepted and wrote checks on behalf of Jeremy, and paid Jeremy a monthly advance of $50,000. Jeremy knew he was due more but was happy to await the official accounting of his royalties (that often comes months after CD and digital sales are reported). He liked the idea of receiving a consistent paycheck and didn't know how to read royalty statements even when he got them. And he never asked.

When no one renewed his recording deal after five years, he turned to his manager for money, who explained that for the past three years, he had actually earned significantly less than $50,000 a month and therefore had eaten up some of the earlier monies that were due him. At the present, the manager estimated that Jeremy had been slightly overpaid by management to the tune of $7,000. Being gracious, his manager said that he wouldn't ask Jeremy to return the money.

That's when Jeremy got suspicious. After five years of $50,000 a month, Jeremy had absolutely no income and except for a home, three cars, and a wardrobe to die for, few investments. Yet Jeremy still had bills.

Jeremy's manager rationalized that he had advised his client to get a good business manager and a good lawyer. Beyond that, he was not responsible for Jeremy's life. Jeremy did have a lawyer and a business manager who received monthly retainers for services rarely rendered.

For the 10, 15, or 20 percent commission paid to this manager, Jeremy deserved a bit more involvement. Yes, people are responsible for themselves. Artists marry the wrong people, invest unwisely, get hooked on drugs and, in general, mess up their lives just as badly as people without managers. But when someone is paid to manage an artist's career, the artist's personal baggage cannot be completely separated from the artist on stage. We can't save people from themselves and I don't suggest that we pry, but we can work to prevent and alleviate problems.

Not all artists want to be helped. They'll request advice and then reject it outright. I'm the first to admit that I don't have all the answers, and the answers I do have aren't necessarily foolproof, but I know more than they do. And I investigate what I don't know. But what do you do if your client doesn't want to listen? I propose that you ask your artist to find another manager—and quickly. These artists are looking for confirmation of what they want to believe or what they already believe. They reject you if you reject their way of thinking, but you will be blamed for their problems whether you agree to their suggestions or not when they turn out wrong. If the artist doesn't want your advice then you are putting yourself in a no win situation.

Don Juan received an offer to perform for thirty minutes as part of a lavish private birthday celebration for a prime minister suspected of terrorist ties in the Middle East. The gig would pay $600,000 plus first-class travel and accommodations for a week. This thirty-minute performance alone would more than double Don's income and would provide a significant $60,000 commission to me, so we definitely needed to discuss this.

Money is a potent seductress and we had both pounced on much smaller offers in the past that required a lot more work. But it turns out that both Don and I knew people who had died in the World Trade Center catastrophe and the country is still reeling from not only that, but other reports of future attacks.

The *LA Times* in 2011 reported that "With Mariah Carey, Beyoncé, and other artists feeling the sting of their private concerts' connection to the Mu'ammar Gadhafi clan, the risks and payoffs of such lucrative engagements come to the surface. . . . Some of these artists may be motivated largely by money and are ignorant of, or indifferent to, political concerns. Others like Sting, who performed at a 2009 concert arranged at the behest of the daughter of Uzbekistan dictator Islam Karimov (known for jailing dissidents and other human rights abuses), see themselves as cultural ambassadors opening new communications channels into closed societies."

We have to live with our choices and there can be consequences in the media and with your fan base. Don Juan decided not to take the money (ouch!), but I wholeheartedly agreed. If he was a struggling artist and the offer was $100,000 to open for a major star under the same circumstances, would our decision be the same? You cross the bridge when you get to it and this time that wasn't our bridge.

The phone rings. Only telemarketers call me at the office after 6:00 PM. Everyone else knows to reach me on my cell phone at night. I decide to take the call and let Don Juan rest until tomorrow. At first I think it's Crocodile Dundee trying to sell me a free vacation in Orlando. But then I realized it must be the famous Jeremy An independent booking agent had called me last week to ask if I was interested in managing the popular instrumentalist. This booking agent had stopped speaking to me last year after a different client of mine abruptly quit the music business causing the agent to lose what had been $500,000 worth of business a year. In an attempt to reopen the doors of communication, this agent had referred the Aussie horn player to me.

"Jeremy, I was expecting your call."

"Yeah, thanks for agreeing to talk to me, mate. You came highly recommended by the one guy I trust."

"It's why I'm here. How's it going?"

"Everything's going great if you read the *Billboard* ratings. But they're telling me the coffers are dry. I'm starting to wonder."

"Well, tell me—what can I do for you?"

"Well, to be frank, my fucking accountant is screwing me. My fucking manager is screwing me. My lawyer, that bimbo bitch, has been screwing me for years but now she's really fucking me, know what I mean?"

"Well I've heard that no one's offering you a new record deal and you're out of money. Do I have it right?

"Those fuckin' assholes—"

"Jeremy, you're really upset, but I need to talk with you . . . calmly."

"You're right, mate. Sorry. When I think about it I get pissed. Man, I've been working my ass off doing more concerts than ever and my CDs sold platinum, not just gold. But I haven't seen any of it in tangible terms. Not one extra shilling or ruble, know what I mean? I've been getting the same monthly stipend for years and now that's gone . . . what's wrong with this picture? I was hoping you could tell me what the fuck is going on!"

"First of all, you're not a poor man. You've made plenty of money. You're just not sure that you've gotten all the money due you. Is that right?"

"Yeah."

"Why isn't your label renewing your deal?"

"Because they're assholes."

"Jeremy, stop it. I'm trying to help."

"OK. My manager tells me I'm too expensive for the label."

"Is that true?

"I don't know. I know I made them a shit load of money so why shouldn't I make whatever I can get?"

"Can I ask what you were asking for?"

"You'd have to ask my manager."

"You don't know?"

"Not exactly. I was asking for the same points but I'm not sure about the advance. I mean Mariah Carey got something like $78 million for five albums. I'm sure we weren't asking for that."

"It seems logical to me that some label is going to want to make money off of your talent. But they have to *believe* they're going to make money. Are you a pain in the ass?"

"Funny, mate. I'm really good about deadlines and I make nice with all the recording company hot shots. If they think I'm trouble, the pussies don't say anything."

"So you think your money has been mismanaged, right?"

"Abso-fuckin-lutely!"

"Jeremy, you're already doing the first thing right: auditing the books. That's going to take some time and cost a bit of money, but it's always beneficial to double check the numbers. In the meantime, have you asked your manager to explain why you're out of cash?"

"He said something about too many crew and staff, but he hired the blokes. He also said I've been making too much money all along. But I know he's got a helluva lot more than me—and that ain't right!"

"To be honest, I'd have to know a lot more details before I could figure out what's really going on, Jeremy."

"What do you need? I'll get it to you."

"If you're willing, I'd need to look at your recording deal, your agreement with management, your royalty statements, your staff list—it's too much for anyone to analyze in a few months, let alone a few days. How about we look at your options from this point on and decide if you can salvage your relationship with your manager or whether you need to move on—if you can."

"What does that mean?"

"It all depends on what your management agreement says. When and if you are allowed to terminate it."

"Hey, I do whatever I want."

In my head I'm saying, *That's why you're in so much trouble.*

Instead I say, "It's always a good idea to avoid going to court if you don't have to. Can I look at the agreement you have with your manager?"

"Sure you'll have it in ten minutes. I'll fax it to you."

"Great. For now, let's not dwell on what's been done to you. You are a very popular performer who makes good music. Hang in there. You're life's not over yet."

"Thanks for the help. What happens now?"

"I'll call you back after I get the agreement. I need to see the 'out' clause."

"What's that?"

"It lets you know how you or your manager can get *out* of the agreement. I'm trying to find out if you have an easy way of leaving your manager or whether we need to go another path."

"So we'll talk tomorrow?"

"Just give me enough time to read the agreement and I promise I'll call you. Just stay calm. And although you didn't ask, this isn't costing you anything right now."

"I like you already."

"OUT" CLAUSES

Every contract should be considered a pre-marital agreement. When things are good, no contract is necessary. When things go wrong, no contract is ever sufficient. A manager's talent is never more evident than when negotiating a quick and fair way to exit out of a deal. The safest way to be sure that your client will not regret signing a contract is to be sure that there are clearly defined methods to get out of a contract after it is signed. This is commonly called the "out" clause. Here are examples of various clauses (with my comments in bold):

Authors: The easiest form is an automatic ending to the deal. In the following example, the contract starts on one date and ends a month later.
Term of Engagement: The performance schedule shall commence on March 7, 2002 with a final performance on April 6, 2002.

Authors: Another form requires advance notice of the intent to terminate a deal. It can require a method of notice or none at all.
Cancellation: Artist may cancel any performance with no less than two (2) months' notice in writing by certified mail or by fax.

Authors: Even when no "out" is available, there can be special considerations such as a job offer with greater compensation.
More Remunerative Employment: Artist has the right to terminate this contract if she receives a bona fide offer for a role in a television show or film. Artist further has the right to terminate this contract if she receives a bona fide offer for any role whatsoever that offers more remunerative (higher paying) employment. Such right will require four (4) weeks written notice.

Authors: "Any reason" gives the Artist the most flexibility.
Early Termination: Artist may terminate this contract at any time for any reason whatsoever, provided that Artist returns any monies advanced and has paid all monies owed.

Authors: It is also essential for a manager severing ties with a client to be sure he continues to be paid for the work he has already started. This too is part of an "out" clause.
Refusal to Perform: Should the Artist refuse to perform his duties as described above for any reason whatsoever other than medical instructions from a physician, manager may terminate this agreement immediately. All compensation including but not limited to commissions will continue to be due Manager for all work completed, in progress, or initiated by Manager on behalf of Artist.

Authors: Artist and manager must have the right to terminate the manager-artist relationship. Yet it should not be arbitrary. "For cause" is the term used for an "out" clause that makes bad behavior the reason for termination. Of course, the definition of this bad behavior must be carefully spelled out.

For cause or breach of contract: In the event Artist has cause for dissatisfaction in regard to Manager's fulfillment of its obligations concerning timeliness, or quality of work, Artist may give notice of such dissatisfaction to Manager. In the event that Manager does not cure such faults as identified by the Artist within fourteen (14) days, Artist may terminate this agreement, provided that all compensation due Manager for all work completed, in progress, or initiated by Manager on behalf of Artist is paid in full.

Authors: A variation can be added to the "For cause" clause. "Breach of contract" is a term that means a significant item in the agreement has not been followed. A breach can be taking more commission than permitted or not presenting a job offer because the manager gave it to his girlfriend instead. Negligence is a legal term, but in simple English it refers to when someone causes pain or loss that would have been avoidable if that person had been paying attention. Gross negligence is an extreme version of negligence.

Breach of Contract and Gross Negligence: In the event Artist terminates this agreement due to the gross negligence, breach or default of Manager, Manager will not be entitled to any compensation other than for work completed.

See chapter 22 (Three Artist-Management Agreements) for other examples of fair or abusive out clauses.

I am not sure if I really want to get involved with a seemingly irrational hothead, but then again, without hotheads and maniacs and other potential psychiatric candidates, there might not be a music industry at all.

Only kidding . . .

Sort of.

Artists have a legitimate reason to be hotheads when they think their money is being mismanaged. Audits are guaranteed in every record deal. It allows an artist to have his personal accountant check the financial data related to his personal income. This means the artist, at considerable expense, must hire a certified public accountant (CPA) knowledgeable in the business to be audited (you don't want your father's tax accountant trying to understand the tricks used in recording royalties). You would normally hire your accountant, with your manager overseeing it, to handle the audit of your merchandising agent or concert box office receipts. Where do you go if the people you are auditing are your trusted manager and accountant? It is possible that no discrepancies will be found, but experience tells us that a good accountant can find a problem anywhere.

Audits are not always the answer. When I was an assistant general manager of a prominent nonprofit production company, I enjoyed reading the CBS recording contract for the cast album of the company's monster hit Broadway musical. I noticed a special clause related to reduced royalties for "compilations and overseas sales." This referenced albums sold on television and other similar albums having one song from each of many shows or artists. Often there would be sixteen songs on what was commonly a ten- or twelve-song album. The contract clause acknowledged that these albums sold for less than current releases and had to divide the proceeds among more songs.

It also said that CBS would provide a one-page agreement for each of these recordings or for any recordings sold in foreign countries. I studied a royalty sheet in the files. It listed eighteen nations and two similar recordings. Yet there were only four one-page agreements. So I called CBS. I was passed on to a young girl in the accounting department who had never heard of our show.

She promised she'd check and get back to me. Only one week later she called and told me that she was assigned to double-checking the royalty statements for the cast album. A week after that a check for $98,000 in unpaid back royalties arrived. This may not sound like much, but back in 1980 when this occurred this was a considerable sum. Everyone at the company congratulated me. Then a second and final check for $98,000 arrived the next week. The producer told me that I had probably made the company more money than I would earn during my career at that company.

The point is that people and companies make mistakes, sometimes major. It doesn't make them crooks until they try to hide the money. Jeremy was not the type to have a friendly exploratory conversation with his management and I doubt he would understand any but the simplest of answers. This was not because he was stupid, but his management had never taught him to participate in his own business affairs.

There are many reasons why Jeremy thinks he's been robbed, but the reasons may not be criminal. An audit will tell Jeremy if he is due any more money. The rest is a mystery to be solved.

Unfortunately, Jeremy's relationship problem with his manager is not an unusual one, or even the worst.

When artists are managed by their spouses, they often trust them so completely that they willingly sign irrevocably bad contracts, perhaps feeling that if they question the manager/spouse, they are questioning their personal marriage as well as their professional one. This blurs the line between a professional taking an interest in the client's personal life and the professional being *in control of* the client's personal life.

When things fall apart in one relationship, it takes the other one down with it. The complications involved in parenting a young talent can be even more destructive. Lawsuits are big news between manager-parents and their child stars. The parent has to decide priorities in the child's life—school or work or rehearsal or playing ball. The money earned can be put in trust for college or spent as it's made, and sometimes on a big house or car. Should children have a say in what happens with the money that's earned? Usually they're not even aware until they're older.

Sammy Davis Jr.'s father put him in his act instead of in school. He's been called the greatest entertainer of a generation. Were we better off for it? Was Sammy better off for it? Parents may be a child's most important advisors, but should they also manage the business, or just watch over it? The mother of famous stripper Gypsy Rose Lee tried to manage her children's career. Brooke Shields, Britney Spears, Shirley Temple, Natalie Wood, the Jacksons, and the Osmonds were all children with phenomenal careers. Am I saying that their parents should not have managed them? I'm not sure. I just know that there are deep inherent problems when the delineations of professional and personal become blurry. When the person becomes unhappy, it helps to have a separate consultant to handle the business, and vice versa.

Ten minutes later, with Jeremy's fax in my bag, I left for home.

Jeremy R. (right) arguing with a concert promoter.

17

The Stuff of Stardom—
Day Two Begins

Opportunities are never lost; someone else will take the ones you miss.
Never be afraid to try something new. Remember amateurs built the ark.
Professionals built the Titanic.

Yesterday was not unusually long, but I had quite a few personal errands to run in the morning so I called Juan and suggested a catered lunch in my office today to go over the information I gathered yesterday plus merchandising and his ever-changing website.

Robert O. asks if he could take notes during our meeting because Don Juan is our biggest star-client and Robert is star-struck. Plus, he is here to learn. I am expecting Robert to be casting off shortly to make a living, but I agree because the more he knows about what Don Juan wants, the more he can help me take care of him.

The design for Juan's website was by one of his close college buddies who lives inside his computer. It was imaginative and exciting and got lots of hits but had technical difficulties and was always crashing. It worked better on some search engines than others, but we wanted full access on even the worst of search engines. I brought in a technician to solve the problem and take responsibility for posting updates and keeping the interactive site trouble free.

The best part was that the technician was so taken with the idea of working with Don Juan that he did the initial work for free. We now pay the technician for work done on an hourly basis. Just because Don Juan is making good money doesn't mean his manager shouldn't be on the lookout for bargains.

Don Juan arrives along with the deli guy. I don't want to discuss insurance over lunch because I need his undivided attention to make informed decisions. So instead I tell him that our merchandise manufacturer is closing shop to start a camp for children with cancer. We still have a supply of t-shirts and caps, but we might want to redesign these things when we choose another company. The old company is shipping us boxes and boxes of our stock and that means we will have to find and pay for storage. We will also be responsible for *fulfillment*, the term used for the people and place that actually does the packaging, shipping, and handling after the order comes in. One of Juan's staff has always been responsible for processing payments, from mail orders or online, in stores or at concert stands. I always checked the staff member's financial and inventory statements for discrepancies. This staff member also took care of sales tax collection, and returns. Juan's accountant checked those figures periodically.

MERCHANDISING

Making money from merchandise is not a 1-2-3 proposition. On the megastar level, there are separate companies that do nothing but sell stuff. The artist makes a royalty off the gross or net income and has little to do with the selling of the stuff. An artist's name, at this level of notoriety, is a commodity that can be exploited for millions of dollars in the same way that the Disney name sells anything attached to it. On the beginner or intermediate level, it is more often a great way to market your client's image, but can cost the client money even when charging inflated prices. Sales are just not large enough to overtake the many hidden costs involved.

If you use a photograph of your artist, get permission from the photographer. Unless you negotiate otherwise, your usage rights are usually restricted to publicity, not profit-making. In one case, a photographer accepted a few hundred dollars for the initial batch, but if we sold out and needed to make another batch, he would receive an additional royalty per item. Storage costs and shipping costs are other surprises that may eat up your profit margin.

Sales tax must be paid. This varies from state to state. The location of your *fulfillment house* determines the applicable sales tax (i.e., if you mail out of California, only California residents pay sales tax; if you mail out of New York, only New Yorkers pay).

Step One: Choose a manufacturer. There are many t-shirt, leather jacket, key chain, etc., companies in New York and California that cater to films, television, theatre and concert groups. You want to ask about the quality of the t-shirts (all cotton, shrinkability—fans seem to notice the difference) and that will affect the cost to you. Printing on one or both sides of a shirt also changes the cost. You should ask if the company will store them for you and provide fulfillment. You must lay out the full cost of manufacturing in advance. $6.50 a shirt means you lay out $6,500 per thousand.

Step Two: You need somewhere to sell the stuff. If your stuff is only available in one small store in your neighborhood, you're not going to sell much. You can move merchandise through a website with a good shopping cart (see Internet box below), retail stores (unless you're a big name, forget it), mail order (postage is expensive) and concerts (a separate topic).

- Concerts: Who's going to sell your stuff? In large stadiums, there are union sellers and the "split" can be 35 or 40 percent of the gross price going to the stadium sellers. You also have to ship the stuff, make many long distance calls to make arrangements, and have the leftovers shipped back. Expensive. At state fairs or smaller concerts, there may be no one available to sell for you, so you have to send your own person—that means travel and hotel costs and a percentage of each item sold to the seller. Of course, if you don't sell a lot, your seller will demand a basic fee and that may leave even less for your profit. And you still may have to ship the stuff to and from the venue.
- Mail Order: A brochure must be designed (fee) and printed (expense). Be conscious of the size and weight of the brochure for postage purposes. You'll need an address or P.O. box to accept orders and you'll still need to have a fulfillment house (or your basement) to store, package, and ship the stuff.

Step Three: You need to advertise, advertise, advertise. If the public doesn't know the stuff exists or where to get it, you're still not going to sell much. Here's a sample of a financial summary page to determine possible profit:

Income:	Concert price per t-shirt	$20.00
Expenses:	Sales tax (varies per state) @ 6.25 percent	$1.25
	Union concessionaire 40 percent	$8.00
	Cost of manufacturing per shirt	$6.25
	Roundtrip shipping UPS ground (slowest)	$0.25
	Photographer or designer's royalty per shirt	$0.25
		$16.00
Net Profit:	(taxable later)	$4.00

Whatever you do to reduce your costs adds to your artist's income (and your commission).

Juan's interest in merchandising is nothing more than cosmetic. He likes the extra income and he likes choosing the design. Our fulfillment house and manufacturers have always advised me that the most successful designs are not always the most interesting designs. Audiences tend to buy white and black t-shirts more than colors. They like photographs. They also advise not to overload your stock with too many different items. The less choice you offer, the better the chance to sell more of what you have. It's also easier to stock and ship. If you have three different t-shirt designs, you must ship various sizes (unless it's a one-size-fits-all) of three different models. It's common to run out of one popular design and have to ship back the others.

It's also counterproductive to offer too many inexpensive items. The public will buy a $5 autographed photo before a $20 photograph t-shirt. Having more than one cheap item is not a good idea. Offering three items together in a discounted package sometimes works.

Juan looks concerned at the idea of storing a lot of souvenirs and asks, "How can we move this stuff so we don't get stuck with it?"

"We can offer discounts. We can also use the stuff for promotional purposes and give it away. You want to donate some of it to the manufacturer's children's camp?"

"We can do some, but I want to make some money off of it. It costs us a lot."

"Your next concert tour doesn't begin for three months. I'm sure we can get rid of it there, but are you willing to wait?"

"Why wait when we've got the website open 24/7?"

"But you forget that someone's got to package and ship the stuff. You'll have to hire someone. Maybe we can find someone with a basement to store it for the same money."

"Well, let's put the offer on the website and see how many people bite."

"Don't forget we offer seventy-two hour turnaround. If someone orders, we're going to have to get it out quickly."

Robert O. interjects, "Depending on the volume, I'd be willing to do some of it and I might be able to get some college friends too. We could all use a little extra cash."

"*Que bueno*! Now all we need is storage." Then he turns to me, "Can't you fit the stuff in your office?"

"No, there's too much. We can rent a mini-storage room, but I'd much prefer to have everything together at some place where it can be processed easily. Robert, see what you can find. And, Juan, I'm going to start a search for another manufacturer. I'll call a few industry friends, see who they use and like."

"Good. Now, what about the Internet? We haven't done much advertising lately."

"We can add some direct links to someone else's website and offer yours in kind. It still may cost something but maybe not. Who's our best bet?"

Don Juan doesn't waste a second. "Ricky Martin, Enrique Iglesias, Janet Jackson, Jennifer Lopez, and maybe Amazon and CDNow."

"We already have links with Amazon and CDNow because they sell your CDs. We can ask for special treatment next month and see what they say. It would be easier if you had a new CD coming out. I'll call Rick at the label and see if he has any ideas for marketing. You already advertise your site on your CDs so that's taken care of. Maybe you should hit a talk show and hawk your website."

"Oh, wow—what about moving some of this stuff on the Cable Shopping Network?"

"It's not that simple. I have a friend in management there. You're probably going to have to give them a free thirty-minute on-air concert. And by policy, they don't sell t-shirts—ever. Beyond that, they want exclusive items or collectibles, something the fans can't get otherwise. And do you know that if we make new stuff to sell on CSN, we still have to pay for all of it ourselves, even the shipping, with no money upfront."

"Well we don't plan to re-order this particular stuff, so it *is* exclusive."

"But they don't want t-shirts."

"Oh. I guess they've got us by the *cojones*. Seems like the net is our best bet and then we'll get rid of anything else at the concerts. Oh, and let's give some away on the radio."

"Right! In exchange for recording the call letters for a radio station ID promo and providing them with giveaways, maybe they'll let you announce your web address. The only issue is if we'll need these station IDs to promote your upcoming concert tour later this year. You don't want to exhaust all your marketing tools now if you're going to need them in a few months."

"Maybe they won't mind. Ask them."

"Will do. Roberto, ask your college station if they have a list of other college stations. See if you can get the college network listings and you get the honor of making lots of phone calls."

"Do you want me to call Marjorie for some marketing help?"

"No, she'll charge us and this is leftover crap. We can do this . . . at least for now. The worst that happens is we wait for concert season.

"The Internet is the most powerful marketing tool we've got. It's international and moving through the industry like a California brush fire. So, let's outline all of our Internet options," I say, getting us back on track.

I am very proud of the shopping-cart system I found for Juan and all my clients. It was inexpensive and it works like a charm. We accept major credit cards. The only problem was that the first person put in charge of processing orders was me. I needed to know how the processing worked so that I could watch over the operations. I especially did not want to be bound to some assistant who was hired to do the work. And since I didn't know how well the cart would do on each of the websites, I wanted to observe firsthand.

SELLING STUFF ON THE INTERNET

Each year the number of customers buying products on the Internet is increasing by leaps and bounds. However, many Internet storefronts lose money or close up shop even though there are millions of shoppers online. As in the real world, if the public doesn't know your store exists, they can't and won't be buying in your store. Advertising is the key in the virtual world, just as it is in the real world.

The only tangible things sold in stores are products and services. Now the Internet has created a new opportunity for artists to promote their images and their names. It can cost $125,000 or more for a one-page ad in the Sunday *New York Times* Arts and Leisure section, but you can reach millions of people over a year with your website at no cost beyond the original website set-up expense. And you can say as much as you want and have as many photos as you wish, sample your music, and offer moving images as well.

But if nobody knows about it, so what?

You can buy email lists that involve no postage costs and can be used over and over again. There are companies that will send out your announcements for you—for a fee. This cost is nowhere near the price of regular advertising and it's environment-friendly since it doesn't use paper.

There are also banners, those annoying flashing ads on someone's web page telling you about a used car loan you can get even with bad credit. By clicking on the banner, you can be linked to the used car website. You can pay for or exchange banners with other websites or pay for premium locations on the home pages of major search engines like Google or Bing.

When you do a search for a subject or title, you're given many choices of websites that may or may not be exactly what you want. Notice the websites at the top of the list. They received priority status from that particular search engine. If you're not an Internet wiz, you may need a consultant to help you set up banners, links, and priority listings.

You need to register the name of your website—it will be the *address* for the world to find you on the Internet. Even more than the music industry, the Internet is the new wild wild West and some fan may already be using the name of your band for his own website tribute to you. If this fan registered your name before you did yourself, you have to find a new one for your website, even though it's your name and even though you may have trademarked it (see *Trademark* box below).

Make sure your web address is printed on your CDs, announced at your concerts and during interviews, on posters, in ads, on your forehead when you walk down the street (only joking, but you get the point). The success of a website does not depend on the cleverness of management, but on the artist's determination and promoter instincts. Talk with your artist.

A shopping cart is the mechanism on a website that takes your order when you buy a product. You click on an item and it is put into your cart and when you are finished shopping, it adds up all your costs, adds shipping and tax, and delivers it to the business "headquarters." After processing it at "headquarters," the order comes back to you for credit card processing and fulfillment. When I first investigated selling product on the Internet, I hired a consultant who found me three well-known companies (headquarters and cart) charging more than $5,000 each to set me up. I settled on a novice company catering to small businesses with an up-front charge of only $500. Luckily I had a technician, because the initial trouble I encountered was overwhelming. In time, my technician developed his own shopping cart. He let us use it without charge so he could point to it as a model advertising his skills and his cart.

It was slow at the beginning—except for Don Juan's site. Juan's products were selling like gangbusters. Juan always has new ideas, although they aren't always good.

"What about panties with my name on them?"

Normally I would dismiss the idea outright but Don Juan could sell anything right now.

"Juan, we may just have too many items to sell. Is there anything you want to drop if we add panties?"

He thinks. "No. Right now they're making too much money."

It's true. Juan is making a good living from his merchandising alone. My other clients are not doing so well. They just don't have his name, his trademark. In Juan's case, we have carefully trademarked his name in the entertainment and merchandise fields. Legally, someone could sell Don Juan cigars without infringing on my client's rights, because items like cigars are a separate trademark category, but they couldn't sell t-shirts or CDs or souvenir panties . . . unless we licensed his name like we're planning to do with a successful aftershave.

Licensing is when you endorse a product with your name. This lends that product a marketing edge. Sometimes the artist will do commercials for the product; sometimes the artist's name goes right on the product itself. I suspect Martha Stewart does not make towels. But K-Mart did very well with a line of Martha Stewart Living towels and other home products. And I suspect neither Lebron James nor Michael Jordan make sneakers, however I suspect they earn a pretty penny for licensing their names.

Imagine finding out that your former lead singer had personally trademarked the group's name and he now can prevent you from ever using the name without him. Don Juan wouldn't have known to trademark his stage name. I did it for him. I could have attached myself to the trademark and he would have been none the wiser. It's been done to many groups. And it will continue as long as artists stay ignorant and the music industry continues without a method to enforce ethical standards.

TRADEMARKS

The name of your group, your personal name, product names, etc., can be the most valuable single item you own. Entertainment unions like Actors Equity require a name search before you can join to be sure that there is only one person with your name working in the industry. Many performers are shocked to learn that they must change their name in order to work. When Miss America/singer Vanessa Williams first joined various acting unions to work in films, television, and on stage, there was already an actress with that name. Even though she was known worldwide by her given name, she had to add the middle initial "L" in order to continue performing under the Vanessa Williams moniker.

Disney, McDonald's, and many other product names would be worthless if anyone could use them on unofficial products. So it is with the name of an entertainer. Imagine going to the movies to see Denzel Washington and finding out that the actor in the movie was a short, white fifteen-year-old using Denzel's name. You might feel ripped off. A well-publicized name is most times more powerful than the product or person. A CD by an artist like Fantasia or Jennifer Hudson can sell a million copies before anyone hears a note. Musical artists are given roles in movies or television or product endorsement because their name attracts a following that translates into money.

Disney and McDonald's are worldwide entities. How do they protect their name in a world of seven billion people? They have attorneys who do a search among all trademarked names registered with our government and even other governments. You can get a trademark in one category of business at a time or in all categories, but each category will cost you the price of a legal search and then the price of registering your name. This takes time.

The kinds of groups that were "put together" by managers or producers like Backstreet Boys, Village People, Menudo, 'Nsync and Spice Girls probably had their group's name trademarked by the manager or producer. That means that the group itself does not get to make decisions about the use of the name. However, it may be possible to the group members to trademark Menudo in Australia if the managers failed to do so. Or it might be possible for anyone to register the trademark Spice Girls for the purpose of designing and selling clothing in Southeast Asia if the producers of the girl group only registered the name for entertainment purposes.

Don't try to do a legal search at home! Pay a lawyer. It's worth every penny. Even with Internet access to trademark listings, it cannot hold up in court and there is no assurance that you've checked every list. A lawyer will give you the assurance you need to build and protect your "property"—your good name.

Those just starting out may not find it cost effective to do a search just yet. However note the expensive price George Tabb paid for not registering his punk rocker stage name Furious George. As reported in *Daily Variety* (March 4, 1999), the book publisher Houghton Mifflin Harcourt sued Tabb to protect its fifty-plus-year trademark on its popular book character Curious George, which Imagine and Universal Pictures planned to turn into a $100 million live-action film. Tabb's band made about $400 in the previous year but had to go to court to defend its name. The courts ruled in favor of Tabb. But the legal costs could not have made him happy. Had he registered his name early, especially since Furious is not Curious, he might have saved himself a lot of trouble and money.

18

Five-Year Plans

Worry is the misuse of imagination.
Do I want to be right, or happy?

"You ready for the interview with *60 Minutes* next week?" I ask Juan.

"I don't know, man. Everything's moving so fast. I'm a little overwhelmed. I thought the purpose of the five-year plan was to keep the career on track."

"Hey, don't complain. That's the price of success. We've changed our plan at least four times since we first wrote it up three years ago. Your career took off like a rocket. What exactly overwhelms you right now?"

"Man, our first plan had things in real time. This is warp speed. I can't write a hit song in twenty-four hours. We used to schedule for three new songs to be written over three months, period. But now you expect me to do that plus all these important interviews, extra concert dates, and now trying to understand all this insurance crap. Man, it's just too much."

I assure him, "That's what I'm here for—to help you." A five-year plan should be the core of any artist's career. Even a bad plan is better than no plan; a bad plan can be changed. Every plan is a living being, subject to growth, wrong turns, enhancement, and disappointment. Those with experience and knowledge can best create a realistic plan because they've watched plans work and fall apart. They know that it is unrealistic to expect the world in a matter of months. Managers not only manage these plans, they help the artist create them.

"So let's look at where you want to be at the end of this year. Let's go point by point and try to find out what is creating the most pressure. We can cancel the interview. We can reduce the number of concerts. We can stall the release of your next CD. Or is something going on in your personal life?"

"I don't have a personal life and that's the biggest problem!"

I guess I hit the right nerve. On the other hand, despite his complaints, Juan is blessed. We have gone through most of the original five-year plan in three years. When we began, the first year looked like a wish list. But it was all possible and Juan wanted it really bad.

A SAMPLE FIRST YEAR OF A FIVE-YEAR PLAN

This is a first-year plan, as developed by Don Juan and his manager.

FIRST SIX MONTHS OF YEAR ONE:

(Note: His first CD was released six months prior to the start of this plan. The CD did reasonably well. The idea is to build on this CD during the first six months.)

- Solidify NY and Miami Latin audiences—appearances in at least ten Latin-oriented clubs (paid or unpaid), interviews on Latin-based radio stations, street fair concerts, CD signings in barrio CD stores, plus one benefit concert in each city.
- Find the right booking agent to concentrate on the college market.
- Develop new stage costumes.
- Take new promotional photos and create a press package.
- Practice giving interviews.
- Create an inexpensive website format and content.
- Send out promotional CDs to university radio stations nationwide and offer phone interviews for any station requesting one.
- Put together the structure of a thirty- to forty-five-minute concert and begin preliminary rehearsals.
- Begin to piece together a concert staff and crew.
- Find and select consultant staff: accountant, lawyer, photographer, and personal financial advisor.
- Banking and savings plan in place with goal of funding his own concert costs.
- Budget in place, to include plans for basic merchandising, website, costumes, photos, etc., as well as lowest acceptable salary/fee structure with highest savings/investment plan.
- Sign on with an affordable medical plan.

SECOND SIX MONTHS OF YEAR ONE:

- Expand audience base—appearances in five large diversified clubs in NY, Miami, and LA.
- Complete thirty- to forty-five-minute concert and hire staff and crew.
- Perform at least ten paid concerts in college market.
- Website online.

- Record at least three new songs for a future CD and collect potential future songs with eye on a hit single.
- Develop sixty-minute show format and physical production ideas for larger show.
- Refine image (clothes, hair) based on a re-evaluation of audience base.
- Perform on two high-profile television shows.
- Put together world tour for next season with aid of booking agency.
- Find commercial sponsorship for next season's tour.
- Open pension plan and research better coverage medical plans.
- Perform in at least two high-profile benefits.

(Note: The manager and artist *must* put medical insurance and pension planning somewhere in the five-year-plan they develop together because the popular music industry is primarily non-union and rarely provides benefits like these. And no one needs these benefits more than a performer traveling around the world, working with unknown promoters under extremely varied conditions.)

Be careful what you wish for, you may get it. Juan seems to have it all right now.

I let him vent about his personal life for a while and then get back to business. I ask him if he wants to work less.

"I'd like to stay home more, but I don't need to work less."

"Well let's redo your plan to include more time at home."

"Great, but how? To be honest, it's hard turning down the money. It may not always be there."

"Juan, you have choices to make and you can make them. Just make sure you won't regret your decisions. If you need a break, we can make it happen. Not getting enough sex?"

"Funny. I could have plenty of these groupies, but my mama taught me to look for someone special. I'm not getting any younger and I don't know how to meet them anymore. They all want 'Don Juan,' not me."

"But you are Don Juan. When you're quiet backstage is when they all fall in love with you."

"Pretty girls make me nervous. I'm only quiet because I don't know what to say. Anyway, that's not your problem."

"Hey Juan, being a big star has its good sides and bad sides. This is definitely part of the bad. You've made plenty of money this year. You can afford to take a rest and concentrate on other things."

"No, I don't want to stop completely. I guess I like the money too much. And it's such a high being on stage, but I want someone special to share the good times after the show. Call me greedy. I want both—dinero y amor. Manage that."

"I can't get you love, but if you need more money and you want to stay home, what about writing a book?"

"About what?"

"You."

Silence. He was thinking.

A lot of celebrities have capitalized on their lives and troubles by writing books. Becoming an author can add another dimension to the artist's image. Not all tell-alls are successful and not all are worth reading, but artists can take control of their lives and careers by presenting themselves as they want to be seen rather than chance the press writing their stories for them.

Superstars will often use ghostwriters and may avoid certain procedures outlined in the box below. However, successful artists not dubbed *superstars* may still have to make the case to the publisher that a book about them is marketable. Hence, managers need to understand the basics about book publishing when working with celebrities.

For artists who are good at public speaking, this can also provide financial help during slow periods in their performing careers. Speakers, especially celebrity speakers, can earn substantial sums for short talks in front of conventioneers, garden parties, political fundraisers, schools, clubs, and what-have-you.

BOOK DEALS

- Writers must submit a proposal that usually includes an outline of the entire book, a few finished chapters, a biography of the author, a discussion about why someone would buy the book and how it differs from other books in its category, and materials like photographs that would be included in the book. This usually must be completed *before* a publisher will offer a contract.
- A literary agent is not necessary, but is usually more knowledgeable about contractual arrangements and has a good understanding of appropriate publishing houses.
- In the contract:
  1. Writer gets an advanced sum of money based on the publisher's assessment of the writer's salability (similar to a record deal).
  2. Writer gets a royalty that kicks in after the advanced sum is recouped (similar to a record deal).

3. Writer must get written permission to use other people's phrases, names, photos, etc.
4. There is a deadline for a first draft.
5. Publisher gets final approval of most works.
6. Publisher may require writer to participate in publicity and book signings.
7. Publisher will return first draft with corrections and suggestions that the writer must then finish within a new deadline.
8. Self-published books, as with self-produced CDs, need some form of distribution. These are often called vanity books, because they are really for the artist's ego, rather than the public. Now that the popularity of e-books is rivaling hard copies, the self-published author must learn how to be sold through diverse distribution methods, including apps and online booksellers.

"Writing a book will keep me too isolated. I'm trying to socialize a little more." Juan's facial expression dismissed the idea a lot more emphatically than his words.

"Well there are other ways of selling your name without you leaving the house. That's why we have a trademark."

A large part of the value of a trademarked name is the quality of the work attached to it and the notoriety and celebrity of the artist. This brings us back to the importance of the music itself, the marketing plan, and the development of a recognizable image. The success of your trademark has little to do with your artist's performing talent—unfortunately.

High standards in front of the microphone will always be the first element of success. It's just not the only element, and by itself certainly will not assure commercial or critical success. True talent does not automatically lead to success. There are too many extremely talented people in the world. After you get past the "being in the right place at the right time" concept, superstardom requires a brilliant business plan. Imagine that: the same principles taught in business schools apply to the arts.

"Aren't we already doing that?"

"Yes, but we can work it differently so we can keep you at home."

I am not suggesting that he take off six months right now. He still has three immediate concert obligations to fulfill. I explain how we could push the merchandise aspect of his career. I suggest we could tape one or more of his upcoming concerts and sell *Don Juan Live at Madison Square Garden* DVDs. He could remix some of his bigger selling singles and re-release them. We could solicit him as the official spokesman for any number of products, particularly targeting the Latino markets.

He's already a songwriter and that's a *big* plus. Juan can spend six months writing songs for his next release and for other artists to record. The commercial market, be it television series, made-for-TV movies, major motion films, TV and radio advertisements and jingles, or billboard slogans, can use his lyrics or music for a nearly inexhaustible variety of possibilities. We could push his publishing agency to find lucrative uses in areas like these. This would pay him music publishing dollars, which is a much stronger and longer-lasting currency.

More importantly, it will keep him at home. He likes that. It seems he met a girl at a party and that was the inspiration for this entire discussion. I just want him happy long enough to get through the next three concerts.

No artist and few managers seem to know much about the machinations of publishing, except that it pays well. Juan figured that if the publishing agent at his record label looked confused, he wouldn't even try to understand the complexity of this aspect of the business. He just took the checks and moved on. Last year, I forced him to listen to my short version of the publishing business.

HOW MUSIC PUBLISHING WORKS

Think of a publisher as an agent for the song with an enormously high commission. The publisher gets half of the song's income.

The most confusing aspect of publishing is the concept that the total income is discussed in terms of 200 percent, not 100 percent. The publishing agency gets 100 percent and the songwriter gets 100 percent. How is that possible, you ask? The answer is that it's really fifty-fifty and this is just the terminology used by the industry. The publisher is getting 100 percent of the publishing share and the songwriters are getting 100 percent of the songwriting share.

If there is more than one songwriter attached to a song, then the 100 percent due the songwriters is divided. How is it divided? Equally, unequally? This needs to be negotiated among the songwriters. Managers can help keep peace by participating in this process. Note that here is another situation where each individual in a group-written song can potentially earn less than the publisher. Songwriters rightfully don't like this.

Before a songwriter jumps up and down wanting to retain his publishing rights for himself, managers should explain that a good publisher is in business to make the songwriter even more money by getting many singers to record the song, by getting a television show to use the song as its theme, by brokering the song for product placement in commercials, by negotiating a great deal with a film, and by looking out for illegal or improper usage of the song.

In some cases, the publisher can get the song recorded when the songwriter has failed because of access to labels and artists. The independent publisher will be proactive because he won't make a dime unless the songwriter does too.

An independent publisher also performs the dreary job of keeping track of royalty calculations from performance rights organizations like SESAC, ASCAP, and BMI, who collect the money from television and radio play, concert halls, muzak heard in elevators and stores, etc. (see box in chapter 19), and then executing the financial paperwork. As with any industry, there are honest publishers and there are less than honest ones.

Songwriters who open their own publishing companies may end up sharing the duties with a record label's publishing division or the film that showcases the songs. In these cases, we're right back to a split of income. Songwriters usually need someone who knows how to manage the accounts and negotiate deals, commissions or salaries. The songwriter pays either way.

The trick is finding someone who is honest and has a track record of placing songs into moneymaking situations. I was once offered a publishing deal for a song I wrote. The publisher didn't like one line in the song and asked if he could have a staff writer redo it. He thought he had a placement for the song on a new artist's album. He wanted half of my composer's share for the work. It was a take-it-or-leave-it deal. As much as it hurt, I left it. It's a hard world of choices. Is it better to give up 75 percent of a hit song, or to stay away from people who seemingly are trying to cheat you? Everyone has a different answer.

Managers who control their artists might see the answer as "Any money is good money" and sell the song. The songwriter may decide to look for another publisher and risk everything. I believe that managers should advise, not control. Right or wrong, the artist should be allowed to make the decision.

The last item on the agenda for today's meeting with Don Juan is insurance. Before I show him my suggested coverage, he proudly pipes up, "I took care of some of this myself."

With a faint look of disgust, I ask, "When did you do that? We just discussed this a few days ago and I was supposed to research all your options, remember?"

"My aunt, who's really more like my mother, has this friend with a daughter in insurance. I figured I might as well learn something on my own before I discuss it with you. Some of it sounded great, but there was a deadline and I know I wanted what she was offering, so I took it."

"Forgive my looking dumbfounded, but what did you get and have you written the checks yet?"

"I bought $100,000 life insurance and signed up for this really inexpensive health plan. I figured we could always add more life insurance later but I needed to be on a medical plan now. The last one I had was a mess."

He purchased term life, less expensive than the whole life I was going to suggest. He signed up for an HMO that was almost as bad as his last medical plan. No wonder it was inexpensive. It has no coverage for travel and limited access to doctors outside his home area. I am pissed.

"Hey man, I know we talked about you looking into the policy situation. But when this little lady ran it down it just made so much sense. Plus she was telling me how I needed to sign up right away to get the great prices she was offering. I appreciate all the work you do, but I figured sometimes I should be doing some of this for myself. I thought I could help you out."

"I'll give you an *A* for effort but it doesn't help me out. In fact it screws everything up. I'm looking at the whole picture from now until five years down the line. You just threw a wrench in the works. Term life is cheaper because it's worth less. Your new medical coverage might be perfect for a domesticated pooch, but you travel the world! You need to be covered wherever you are in the world. You think you saved yourself some money. You'll go broke real quick saving money this way."

"Sorry man," he says, but I can tell he isn't sorry. He looks embarrassed and maybe a little irritated. "Can you get me out of this?"

"Probably," I say, but I think, I ought to let you eat this one. "Let me see what I can do. Ask her to call me tomorrow."

"I don't know if I kept her phone number."

"Ask your aunt or look on the receipt," I condescendingly suggest.

He stays sullen. I stay pissed.

Robert O. adds, "I'll call you tomorrow, Mr. Juan, to get the number from you."

"Thanks," he says to Robert. Then he says to me, "We'll talk about some time off next week, OK?"

"Absolutely. And we'll get this insurance mess cleaned up."

"I'm really sorry and thanks. You know you're the best, boo boo."

Robert O. smiles, knowing that is Juan's funny name for me.

Meeting over.

Juan a.k.a. Don Juan

19

Dueling Divas

People grow old when they desert their ideals. Years wrinkle the skin, but to give up enthusiasm wrinkles the soul.
The only real aging process is the erosion of worthy ideals.

After that rousing lunch, I decide to check my emails, something that is second nature to other people I know who check hourly. Good thing. Robert O. has been efficient once again and returned a call from Dana Goode who wants to meet with me as soon as possible. "As soon as possible" will be in about fifteen minutes, just enough time to look at the Express Mail delivery that came during lunch, glance at new faxes, and hopefully take a bathroom break.

Max X. has lost no time sending me all the documents he had—more than I asked for. And some of them look like originals. I ask Robert O. to make copies immediately and to file the originals in a safe place to be returned to Max, whether he comes in or we wind up mailing it. The dozen or so faxes include requests for my clients to perform in three benefit concerts for cancer, AIDS, and MS. Other faxes and emails ask for items to be auctioned at charity events benefiting a firehouse, a hospital, and a pre-school beauty contest.

There are two radio interview requests for BoyBand from the Seattle promoter. They want all of the guys on one line this Thursday at noon their time, which is three o'clock our time. Normally we arrange interviews one performer at a time. Coordinating schedules is hell, so we don't try it. I'll get Robert O. to find one of the guys to call the radio station at the appropriate time. I have the guys make the calls, even the long distance ones, because they can call from wherever they are, with minimal interruption of their personal lives. Or one of them can always come into my office and the station can call him here.

There is an email offer for BoyBand to be in an independent movie. The band would be performing in the background during one scene, and in another scene they would be introduced by the fallen hero to a kid with a terminal illness. So they would be playing themselves and get a few lines. The star would be a famous wrestling personality who had bombed in one previous movie. Decisions, decisions . . . The opportunity to debut a new song in the film did not escape me. The guys would make the final decision but they would have many questions. Right now, I need to get more information before presenting the movie to the band.

This would be their first film and they would have to decide if this would be the best way to make their debut. They would have to join SAG unless the movie was being produced non-union. Would the guys want to work without union protections and benefits? And there might be political ramifications for doing a non-union film.

I meet every month with BoyBand in my office. In the meantime, I'll have Robert O. email them whatever information I can get about the film so they can think about it.

Sonny Redd emails me his schedule to make sure that our tax-paying party does not create a conflict for him. It would have been easier to just call and make the date with Robert O. but now I have more information than I need. I tell Robert O. to call him back and make a date.

One fax is a fan letter for Don Juan that will be forwarded to him (how did they get my fax number?). One new email is from an erotica company wanting to make a Don Juan life-sized, blow up, anatomically correct doll. What can I say?

Robert O. sits with me while I go through the emails. This way he can see and hear my reaction and I can assign him appropriate tasks. He can be working on these items while I am meeting with Dana. Shortly after sitting at his desk, I hear him bellow, "Dana's here!"

I walk out to greet my ex-client and see Robert's jaw drop open. That's when I notice the woman with Dana. It's Pollyanne Heart, a feisty forty-something country star whose call I've been anticipating. I certainly was not expecting her to show up with Dana. Dana immediately explains that the two of them are old friends and are going to collaborate on a new CD.

Dana Goode was the lead singer of Goodness with her three sisters who rocked the 1960s charts along with the Supremes and Martha Reeves and the Vandellas. The group faded before 1970 but worked in the nostalgia market for another twenty years. Eventually they all left the business for families or steady work. Dana is itching to be back on stage. She wants me to help her revive a career.

She looks great, almost as enticing as Tina Turner. She's almost as old as Tina Turner, and in this age-conscious industry, this will be an additional challenge for a comeback. I sit them down and excuse myself to answer nature's call.

When I come back, I kiss Dana and asked about her sisters.

"Sasha and Debbie are doing great with a line of cookies that they hope will take off like Famous Amos did once upon a time. Leslie is busy helping to raise her six grandkids. Her children are flying all over the place attending conventions of every assortment, medical, educational, information-age, and musical, of course. I told Leslie she should come back with me, but she suffers from loss of hearing, about 15 percent in her left ear and 35 percent in her right. She's pretty bitter about that. I told her it didn't have anything to do with us singing. It's not like we were screaming; we did classy club dates and the speakers weren't blaring. I told her if she could hear those babies, she could still perform."

Pollyanne chimes in, "These days the monitors on stage can make you deaf during the ballads. I worry about that all the time."

OCCUPATIONAL HAZARDS

Singers and musicians need to learn more than musicianship from their teachers and coaches. Similar to playing professional sports, musical performance is a physical activity requiring preventative care for career longevity.

Several studies have shown that many musicians including orchestra players, have hearing loss due to high sound levels. This is due in part to the higher decibel levels at which music is played today and to the greater emphasis given to the louder brass instruments. In addition, the type of hall and the orchestra position can be important factors.

Singers can develop a variety of problems with their singing voices. Some of these include vocal cord problems resulting from overuse and misuse, artificial fogs and smoke on stage, stage dust, infections, etc. Minor and temporary respiratory irritation, not normally considered a problem for most people, can drastically affect voice quality and result in major problems for singers.

Instrumental players can develop a variety of problems. Again, overuse is a major cause. The problems can include inflammation of the muscles, tendons, ligaments (tendonitis, arthritis), disorders of muscle control, and entrapment of nerves due to inflammation of surrounding tissues (e.g. carpal tunnel syndrome). These injuries can be permanently disabling. Many of these problems result from repetitive motions of particular parts of the body. Examples include tendonitis of the arms in string players, and right-hand problems—especially of the fourth and fifth fingers—in pianists. In some instances, injuries occur because a musician is working beyond his or her physical capabilities.

Solutions to the noise problems have included special earplugs and plastic shields behind the most exposed musicians. Solutions to the other types of musician's occupational hazards include good posture, holding the instrument properly, and good practice technique. In particular, length of practice time is important. If you experience pain, stop immediately and seek medical help instead of simply ignoring the pain. If an injury occurs, treatment can include adequate rest, proper exercises and other physical therapy, medication, and sometimes surgery.

Take your career seriously. Care for your health and insist on healthy conditions.

Pollyanne adds, "Nothing against Leslie, but I reckon Dana should go solo."

"I guess that's why she came to visit me today," I smile.

"That's a big part of why I'm here, but there's more. I've been writing songs and Pollyanne is going to record one of them on her next CD! I'm going to come back and I'm going to come back big and I want you to manage me."

"I'm looking for a new manager too."

Pollyanne's outburst is a surprise to both Dana and me.

"You're leaving Dick?"

"He let me go bankrupt. I want to know where all my money went, dang it!"

Here we go again with the hit tune of the week: the missing money blues. I know Dick is a good and respected manager so I suspect that Pollyanne is responsible for her own condition. I am not sure if she is seriously looking for a new manager or if she's just looking for some attention during this meeting. I decide this is Dana's meeting and I should pay appropriate attention to her.

"I think you two will make a great team. Are you going to perform together on the song?"

"What a great idea! We didn't talk about that. What do you think, Polly?"

"I have a better idea. You sing backup on the entire CD and one song will be our duet. You know I love you but your song is all mine, honey."

Dana asks, "Do we need to get some of this in writing?"

"First things first. Have you registered the copyright for the song?"

"No, not yet."

"You're also going to want your own publishing company."

"I've got a great name for my company . . . Heartfelt," Ms. Heart interjects.

"I going to call mine Very Goode Publishing," Dana chimes in.

There is definitely some competition going on between these two friends. It makes me wonder if their teaming up will backfire. I know that Dana is sincerely excited about getting back into the business. I have no idea what is really on Pollyanne's mind.

I call Robert into the room and asked him to get me a copyright registration form. "I'm going to need you to give Robert all your pertinent information so we can fill out the registration."

COPYRIGHT REGISTRATION

Phone:

Copyright Public Information Office: 202-707-3000, (TTY: 202-707-6737)

Forms and Publications Hotline: 202-707-9100

Leave a message on the recorder and they will send you the forms (in two to three weeks).

Forms can be downloaded from website if you have Adobe Acrobat Reader installed on your computer.

Address:

Library of Congress, Copyright Office

101 Independence Avenue, S.E., Washington, D.C. 20559-6000

Website: www.loc.gov/copyright

To view official records of your copyright registrations (registered after Jan 1, 1978): go to above website and click on Copyright Office Records.

Fee:

It changes. At this time, it's in the $35 (email) or $65 (mailed in) range per application. You can copyright one song at a time, or an entire album of songs as a single entity. You can copyright the CD itself (which is different than the songs that are on it—see below.)

It may take up to 3.3 (email) or 11.5 (mailed in) months to receive a certificate of registration after the office has received your application. Your work is still protected even without this certificate. Copyright law does not require a piece of paper from the Copyright Office. Technically your work belongs to you because you created it. And the law protects that automatically.

The only problem occurs when others challenge your ownership or claim that they own it. The easiest method to prove your ownership in court is a copyright certificate. That's a real advantage.

Still if your work is in physical form (DVD, CD, video, etc.) and you have proof that it existed before the challengers had it, your rights are probably secured. Nevertheless, proving your ownership can be difficult if all you have are some friends who heard the tape or an unopened envelope dated by the post office containing a copy of your work, etc. And lawyers do not recommend that you rely on these methods.

Panic is never helpful. Ignoring the value of protecting your rights by forgetting to fill out a simple form is stupid.

Pollyanne asks Dana, "Are you going to join BMI or ASCAP? I belong to ASCAP."

"What's the difference?"

I respond as simply as I can: "All the performance rights organizations monitor and collect fees from radio, television, elevator and supermarket muzak, jukeboxes, club play, live shows, etc. They each pay you about the same amount of money. It's the scheduling of payments that differ. One pays the songwriter and the publishing company a lot of money in the first most active years and a smaller amounts over time; another spreads out the payments more evenly and over a longer period."

SESAC/BMI/ASCAP—PERFORMANCE RIGHTS ORGANIZATIONS

If your artist is a songwriter, there is enormous income potential from hundreds of sources, the most obvious being CD and digital sales and live performances. You know how the performer gets paid, but what about the songwriter? The songwriter signs up with one of these three performance rights organizations: SESAC, BMI, or ASCAP.

They act like the Nielson ratings for television shows by monitoring a worldwide sampling of radio stations, live venues, jukeboxes, elevator music companies, television shows, and more.

For example, a dance club might pay a flat fee of a few hundred dollars each year for "music rights" to a combination of the three organizations allowing them to play whatever songs they want all year long. The organizations may or may not survey the exact songs being played at the club and then, added to the other polling numbers they collect, calculate which songs are being played the most. Based on that, those most played songs get the most royalties when they divide up all the fees among all of their member songwriters and publishing companies.

Sometimes you will see in an international booking contract, "the promoter agrees to be solely responsible for visas, working permits, and music rights." It is taken for granted that the "music rights" payment has been paid by the promoter in the U.S. (although it might be a safe measure to include it in all contracts). Overseas, you cannot be sure that BMI, ASCAP, or SESAC has secured jurisdiction in the venue you are playing, so the promoter rents the hall and then you find out after the gig is over that you're being asked to cover the cost of performing your own materials.

In response to the question, "Do I need to have these organizations at all?" I simply ask, "How can you monitor the use of your songs in thousands of locations every day, and if you could, how would you convince them to pay you?" Don't argue; have your songwriter client choose one of these organizations, pay the membership dues, and fill out the forms for every song written.

Don't be intimidated. Call the organization for information whenever you need it. They are nice people who understand their world a lot better than most artists or managers. BMI (Broadcast Music Inc., www.bmi.com), ASCAP (American Society of Composers, Authors and Publishers, www.ascap.com), and SESAC Inc. (www.sesac.com) have offices in New York and Nashville. BMI and ASCAP have Los Angeles offices as well. ASCAP is also in Chicago.

The significant loss of CD sales due to Internet access to music signaled a revolution in the music business. It hit hard and without warning. No one predicted its impact would be so revolutionary. Staying current with industry changes is important. And it is very important to negotiate a rate for Internet use in every new recording deal, especially because the record label isn't being paid at the same rate as a CD retailer like Target or Walmart.

I suggest that Dana make another appointment to discuss the details of our trial agreement. She asks if I can recommend a lawyer to help her form a publishing company. Depending on the career plan we devise, she may need a whole new support staff because of the length of time she has been away from the business. With a few exceptions, the old staff from the Goodness days has retired, relocated, or died. She wants new blood to go with her new attitude.

Pollyanne looks perplexed and wonders who Dana would need at this point.

"Well for one thing, she'll need to decide on a lawyer, a booking agent, and an accountant she likes. If she decides to perform, she'll need a road manager and perhaps one or two traveling crew members."

"You mean she chooses them? My manager Dick always has me use his people. And they tell me what I need to do."

Dana pipes up. "Oh, no. I'll be telling them what I need them to do. They work for me."

"How does that happen?

"You're paying them, aren't you?" Dana challenges her. I stay quiet.

"Dang, this is news to me. It makes so much sense. Why didn't I know this?" Pollyanne turns to me. "You know I'm really not as stupid as I sound. I just work so much that I don't have time to deal with all of this."

"Do you like the people Dick has you working with?" I ask her.

"Some of them, but some of them intimidate me."

I realize that Pollyanne is dominating my time with Dana, but it is helping me learn a lot about how determined Dana has become. I like her and her new attitude.

Dana tells me that she met a few people she liked backstage at a Maxwell concert and maybe she wants to work with them. Her sisters have a great accountant for the cookie company, but she isn't sure if that accountant knows anything about entertainment. I suggest that we invite her to lunch to find out. Dana agrees to call the accountant herself. She's definitely going to be involved in her own career building.

It's premature to discuss employment with Maxwell's musicians and crew until we have dates. It makes sense to find a road manager somewhat early to be sure he is available and interested. Maxwell's road manager might also work with other acts and might not be looking for additional commitments. At this point, we are putting the cart before the horse. Dana doesn't have an act yet. She will need new band arrangements if she wants live musicians or she will need an engineer to record tracks if she wants to go out on the road without a live band. These are artistic choices with financial ramifications.

BUILDING A DREAM TEAM

Choose professionals with a talent for communicating, people who believe that strength and power comes from imparting knowledge, not withholding it. If you can get a sense that someone thinks like an educator (without a condescending tone) and has the patience to explain in simple words what she knows, then you have found a potential team player. Of course, above all, make sure you are dealing with knowledgeable and experienced people.

Depending on artistic choices and finances, an artist might need some or all of the following (note: most of these people are consultants and would not necessarily be on the artist's payroll):

Accountant / Business Manager (payroll, bills)
Legal representation (firm vs. independent)
Tour / Road manager
Booking agent
Production designer
Personal stylists / costume designers
Choreographer
Design team (lights, scenery, props)
Press representation / marketing / publicity
Technical crew / roadies (lights, sound, stage)
Backup singers / musicians
Musical arranger / musical director
Personal security
Travel agent

QUALITIES TO LOOK FOR

Has many good and trusted contacts.
Levelheaded and clever.
Works toward a common goal.
Develops team members' skills.
Efficiently uses time and talents.
Embraces diversity.
Is committed to continuous improvement.
Builds morale internally.
Performs effectively and produces results.
Accepts praise *and* criticism.
Cooperates rather than competes.
Maintains a positive attitude toward everyone's ideas.
Stays on task.
Uses resources wisely.
Communicates openly.

Teaches and learns from one another.
Resolves conflicts effectively.
Welcomes challenges.
Shares pride in its accomplishments.
Celebrates successes!

I ask Pollyanne about her concert plans. She explains that she is about to begin a new series of recordings and will probably stay off the road for a year.

"How do you like your road manager? Maybe Dana can use him to help her put together her show since you won't need him for a year."

"Her. Rachel is a *her*. I like her but dang, she can make me feel stupid sometimes. And she can be pretty scary."

Dana says, "But is she any good? Nobody scares me and I know what I know."

"Oh girlfriend, Rachel is really good. She's too good, almost perfect. She works a computer like you've never seen. She knows lights and sound and doesn't take crap from the union guys or management."

"That's a glowing recommendation. Would you mind if Dana calls her? Are you okay with that, Dana?"

"She sounds great. Our last road manager was a joke. I was just so happy to be on the road, I didn't know it then. He knew nothing about computers, slept all day long, never remembered to call us when the limo was on its way and gambled. I don't think he thought he was paid enough."

Pollyanne asks, "Isn't there a minimum amount they all get paid, like in some union?"

I answer, "There are no unions for road managers or any of your staff. They don't have to get dinner breaks. They don't have to sleep. They can be paid as little as you can get away with. We paid him what he was worth—very little. If you remember, he was great the first year when you and your sisters did the long summer tour by bus."

"Oh I remember that tour. It was great, except for Birmingham. The promoter tried to put us in this flea-infested flophouse when our contract said four-star hotel. I think Mule burned out quickly. Our mistake was keeping him on so long."

"Mule? Was that his real name?" Pollyanne sounds amused.

"Sam-mule. Samuel. We called him Mule because he said we treated him like a mule. He used to work with men and they carried their own bags, but me and my sisters are too ladylike." She and Pollyanne burst into laughter.

"Before Rachel, my manager Dick hooked us up with Angel who was a real devil . . . I had the best time with Angel, but he wasn't good for me. He kept me out all hours of the night and I knew I didn't have any business staying up like that. By the time I crashed, around 4:00 AM, Angel was just getting started. He was a pure slut."

Dana seems interested. "Was he good looking?"

"Dang it Dana, now don't think what you're thinking. We went out drinking and that's all. Well, that was all for me. I think Angel was a sexaholic. He found a different girl at every port and I don't think he ever knew any of their names. He called them all *Baby-Girl.* 'This Baby-Girl wouldn't leave me alone last night . . . I met this Baby-Girl . . . Me and this Baby-Girl was knocking boots this morning . . . ' It would've been funny if it wasn't so triflin'. He'd show up just as the limo was arriving to take us to the airport. Dick saw him with me one time on a plane dressed in a torn t-shirt and stained shorts and almost fired him on the spot. Angel was cute in the face but he brought my image down."

"So wait a second," Dana says, "Y'all fired him because of a fashion statement?"

"Basically. 'Cause he could work a soundboard; in those days he was both road manager and soundman, and he was strong. Like I said, he kept me out late and that brought my show down. So Dick fired him and got Rachel."

"So tell us about Rachel," Dana suggests.

"Rachel does everything she's supposed to do and by the letter. The worst part about Rachel—she is so pretty. I can't stand it."

ROAD MANAGERS/TOUR MANAGERS

Road managers are perhaps the most important staff person for any artist who performs and/or tours. In theatre I compare them to a production stage manager. For the manager, the road manager is your eyes, ears, muscle, and savior out of town.

There are times, especially for a just out of the stable band, when a road manager can double as the artist's manager, sound person, lighting director, travel coordinator or agent, designer, and road crew. As the artist gets "bigger," there will be a need to divide the duties, traveling with separate sound and lighting crew, etc. Until then, the road manager is a great substitute.

The problem, of course, is that most road managers, as with managers in general, don't know a lot about some of the things in their job description. It is in the artist's interest to find out what the road manager is good at and to either train him where he is lacking or keep him away from those responsibilities which could endanger the artist's business.

His duties can include everything *and* the kitchen sink, but most will set their own limits based on their personality, likes, interests, control issues, abilities, and salary. As with almost everything else in the music industry, there are no rules, no requirements, and few standards except for those that a self-respecting road manager has made for himself.

Primary responsibility is getting the artist and crew safely to the venue and back. This can mean air, bus, car, truck, limo, train, whatever. This can mean carrying luggage and equipment or assigning it to someone else. This means having cash for everyone's tips—bellhops, luggage attendants, waiters, and airline personnel. The road manager handles group check-in at hotels, at the airline desk, at the venue. He arranges hotel and dressing room assignments. He makes wake-up calls and sends out schedules that he's made himself.

He represents the artist and manager with the promoter, the promoter's production manager, the technical crew and the venue's box office, backstage staff, and security. Helpful attributes include attention to detail, knowledge of budgeting, computer expertise and *tact*. He "advances" the entire show, which means he calls weeks ahead to speak with the promoter and the venue's technical supervisors to be sure that the artist's technical needs can and will be met.

Coordinating meet 'n' greets and handling the media are also part of his duties. He makes sure the hotel arrangements are secured and satisfactory, that backstage food nuances are understood, and, if provided, that airport pickup arrangements are known. He coordinates the times that he and the crew can be on stage to set up the show and when a sound check can take place. This does not always coincide with airline flight arrivals and adjustments may have to be made.

When the artist is napping at the hotel after a long flight, the road manager is at the venue working. When the show is over, the road manager is supervising the packing of equipment and writing the next day's schedule. When the artist has a problem or causes it, the road manager is there to solve it. When the promoter creates a problem, the road manager negotiates it or contacts the manager back home.

And when there's money to be picked up just before the concert begins, the road manager collects it and holds it and arranges for its safe delivery to a bank.

Above all else, be sure your road manager is honest and that his personality brings out the best in the artist and staff. Attitude isn't everything but it can make or break a crisis. Whatever goes wrong on the road will come back to bite you.

The road manager can be treated as your partner or your right hand man. That's up to your style of management. But treat him well. If you've got an artist that's a handful, he'll be abused plenty without you adding to his troubles.

Where do you find road managers? Usually through word of mouth, calling other artists for references, ads in trade papers, associations and lists on the Internet and in trade magazines like *Pollstar*. You might even try the Stage Managers Association through Actors' Equity Association. Many stage managers are very experienced at touring large Broadway shows with well over a hundred people on staff; a band tour might be a piece of cake for them.

The meeting is wrapping up when Pollyanne asks, "When can you and I get together for a private chat?"

"I thought you were just joking about leaving Dick. But if you're serious, we can talk next week. And Dana, we should maybe meet again at the end of this week to get the ball rolling on your publishing company. You can sign the copyright forms then, but don't forget to bring in a copy of the music and your checkbook."

"I don't have anything on paper except the words, but I have a tape of me on the piano."

"Then bring that with you and we'll send it off. Pollyanne will get you Rachel's phone number and let me know when the two of you are going to get together. I'd like to be there."

"I'll be there too," Pollyanne says.

Why am I not surprised?

As soon as the ladies leave, I invite Robert O. in with the latest batch of telephone messages. There are a number of messages from BoyBand's booking agency, Don Juan's road manager, and the Redds have decided on a date for our tax-paying party. None of them say urgent, so I call Max X. first. I'm hungry, so I grab some of the leftovers from lunch with Juan.

Max X. is home and he sounds a little groggy. "Hey man, wassup?"

"You sound like you were sleeping. You want me to call back?"

"Nah, that's alright. I was sleeping, but I need to get up. What time is it?"

"It's ten after four."

"PM?"

"The afternoon, right. Look, I can call you back."

"I'm up," he says, sounding more awake. "What you got?"

"There's something you can do right now that can save you some money with your manager. Your manager is taking 20 percent of the gross and the four of you each get 20 percent of the net. The RRU Corporation holds the 80 percent that is supposed to go to you guys. It then pays your bills and production expenses—expensive things like rehearsal space, airfare, ground transportation, lodging, business and legal costs, insurance, etc. Then you four get to divide up whatever's left over. That's why your manager ends up with more than anyone of you guys. Of course, he's got office expenses, but they're nothing compared to your bills.

"Now I know you said that you're the only one in the group complaining now, but if you explain this to the other members and they understand that this arrangement puts you all at a decided financial disadvantage, you can go in to your manager as a unified group and demand that the contract be amended so that he gets his percentage of the net too. You won't get back what you've lost, but you won't lose any more and you'll know how to avoid this type of thing in the future.

"If your manager says no he won't do it, then tell him you won't be doing any more gigs. Your contract is up in December anyway, that's just a few months off. Then you can renegotiate your contract with him or get another manager."

"And if the other guys won't go in with me?"

"Go in on your own, but try to reason with the others. There is strength in solidarity."

"Cool man. I heard you were good. You're fast, too."

We agree he will call me after he talks with the other members of RRU.

"If he gives us any flack, we might be looking for new management. You think you could take us on if it comes to that?"

"We'll talk about it if it comes to that."

"Thank you, man, so much. You just made my day."

He just made my day by saying that.

Dana Goode of Goodness in her dressing room

Country sensation Pollyanne Heart

20

Crisis at 3:00 AM—
Day Three

I like my attitude problem.
Obstacles are what you see when you take your eyes off your goals.

I finish my calls, fix two clauses in one of Don Juan's performance contracts, and get out of there. One of the advantages of this kind of management is that your hours are erratic, but you have some control over the hours you want to work. I like going to the grocery store during the day and working on contracts late at night. But since I have no other contracts to write or review, I've got a free evening tonight . . . when did this last happen? I can't recall, but I'm going to love it. Other nights I might go to a concert or a show with friends, celebrity clients, or an occasional date. My ex-wife left a message on the machine asking if I thought I could get an autographed photo of Don Juan for her new best friend's birthday, which is Saturday. I bet she likes him better than she ever loved me. I know she treats him better. Anyway, I've got a file of pre-autographed Don Juans. I'll sign her friend's name and mail it off tomorrow.

I catch up with the news, order a pizza, eat half, and wash it down with some lovely merlot. I watch part of a bad movie on cable and retire about half past midnight, which is really early for me.

My cell phone wakes me up about 3:00 AM. I leave it on while it recharges in the rare event that one of my clients is having an emergency. I've gotten calls bearing the news that the road manager is taking band members to the hospital, that the promoter is trying to stiff my artists, that canceled airline connections have made it impossible for the artist to arrive for the concert on time, that the artist is in the midst of a drunken binge, as well as hysterical calls from overworked artists about absolutely nothing—all of which have come after normal work hours and all of which I consider part of the job.

This time it is a call from California.

"I'm in a fucking jam, man! Can you bail me out?"

"Who is this?"

"It's Jeremy, man. I couldn't reach my manager so I hope you don't mind I'm calling you."

I glance at the clock. "Where are you?"

"In Los Angeles at the Forum."

"What happened?"

"The damn promoter lost his fucking mind! He got up in my face ranting about how he wasn't gonna let me leave this fucking shit hole if I didn't pay the fucking overtime for his fucking slow-as-molasses tech crew. Well that pissed me the fuck off and I told him to fucking kiss my ass. One thing led to another, and I punched the pussy in his fucking pretty boy face!"

"Jeremy, you're doing it again, man. Take a deep breath and talk to me slow."

"I can't. They called the police and they're having me arrested!"

I have the clarity of mind to ask him for his cell phone number in case we're disconnected. For the life of me, I can't figure out why he thought he should call me.

"Hey, Jeremy, where's your road manager?"

"He's in the other room trying to smooth over the asshole promoter. Let me tell you what happened. You tell me if I'm in the wrong."

"Well, if you hit someone, you're in the wrong. No question about that."

"Yeah but he was holding me hostage and trying to steal $3,000 from me! What was I supposed to do?"

"You were supposed to let your road manager handle it. That's what you should've done. But I guess you don't need me to lecture you. You know it's three o'clock in the morning here."

"Yeah, I'm really sorry but my manager is never around when I need him."

"Do you often call him at 3:00 AM?"

"Sometimes. Well, not too often."

"He's probably hiding from you." Well, I think I'm funny but Jeremy doesn't.

"Man, you getting on my case too? Shit, I'm going to jail and no one's helping me."

"Jeremy, your road manager is helping you. And if he can find your manager, he'll help you too. I don't know what you want me to do."

"Just listen to what happened."

Jeremy R. was the opening act for a famous rock band that night. It seems that the promoter was afraid of paying union overtime in the heavily unionized LA Forum. A rental agreement at these larger venues includes stagehands, ushers, and other staff until 11:00 PM. So the promoter smartly included a contractual clause that said Jeremy's show should be fifty to sixty minutes long. The headlining rockers were supposed to play for seventy-five minutes. There would be a twenty-minute intermission when the crew would clear the stage of Jeremy's band and set up for the final act. The show was supposed to start at 8:00 PM. If all went well, the show would end around 10:35, not risking the 11:00 deadline.

The contracts also said that each act was not to go over its allotted times. If one of the acts played too long, and if the show went into overtime because of it, the act could be fined the cost of whatever overtime charges the arena imposed. Jeremy said he was aware of the clause and did his usual sixty-minute show.

But the show started twenty minutes late, not due to any fault of the performers. And the union stagehands needed thirty minutes to change the stage at intermission, not twenty. So when the headlining act began their set, it was already nine forty-five. There was exactly seventy-five minutes left for the headlining act to play a seventy-five minute set. The show went into overtime by one and a half minutes.

After the concert ended, the promoter and his security guards asked to meet with both acts. He told Jeremy that he had timed his act at sixty-one and a half minutes. He would therefore have to pay at least half of the cost of the overtime. The other act would have to pay the rest since they should have cut their show short to end before 11:00 PM. The overtime incurred came to almost $7,000. The Forum has a large crew and they are guaranteed a full hour even if they only work one minute.

Jeremy refused to pay, but the promoter was blocking the door to the dressing rooms and wouldn't let anyone leave before they agreed to return $3,500 of the cash paid to them just before the show.

Jeremy yelled. The promoter yelled. Jeremy punched the promoter in the face. The police were called. While security guarded the door, the road managers tried to do damage control in the next room with the promoter and Forum management.

Again I ask, "Jeremy, I'm not your manager. I'd love to help but what can I do?"

"How about paying my bail?" He starts crying. "I don't want to go to jail. All I did was play my regular show. I don't know if I went over the limit. I don't think I did."

I interrupt. "Even if you did, you don't owe the promoter a penny. The concert started late, the intermission went long, and the star act wasn't told to cut it short by the promoter's people. The promoter's stage manager could have warned the last act to cut one song. Every-thing would have been fine."

"So I'm not at fault?"

"Not in my opinion. But I don't have any say in this."

Jeremy interrupts. "John just walked in. I'll call you back."

"Jeremy! Jeremy!" Jeremy hangs up. It's almost 4:00 AM.

I sleep with half an eye open expecting the phone to ring as soon as I go into deep sleep. Jeremy never calls back. But at 4:30 AM, the airlines do.

The domestic airline handling this morning's flight for Don Juan and his entourage has been cancelled. Not because of local weather or terrorism, but because there's a storm in another city preventing the aircraft from making its New York City connection. This is, of course, a recorded message with no information about how to fix the problem.

The flight to Las Vegas was originally due to leave JFK airport at 12:15 PM for a show the next night. We booked these seats two months earlier to save money and to get the better seats. Delays are common and so Don Juan spends his extra time in the airlines' executive lounge almost every flight. But cancellations create different problems . . . at 4:30 AM. If I can get him a new flight today, he can still make his show and have some time to rest.

That's why I still use a travel agent instead of an Internet discount website. First, I don't want to have to buy ten tickets myself and worry about precise seating, as required by the entourage and star. Second, I need someone with "connections" in the travel industry to get us special treatment, especially with last-minute travel arrangements for ten. And to make sure we get the refunds or credit on the tickets that were cancelled.

I immediately email and text our Chicago travel agent, who is still asleep since it's only 3:30 AM there. This will alert him to call me the moment he awakes. Having his private cell is essential in this business. I also contact our road manager and have him call and/or text everyone so they know the flight is cancelled and should be awaiting our instructions, keeping in mind that we are trying not to wake them up . . . yet. Ground transportation has to be alerted as well.

After hours of research and negotiations, and numerous emails and calls repeatedly telling everyone to be patient, we finally get a new flight later that afternoon from a different airport and two different airlines (because there was insufficient seating on any one airline).

In many cases, the road manager secures travel arrangements, and not the business manager, but that's not how I roll for Don Juan because he alternates road managers and he needs consistency.

In the middle of all of this, I call Jeremy's manager and find out that John, Jeremy's road manager, made a deal with the promoter to avoid jail time for Jeremy. Everything is now fine. I never find out how much money, if any, they paid.

UNIONS/MUSICIANS

Unions are both a curse and a blessing depending on your situation. On Broadway, there are over a dozen different unions, all with different rules, conflicting lunch hours, and a wide range of health and pension benefits.

On concert tour, although non-union personnel may not actually work all day long, they are on call twenty-four hours a day. They miss meals; they can't find time to take showers. They are sometimes unfairly docked money out of an already small paycheck without recourse. Often they travel all night on a school bus to be dropped off at the venue, where they pay for their own coffee (if they can find any) and begin work immediately setting up scaffolding and lights while the artist and management fly into town and go directly to a five-star hotel to rest.

Some staff people never get medical insurance. If they want to work, they work at the discretion of the show's producer and can be fired at any time without even a return-trip ticket home. To the extent that unions protect workers from abuse, they are a blessing. To the extent that they turn one minute of overtime into a $7,000 fiasco (as in Jeremy's case above), they are a pain in the butt.

Of course, some tours have caring management and some producers and promoters go out of their way to be fair. Managers should never forget how much someone who operates with fairness and consideration is appreciated. Even though staff may not need to be protected from the well-intentioned boss, unions still serve a purpose by helping to standardize the business and create a minimal level of decency for an industry. On the other hand, union costs can kill an otherwise successful show.

Quoted directly from a Local 802 (NYC musicians) brochure entitled "Shine a Light on Dark Dates":

When I play a non-union date, I get cash in my pocket. What am I missing out on by not playing union? Plenty. When you record union, you get guaranteed wages, pension, and health contributions. You also get Special Payments and protections if your recording is ever used in a new format. When it's not union, once you've given away your music, you've lost all control over it.

Unions have negotiated for jurisdiction in certain venues. You're going to have to be prepared to deal with them in the larger venues like Madison Square Garden and Radio City Music Hall. Rock bands may not know that they are considered non-union musicians when they play these performance halls and may be contacted and asked for dues and/or asked to join. This happens in Canada too. Some U.S. states are right-to-work states meaning that no workers can be required to be a member of a union and cannot be denied work because of being non-union.

The American Federation of Musicians (AFM) is only one of many national unions with regional Locals in hundreds of cities. Stagehands, truckers, concessionaires, box office personnel, ushers, security guards, and more may affect your concert.

Artists have various unions: SAG (Screen Actors Guild), AFTRA (American Federation of Television and Radio Artists), AGMA (American Guild of Musical

Artists), AGVA (American Guild of Variety Artists), and AEA (Actors' Equity Association). An artist who finds that her hospital bills are covered because a union required the record label to pay into the welfare fund will give thanks. The same artist will curse the union requiring large membership dues at a time when the artist's career is nonexistent. The artist who does one film and never works again resents having to join. That same artist will be grateful for residual checks received years after the movie has been exiled to and discounted by Amazon.com.

The recording industry is also governed by union minimum payment schedules and regulations. Since the leading performers on an album are paid more than minimum, the pay rates are usually irrelevant to your artist. However, it will affect background singers and musicians.

AFTRA has complex payment rules for recording artists, probably because of how complicated it is to determine the value of each artist's contribution to a recording.

Until you get a recording deal, or work in a large venue, the union doesn't care about hassling you. Still there are benefits to belonging to a union, and as a manager you should make sure your artist thinks about joining up.

Whatever your take on unions, they are a reality. It makes sense to ask about union jurisdiction and to try to understand that union's regulations wherever your people work.

For the record, there is a difference between unions, associations, and guilds. Unions have legal authority to negotiate and *enforce* working regulations for its members. Associations and guilds organize artists but can only *suggest* working guidelines to employers and members. Examples of well-known organizations that are not unions include NARAS (National Academy of Recording Arts and Sciences), GMA (Gospel Music Association), CMA (Country Music Association), RAC (Recording Artists Coalition), NAS (National Academy of Songwriters), SGA (Songwriters Guild of America), and the RIAA (Recording Industry Association of America, Inc.).

21

Who Would Ever Guess?

Don't have conversations with people who aren't there.
'No' is a complete sentence.

I drag myself into the office about 10:00 AM with a large black coffee and a buttered bagel. I'm not expecting Robert O. until one o'clock or so because he has finals. So I check the machine for messages and my calendar for appointments while I munch on my continental breakfast. The most urgent thing I have pending at the moment is getting Don Juan's autographed photo mailed off to my ex. I sit at Robert O.'s desk writing "Happy birthday Beverly! Love," over Don Juan's signature when the phone rings.

It is a teary Aurelio from BoyBand bearing bad news. Jasper, BoyBand's second blond boy from the left with the thin but melodious falsetto voice, was killed two hours ago in a plane accident. He had taken a separate flight from the other boys because he wanted to stay in Phoenix a few hours longer to surprise his mother on her birthday.

Death shakes up any group. Young people believe they are invulnerable and immortal. One theory is that that is why they take drugs and have unprotected sex in greater numbers than older people. The other theory is they are still immature.

Imagine being eighteen years old, having a hit record, heading out on an eleven-month world tour, and being told that you would be paid a monthly allowance of $25,000. Can any "normal" kid be psychologically ready to understand the implications? First reaction, of course, is "Hooray, I'm rich." Then the excesses can become surreal. After their first year of touring and being treated as royalty, my clients BoyBand had begun to believe they were gods. To some of their fans, they were.

Members of England's royal family are carefully educated and prepared in the ways of royalty. And some of them still have major problems. Rockers have no education on how to live the lifestyle of the rich and famous. BoyBand began with an eighteen-year-old's level of maturity (or immaturity, if you prefer) and got sex, drugs, and money thrown at them. Why would they think it would ever end?

In most cases, it ends long before they do.

Music's premature deaths—Michael Jackson, Jim Morrison of the Doors, Kurt Cobain of Nirvana, Mama Cass of the Mamas and Papas, John Lennon, Tupac Shakur, Biggie Smalls, Elvis Presley, Aaliyah, Lisa Lopes of TLC, Luther Vandross, and dozens more—flash through my consciousness. Some of these were drug overdoses, some accidents and some murders. It doesn't really matter what the cause was. They were all premature and they all had everything and nothing to do with their celebrity in the music industry.

I'm prepared and very aware that I can *never* really be prepared for the intense emotional and professional challenges I will face in the next week. The press, the family, promoters from upcoming gigs, financial decisions, legal complications—I will be the de facto executor of Jasper's professional will. I'm hoping that the boys themselves have learned a lot and matured even more over their years of success.

I'm hoping that after the shock of Jasper's death, they will come prepared with answers to my questions. Do we replace Jasper or go on with a four-member group? If we replace him, will the new guy be an equal partner or just an employee? I have to review the group's shareholder agreement to assess what part of the group's assets belongs to Jasper and his estate. How will the loss of these assets affect the financial security of the rest of the members and their plans? Will there be in-fighting over money? Will it lead to someone quitting or possibly the break-up of the group altogether?

Death affects people and careers in strange ways.

PREPARING FOR THE DEATH OR RESIGNATION OF A BAND MEMBER: THE SHAREHOLDERS AGREEMENT

The unexpected is the enemy of financial and career stability. Yet one of the few things to be sure of is that everyone will be visited by the unexpected. No one expects to die today or tomorrow. We think death will come—but much later.

If someone dies before you've put legal guidelines in place, it is almost guaranteed that there will be disagreements, confusion, and legal challenges. A legal challenge could freeze any activity for the group indefinitely. That means no income, no work, and, eventually, no group.

Since a band is a business just like Sony, General Electric, Disney, or Ford, understanding how big business works can help you avoid catastrophe. The shareholders (owners of the company) approve by-laws that describe how they and hired executives will operate the company and how decisions will be made. They also determine how people get paid, perhaps with weekly salary checks, perhaps with ownership shares in the company, some with special deals, others by general categories. On a smaller scale, this is true of musical acts as well; some people get paid by commissions, salaries, fees, or special deals. Because of the variety in payment and status, these companies develop rules for dealing with someone who quits, is fired, or dies. This is called a *shareholders agreement*.

Obviously this is not the first thing a band discusses. Before hitting it big, usually their only priority is the creation of music and the promotion of the group. A struggling band may see no reason to bother and may fight a manager's attempt to write an agreement. Nevertheless, there are small things a manager can do along the way to prepare for someone leaving the group unexpectedly.

When the band writes a new song, ask "Who wrote the music?" and "Who wrote the words?" Try to determine if one person wrote more than another. Put it in writing, even on a blank piece of paper, and have them all sign it. This can be the basis of an agreement later. If a number is choreographed or costumes designed, determine who gets credit for what. There is also an issue as to legal ownership. While the band members are in good spirits, they are more likely to agree that creative work is the property of the entire group rather than just one person. That way, if someone leaves the group, the number and the look remain with the group. Writing it all down is a safer bet.

When the group starts to earn a decent income and starts to save money, the manager should try to write a complete shareholders agreement. Your lawyer will provide samples from other companies, but my experience is that these sample documents are much too complicated for the workings of a musical group. Try to write your own agreement using a list of "what ifs" based on your understanding of the way your clients think and behave. Then let an attorney check it over before anyone signs it.

There is no correct way to write one. If the band has saved $50,000 in a money market account and owns publishing on three songs, how do you divide that among five singers? One band decided that the deceased would get one-fifth of all available cash, but that the publishing would continue as a separate business run by surviving band members after a member's death. All costumes and equipment would also belong to the surviving members. The deceased's estate would continue to earn a share of any profits from the publishing. The deceased would not be entitled to money from the sale of costumes or equipment.

Another band decided that when just one member dies, everything would be liquidated, including the publishing company, and the band would officially go out of business. All five members would get one-fifth of whatever came from the sale of the publishing, the cash, the costumes, etc. Their agreement said that any surviving members would own the band's trademarked name. The band would then be able to form a new corporation but continue to use the old name.

There are major omissions with both of these plans, but at least these bands had a plan that might prevent courtrooms and legal battles.

Some questions to be answered in a shareholders agreement: How many votes belong to each owner or hired hand? Who can approve and change these rules? What's the procedure for changing the rules? How does someone new become a voter or an owner, and how does someone lose his vote and ownership? What does the company consider its assets, and what is not owned by the company? What does the company owe an owner/shareholder as opposed to what is owed to a hired hand upon death, termination, retirement, or resignation? What must happen to dissolve the company/band? Who owns the band's image, songs, stage numbers, and trademarked name? Will an accountant or manager oversee financial determinations needed to carry out this agreement? These are extremely difficult questions. Start with the best solutions you can imagine and be prepared to update or rewrite it on a regular basis.

A lawyer is absolutely necessary to review the language and check for legal omissions but the responsibility of drafting the blueprint of the agreement belongs to the manager and the band members together.

I hang up the phone just as a young, thick-lipped, raven-haired, voluptuous woman struts in on high, black-and-rhinestone stiletto heels. She must have been poured into her black spandex body suit with black leather and rhinestone money belt. She looked like a curious mixture of Angelina Jolie and *Star Trek: Voyager*'s Seven of Nine (Jeri Ryan). She notices the photo I am autographing.

"You always forge your celebrity clients' signatures?" oozes from her lips, even before "Hello" or "I am" or "Are you . . . ?"

"I never forge a signature," I answer. "I'm personalizing a pre-signed celebrity photo."

"Oooo, can I get me one of those?" she playfully pouts.

"Sure," I say and finish writing the greeting, address an envelope, slip the picture, with a cardboard support and a brief note, inside, seal and stamp it, and put it in the out box. All the while, I ignore this dark and lovely stranger-lady who's perched her curvaceous hips on the edge of my desk regarding me like she has something I want, instead of the other way around.

And maybe she's right, but I have other things on my mind. I'm anxious to find out more about Jasper's accident and call his family and each of the guys and offer my help. As a manager, I've had to learn how to deal with death in a detached manner. There's always time to fall apart privately, but the job requires a level head in all types of crises. So although I'm intrigued, she is a distraction.

During the silence, I hear her softly chuckle. I get another photo from the files.

"What's your name?" I ask with a pen poised to write.

"Fanny," she says, then stands up, bends over and wiggles her perfectly round derriere in my face.

"Good name," I say and we both laugh. "What can I do for you, Fanny?"

I hear that soft chuckle thing again.

"You can announce to your boss that I am here with a little proposition of musical representation for myself and my multi-talented husband."

She doesn't know who I am. She thinks I'm the receptionist since she found me at the reception desk, so she's not coming on to me to gain my representation. And she's married— so why is she coming on to me at all? I've seen it time and time again. To get a foot in the door, performers will charm, explain, plead, and reveal intimate details to anyone connected to the business who will listen. This isn't the first time a performer has flirted with me, and I am sure it won't be the last.

Believe it or not, I've never broken Rule #4: never play in your own backyard. There's no chance that anything will actually happen, so I feel reasonably relaxed.

"I don't know how to jump-start my career. I had a production deal but they jerked me around. After serving two years on that plantation, I finally got out with the help of an expensive lawyer. But I've got a demo CD of five songs I think can be mega-hits with the right marketing. I'm all ready to hit the road with my husband as my roadie and your boss as my manager."

A production deal "plantation"—she phrased that well. Production deals can be bad news.

I come around to the front of Robert's desk now that I'm about to begin the interview.

"What's your style?"

"I keep it funky."

"What about costumes?"

"I'm always in costume."

"Can you dance or play an instrument?"

"I can do a lot of things. And what I don't know, I'm very willing to learn. I like new tricks."

"Are you solo or part of a group?"

"Sometimes I'm alone or with a partner, but my absolute favorite is in a group."

"What are you talking about?"

"What are *you* talking about?"

I can tell she's enjoying taking me for a ride but we are getting nowhere.

"Do you have your own musicians or do we need to put a band together for you?"

"Let's put it together."

"How much money do you have?"

"How much will you cost?"

"I'm trying to . . . "

"I know. I'm sorry. I've been a bad girl. You can spank me if you want."

"Stop." I have had enough. "I can't help you, Fanny."

"Yes, you can. And we both know you want to. If you didn't, you'd have gotten your boss like I asked you to."

"I am the boss, and I only work with serious artists."

"You're the boss? Well, hot damn, I heard you were good, but nobody told me you were also cute as a button."

"Thanks. I've got a pressing matter . . . "

"At least listen to my demo and meet my husband," she cuts me off, taking out a CD in a clear plastic cover from her belt pouch. The picture on the disc is what I presume to be her logo, a close up of her buns with a continuing string of the letters F-A-N-N-Y outlining the bottom curvature of her cheeks.

"Cute," I say, meaning it, then add, "I promise I'll listen to this. Call me next week."

"Cool." She looks carefully in my eyes for sincerity and finds it, then leaves with the photo and the soft chuckle thing.

I was sincere because I really think her packaging concept is clever. It's simple, erotic but not lewd, and, most of all, memorable. Tushes sell on BET and MTV daily. She might take it to a whole new level. You've got to have a gimmick to stand out, and that logo alone gives me a glimpse of her vision—and I like it. If her CD is good, I'll schedule a serious dialogue next week.

As soon as the door closes behind her, I leave messages for the other three BoyBand members expressing condolences and asking them to call me at their earliest convenience. I am sure some of them are home but not answering the phone. I'm not sure that the press knows about this, since no one from the media has called me yet. I want to get the guys together to plan a response to the press tsunami and the expected flurry of calls so we'll all be on the same page with the same information. I also want to go over the types of questions the press will more than likely ask, including "Will this break up the group?" or "Was there friction between Jasper and you guys? Why wouldn't he fly with you?" In general, some press people look to provoke dramatic emotional responses since they make great headlines and sound bytes and sell papers.

I call Jasper's mother, but she isn't answering either. I go to the files to retrieve the group's shareholders agreement and I decide to write a draft of a press release to show to the guys and their press representative when we meet later. I'm composing my response to the inevitable first press call anticipating the worst, a gossip rag, when a man walks in saying "Hi. I'm Angel . . . Fanny's husband."

He appears to be maybe twenty-five years her senior with long salt and pepper hair and beard. He's distinguished looking, almost aristocratic—above the neck. His big belly makes the waistband of his jeans ride dangerously low and push his t-shirt way up until it almost looks like a halter. His biceps bulge like his belly.

"I know you haven't listened to my wife's demo yet. I just wanted to meet you and find out a few things."

"I don't mean to be rude but this is a terrible time. Can we talk next week? Please."

"Look, my wife wants you to be her manager and I want her to have everything she wants," he says, ignoring my dismissal. "For the record, I used to be her manager. I'm the one that arranged that lousy production deal. I'm going to make it up to her because she's good. I've got $6,500 in savings and another $17,000 in investments I'm willing to chance on her career. I've been in the business for over twenty years and I can put together almost any kind of tour crew in a minute. I know Fanny well. I know she flaunted her body and then apologized for being a bad girl. She probably asked if you wanted to spank her, didn't she? I told her you might not roll like that so I came up here to tell you that Baby-girl's not the only one with something to shake at you, know what I mean?" He reaches over and playfully pinches my nipple.

I smack his hand, get up and open the door, insisting, "This is a terrible time. We'll talk next week. I promise I'll listen to the demo. Thank you." I nudge him out without giving him a chance to respond, then lock the door behind him.

From the hallway he yells, "Thanks. We'll see you next week. Baby-girl will let both of us spank her then!"

I'm not angry, but I have no time for this crap. Some acts are afraid of a casting couch and it seems some acts insist on it.

Then it hits me. "Baby-girl?" "Angel?" "Experienced, strong as a bull, and over-sexed. . ." This must be Pollyanne's ex-roadie. Angel has a reputation for hard work and talent and though he parties hard, it never interferes with business on the road. Pollyanne couldn't handle him, but Fanny seems to have no problem there. If she's got any talent at all, I'll have to decide if they're worth the headaches I know they'll cause. Then again, compared to many other artists in this pop/rock game, they're still pretty tame.

PRODUCTION DEALS

A significant financial return is the only reason a businessperson invests in an entertainer. Most investors want a guarantee that they will make a profit. Some are gamblers and will take the risk, but only if the potential financial return is huge. What does the artist have that can *guarantee* an investor will make money? Nothing.

Think this through. An artist needs financial backing. The artist has nothing that guarantees a return of this investment. Any investor is going to want *a lot* in return for the money. Maybe they expect to become the manager. Maybe they expect their money back before the artist gets a penny. It's the age-old concept of a loan from organized crime. They expect that you pay up or they take your business, or both. That's the financial concept behind many production deals offered by record labels.

Let's see this from the artist's viewpoint. A recording label sees your performance and offers a deal. However, you're surprised to see that it's not just a recording deal, it's a production deal. The agreement says that the label will produce and distribute a CD and video, provide management, book a concert tour, arrange for photos and press representation. The label, it seems, is committed to making you a star! What could be more exciting? So you sign.

Consider how much money the label is investing in you. What if you're not a big success? The label would lose a lot. Of course, the label expects you to work super hard and to follow the directions of its people. They want to see a return as soon as possible, so you'll spend a lot of time doing what's needed.

A small independent label won't be able to lay out much money, so you're going to have to find a job—but it can't get in the way of the label's schedule for you. Maybe you can negotiate a bit more money up front, so you turn to your manager. He works for the label. Well, there goes that. Even from a major label's million-dollar production deal, you probably won't get much, if any, salary because the money is spent for *production.* You may have to live dirt-poor for a while. But so what? You're going to be a star.

The people at the label tell you you're going to need some new clothes for the photo shoot. No problem. Of course, you've got to pay for the clothes. That's okay—they paid you a small amount of money up front as an advance on future royalties, so you'll let them take it out of that. You later find out that the cost of the photographer will be deducted from future royalties, as will the press rep, the CD costs, and the video. The manager, supplied by the label, also takes his commission from the money you're supposed to get up front.

A few months later, you've got a CD. There are a few club dates scheduled, an exciting release party, some press interviews, and distribution plans set to happen over the next few months. No money yet, but that's OK. You're living at home with your parents and you'll be able to get a temp job next month when things calm down.

The video comes out great and two months later it plays on cable TV. You think, "Here comes the payoff!" The CD peaks on the *Billboard* charts at number fifty-four. The label is happy, but not enough to move ahead with a second CD. That's OK. Another label will want you now that you've had a song that's made the charts. Except the production deal says that you belong to the label for at least three CDs or three years, whichever is longer. The deal also says that the label doesn't have to produce another CD if it doesn't want. And the label has decided that its investment in you was just enough to cover its financial costs plus a little more. It anticipates that you're not worth a second risk.

After subtracting all the costs of your production deal, the label doesn't owe you any additional royalties, your manager tells you. You get to keep the few thousand dollars you were advanced. He shakes your hand and says, "I really liked your sound. Best of luck."

So was it worth it? Everyone can make his own decision. Could the deal have been made better? That's where an independent manager could have helped. That's why an artist needs to find an advisor to explain the deal and negotiate whatever can be negotiated up front.

A manager's responsibility should be to protect his client, first and foremost. Conflicts of interest (working for two bosses: the label and the artist) can tie the manager's hands. Knowing how to set up a deal that doesn't look like the above production deal is a talent that each manager should learn in business school, in consultation with a good lawyer, from financial advisors, or in real life. Advising a client not to sign a deal like this may cause a rift between manager and a desperate artist, but signing it can be death for the artist. It's the space between a rock and a hard place.

Don't blame the record label. They just want a return for their bucks.

The phone rings. I let the machine pick up in case it's the press. I'm not ready. It's Preston from BoyBand. I am about to pick up—until I hear the start of his message. "Hey man. Returning your call. I made a decision. I'm leaving the group. I've had it with these idiots. It's not just because of Jasper, that's horrible what happened to him, but he made me realize it's the right time. I'm going solo. I've been working on a production deal on the side almost a year now. I wanted you to know before I tell everyone else later today. So just make sure I get the same piece as Jasper and write me out. Call me about the funeral. If they ask, I don't want to be a pallbearer." *Click.*

I have a sudden thought about the barnyard of characters I manage. I lose sleep even over the people I don't manage, like the Jeremy's in the world, who will probably never call to say "thank you."

I am pissed at Preston's attitude and the arrogance of many of my clients. I'd like to tell them how rude they can be and how ugly and destructive their narcissism is. I'd like to tell Preston that he isn't entitled to the *same piece* as Jasper because the shareholders agreement says you get one thing if you *die*, but much less if you *quit*. I have no energy to try to convince him to stay, but I know that's exactly what I'll be spending all week doing. Tomorrow I may be in better spirits, but right now I want out myself.

I want to gather up half the recording world and tell them to stop being so small. I am so tired of handholding these old children. And the thought of adding Fanny and Angel to my roster of clients is nauseating. Love of music is one of the things that drew me to this profession; the money potential sold me on this career. Twenty-five years of listening to grown people whining, begging, backstabbing, and blaming has started to make all the benefits fade from view.

I slip Fanny's CD into the office player with the hopes that it will be bad enough to eliminate her from consideration. Just then Robert O. walks in, listens a minute and says, "She's good. She's real good."

"Shit!"

The phone rings and my ever-efficient intern grabs the receiver and after his basic salutation, I hear, "He's right here . . . Oh . . . OK sure, I'll tell him. Yeah, later."

Robert O. asks, "Who's Jeremy?"

"What did he want?" I ask with disdain.

"He said, 'Thanks for last night.'"

I'm stunned. Jeremy just tossed me an unexpected pearl. I am instantly restored. "Let's do lunch, Robert."

Robert O. grins and asks, "Long morning?"

"The usual," I laugh, ushering him out the door for a midday meal and an earful.

Mama told me there'd be days like this.

L–R: Aurelio, Jasper, Preston, Randy, and Donald a.k.a. BoyBand

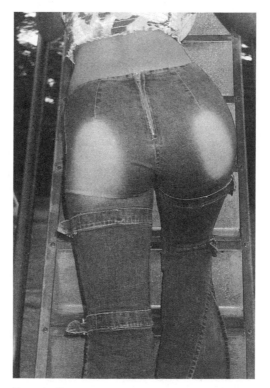

Fanny's "low-go"

Coda: Syra Says (The Most Important Advice)

Have you ever noticed that people who do things get most of their criticism from people who do nothing?
Real leaders are ordinary people with extraordinary determination.

What kind of personality makes a good manager? Aggressive, responsible, charismatic, diplomatic, creative, perceptive, quick thinking, intelligent, skillful, and a whole host of scout traits will certainly be helpful. Some things you'll start out with, and some things you'll develop along the way.

What kind of skills do good managers need? Good communication, basic knowledge of legal and financial issues, Internet savvy, being resourceful (resources include friends, family, associates, Facebook friends, business contacts of all kinds), and most essential of all: typing and computer skills. I remember working for several older managers who hired me in an executive role but needed me to turn on their computers, write their letters, and retrieve data simply because they didn't know how to do it themselves. They were administratively challenged. A good manager, road manager or stage manager must be able to conduct business at 2:00 AM as well as at 2:00 PM, anywhere, with or without assistance. A manager without some combination of cell phone (iPhone or BlackBerry) and a laptop is a dinosaur. Today's manager needs to be familiar with today's game methods. But spending money on tech toys is not a substitute for knowledge, creativity, and experience—true for both managers and artists.

If after reading this book, you can't remember everything, here is the most important advice to protect yourself in this potentially lucrative and dangerous business:

1. The Oxygen Mask Principle (chapter 8).
2. "Out Clauses" in every contract (chapter 16).
3. Arbitration clauses in every contract whenever possible (chapter 22).

4. Acting busy isn't the same as doing something worthwhile; managers are not personal assistants for their artists.
5. Aspiring managers should apprentice under other managers before starting out on their own.

The truth is that an artist can make career advancements without a manager, but rarely can an artist foresee the major obstacles ahead and break through these obstacles. That is the true value of a manager.

These five points protect both you and your artist. Otherwise, the manager will drive himself crazy with work and still notice that he and his artist are getting nowhere and not earning money.

I guess every relationship, management or marriage, has snags. Almost always they begin with a basic understanding and are sealed with a contract. But if things fall apart, and Humpty Dumpty can't be put together again, then move on. Be proud of your accomplishments and do something good with somebody else.

You see, a business life and a personal life are not that different. I believe that you must discover who you are and the standards that will govern your life. Then carry that with you every minute of every day into your business dealings and relationships. Honesty is not part-time. Sincerity cannot be faked—for long. Being happy in your own life finds its way into every deal, every success, and every failure.

Pressure and stress make you ill. Yet management is a crisis-oriented job. Finding your own inner peace before you answer a crisis phone call should be the goal of every manager. Finding the time to be happy is as important as anything you do for your client.

Mitch's mother, Syra (pronounced "sigh-rah"), planning a family celebration at a local catering hall, asked that they assign a maître d who would smile and be pleasant throughout the event. The hall's manager was surprised by the request. Syra explained, "I know you must do a lot of these affairs and one dinner must seem just like another, but I have only one party and I want it to be beautiful. I've seen many affairs ruined by a cranky employee and I want to be sure that the person in charge of my party is friendly."

Syra's point holds true for managers and artists alike. Performers should remember that, even after doing the same show two hundred times, there are audience members out there who are seeing them for the first and only time. Priced sometimes at hundreds of dollars, a great concert or a mediocre concert may be remembered for a lifetime.

A manager in the popular music industry may work with many clients during a career and one client may seem very much like the next after a while. The manager should never forget that artists see their careers in passionate and personal terms and the manager can change someone's life for the better or the worse with just a smile and a supportive word.

Understanding what artists need is the foundation of good management. They need you to be educated and honest. You need them to make a living.

The phone rings. It's George at CAA calling me back after hearing about Jasper's death. The news about Jasper shocked him as much as it did me, but he still has to relay all concert inquiries. He just got two new BoyBand offers from promoters in Japan spanning a two-week frame three months from now. He will of course email me details but he wants to find out if I think the boys will be available by then. We discuss the cancellation of the next few concerts and table the decision about Japan until we know more.

The phones had been quiet for the past hour. It gave me time to reflect, find out more about Jasper's accident, and prepare a preliminary response to the press.

But business does not stop. George also has a request for six comp tickets to Don Juan's next concert for some agency executives. He asks if we could meet with Juan sometime next week about a new tour of South America. Robert interrupts to let me know that there is a promoter on the line from Seattle who wants the OK for a local Kirk Franklin-styled band and radio station DJ to open for the Redd Family when they're in Arkansas next month.

I grab the next call before Robert gets to it. It's a reporter about Jasper. I politely say nothing except that a press release is being prepared. I promise to email it to him. Rule #5. Three BoyBand members suddenly walk in, hug me, and sit down. We talk about Jasper for over an hour. We laugh. We cry. We discuss his life and death and music. He is a fallen artist. Our brother. Our friend.

Management is not always about business.

Interlude of Photographs: Real-life Managers with Their Artists

While the people in the photographs printed elsewhere in this book are actors and models portraying fictional characters, this section contains photographs of real people.

Managers by nature and profession stay behind the scenes away from the spotlight. In the interest of putting a human face to the profession, a few professionals agreed to appear here with their artists.

Unlike the stereotypical Hollywood image of the cigar-chomping, loudmouth manager of yore, these photographs provide an eye-opening perspective on the look of today's crop of professionals.

We thank them.

(These photographs do not represent an endorsement of the authors' opinions and commentary in this book.)

Vanilla Ice and Tommy Quon, 1990 (Photo by Roz Levin)

Clockwise from top left: Brian McKnight, singer/songwriter Cherokee, and Herb Trawick, CEO of Trawick Group

Nedra Carroll and Jewel on tour in Rome, Christmas 1998

Left to right: O-Town's Erik Estrada, Jacob Underwood, manager Mike Morin, Trevor Penick, Ashley Angel, and Dan Miller

Left to right: Petula's Manager Bill Goodman, Petula Clark, Tony Award–winning actress Donna McKechnie, and actor George Coe

Randy Travis and wife/manager Elizabeth catching a show on Broadway

Lou Robin with Johnny Cash visiting a gold mine, two hundred miles
outside of Perth, Australia in 1972 while shooting a TV special

Richard Dieguez, Esq. with Lisa Lisa at a New York City hot spot

Terry McBride manages Sarah McLachlan, Dido, Barenaked Ladies, Coldplay, Sum41, and Avril Lavigne

Omer Pardillo and Celia Cruz

ATPAM's president Maria Somma, press representative Jim Baldassare, and secretary-treasurer Gordon Forbes

Mitch Weiss surrounded by the Village People circa 1994 (Photo by Carol Rosegg)

Contract
Analysis for
Managers and
Artists

22

Artist Management Agreements with Analysis

Don't just copy your forms; understand them first.

Authors: Three separate examples of agreements between the artist and manager are provided below. The variety of styles in these agreements is evidence of the greater variety in management styles. We, the managers, are supposed to be here for artists, so I see no excuse to begin a potentially lifelong relationship without clear, straightforward language that tells the artist that the manager is trustworthy.

While I am not a member of the Conference of Personal Managers, I had a client who was given the Conference's sample agreement to sign in the late 1980s. I don't like the form or substance in the agreement. It is not artist-friendly. Still, some managers use it and therefore I present it here with my comments.

A second agreement prepared by a manager's legal counsel and signed by at least one artist I know, is also problematic. Someone may like its format so I include it here.

I recommend a simple letter of agreement format that must be individualized for each artist. This sample agreement is presented as a third alternative.

SAMPLE #1

CONFERENCE OF PERSONAL MANAGERS AGREEMENT
Between [Artist's Name] and [Manager's Name] dated [Date]

Authors: This agreement is written as a letter from the artist to the manager, with the artist asking the manager to please help provide "advice, counsel, and direction."

Paragraph 2 states the number of years that the artist is hiring the manager and implies that the manager should only advise the artist when requested.

I desire to obtain your advice, counsel, and direction in the development and enhancement of my artistic and theatrical career. The nature and extent of the success or failure of my career cannot be predetermined and it is therefore my desire that your compensation be determined in such manner as will permit you to accept the risk of failure and likewise benefit to the extent of my success.

In view of the foregoing, we have agreed as follows:

I do hereby engage you as my Personal Manager for a period of [. . .] years from the date of this agreement. As and when requested by me during and throughout the term hereof, you agree to perform for me one or more of the services as follows: advise and counsel in the selection of literary, artistic and musical material; advise and counsel in any and all matters pertaining to publicity, public relations, and advertising; advise and counsel with relation to the adoption of proper format for presentation of my artistic talents and in the determination of proper style, mood, setting, business, and characterization in keeping with my talents; advise, counsel, and direct in the selection of artistic talent to assist, accompany, or embellish my artistic presentation; advise and counsel with regard to general practices in the entertainment and amusement industries and with respect to such matters of which you may have knowledge concerning compensation and privileges extended for similar artistic values; advise and counsel concerning the selection of theatrical agencies, artists' managers, and persons, firms, and corporations who will counsel, advise, and seek and procure employment and engagements for me.

Authors: This paragraph gives the manager decision-making power for the artist in the areas of publicity, artistic material, contract signing, check writing, signing and cashing, and hiring. It says that, once given in this agreement, the artist cannot take back any of these powers. You know how I feel about this. It's a terrible idea for the artist and can leave the manager vulnerable for accusations of misuse of funds, theft, and abuse. For some reason, it also mentions that the manager does not have to make loans to the artist but, just in case, can deduct these loans from monies payable to the artist. Another bad idea. Any time the manager makes a loan, he should write a separate loan agreement with details spelled out.

You are authorized and empowered for me and in my behalf and in your discretion to do the following: approve and permit any and all publicity and advertising; approve and permit the use of my name, photograph, likeness, voice, sound effects, caricatures, literary, artistic and musical materials for purposes of advertising and publicity, and in the promotion and advertising of any and all products and services; execute for me in my name and/or in` my behalf any and all agreements, documents, and contracts for my services, talents, and/or artistic literary and musical materials; collect and receive sums as well as endorse my name upon and cash any and all checks payable to me for my services, talents, and literary and artistic materials and retain therefrom all sums owing to you; engage, as well as discharge and/or direct for me and in my name theatrical agents, artists' managers, and employment agencies as well as other persons, firms, and corporations who may be retained to obtain contracts, engagements, or employment for me. You are not required to make any loans or advances to me or for my account, but in the event you do so, I shall repay them promptly, and I hereby authorize you to deduct the amount of any such loans or advances from any sums you may receive for my account. The authority herein granted to you is coupled with an interest and shall be irrevocable during the term hereof.

Authors: The artist is quoted here as promising to work hard to promote the career and money (implication is that the manager can't make money unless the artist does and this makes sure that the artist knows what the manager expects, even though it's written from the artist's point of view). It doesn't say that the manager will work hard. Artist then agrees not to work with anyone that the manager doesn't approve. Artist also promises to send all job information and money through the manager. (In parentheses, the artist understands that the manager is not about getting jobs, only advice.)

I agree at all times to devote myself to my career and to do all things necessary and desirable to promote my career and earnings therefrom. I shall at all times engage and utilize proper theatrical agents, employment agencies, or artists' managers to obtain engagements and employment for me, but I shall not engage any theatrical agents, employment agencies, or artists' managers of which you may disapprove. I shall advise you of all offers of employment submitted to me and will refer any inquiries concerning my services to you, in order that you may determine whether the same are compatible with my career. I shall instruct any theatrical agency or artists' manager engaged by me to remit to you all monies that may become due me and may be received by it. (It is clearly understood that you are not an employment agent or theatrical agent or artists' manager, that you have not offered or attempted or promised to obtain, seek, or procure employment or engagements for me, and that you are not obligated, authorized, licensed, or expected to do so.)

Authors: Manager is an independent contractor, can work with any number of other artists, and is not required to do anything but advise the artist unless specifically requested by the artist. If the artist thinks the manager should do more, the artist must send written notice and then the manager has fifteen days to get going on the work

requested. The manager never has to travel or meet with the artist anywhere other than the office and if the manager does travel, the artist must reimburse travel expenses.

This Agreement shall not be construed to create a partnership between us. It is specifically understood that you are acting hereunder as an independent contractor and you may appoint or engage any and all other persons, firms, and corporations throughout the world in your discretion to perform any or all of the services which you have agreed to perform hereunder. Your services hereunder are not exclusive, and you shall at all times be free to perform the same or similar services for others as well as engage in any and all other business activities. You shall only be required to render reasonable services which are called for by this agreement as and when reasonably requested by me. Due to the difficulty which we may have in determining the amount of services to which I may be entitled, it is agreed that you shall not be deemed to be in default hereunder until and unless I shall first give to you written notice by Certified Mail, describing the exact service which I require on your part and then only in the event that you shall thereafter fail for a period of fifteen consecutive days to commence the rendition of the particular service required. You shall not be required to travel or to meet with me at any particular place or places except in your discretion and following arrangements for costs and expenses of such travel.

Authors: Legalese mumbo jumbo describing all the ways that the artist can make money for which the artist will pay a management commission. It is based on gross income and makes no exceptions for monies that go for the artist's travel, hotel, or other expenses. It also discusses that commissions continue to be due even after this contract expires, and makes sure that the artist knows that commissions are due for stocks, shares in someone's business, etc.

In compensation for your services I agree to pay to you, as and when received by me, and during and throughout the term hereof, a sum equal to [. . .] percent of any and all gross monies or other considerations which I may receive as a result of my activities in and throughout the entertainment, amusement, music, recording, and publishing industries, including any and all sums resulting from the use of my artistic talents and the results and proceeds thereof and, without in any manner limited the foregoing, the matters upon which your compensation shall be computed shall include any and all of my activities in connection with matters as follows: motion pictures, television, radio, music, literary, theatrical engagements, personal appearances, public appearances in places of amusement and entertainment, records and recordings, publications, and the use of my name likeness and talents for purposes of advertising and trade. I likewise agree to pay you a similar sum following the expiration of the term hereof upon and with respect to any and all engagements, contracts and agreements entered into during the term hereof relating to any of the foregoing, and upon any and all extensions, renewals, and substitutions thereof and upon any resumptions of such engagements, contract and agreements which may have been discontinued during the term hereof and resumed within a year thereafter. The term "gross monies or other considerations" shall include, without limitation, salaries, earnings, fees, royalties, gifts, bonuses, shares of profit, shares of stock, partnership interest, percentages and the total amount paid for a package television or radio program (live or recorded), motion picture or other entertainment packages, earned or received directly or indirectly by me or my heirs, executors, administrators, or assigns, or by any other person, firm, or corporation on my behalf. In the event that I receive, as all or part of my compensation for activities hereunder, stock or the right to buy stock in any corporation or that I become the packager or owner of all or part of an entertainment property, whether as individual proprietor, stockholder, partner, joint venturer, or otherwise, your percentage shall apply to my said stock, right to buy stock, individual proprietorship, partnership, joint venture, or other form of interest, and you shall be entitled to your percentage share thereof. Should I be required to make any payment for such interest, you will pay your percentage share of such payment, unless you do not want your percentage share thereof.

Authors: If the manager has a partner and one of them dies, this agreement continues as if nothing has changed. If the manager dies, his estate gets only one-half of the commissions that would have been due to him when he was alive.

If this agreement is with a partnership, the death of a partner shall not affect the agreement in any way. If it is with an individual, then, as to my gross monies or other considerations earned after your death from engagements, contracts, and agreements commenced, entered into, or substantially negotiated prior to your death, I shall pay to your estate a sum equal to fifty percent (50 percent) of the percentage hereinbefore specified for the duration of all such engagements, contracts, and agreements and any extensions, renewals, and substitutions thereof.

Authors: If there is a dispute, it gets sent to arbitration. The loser pays all the legal costs.

In the event of any dispute under or relating to the terms of this agreement, or the breach, validity, or legality thereof, it is agreed that the same shall be submitted to arbitration to the American Arbitration Association in [insert New York City or Los Angeles], and in accordance with the rules promulgated by the said association, and judgment upon the award rendered by the arbitrator(s) may be entered in any court having jurisdiction thereof. In the event of litigation or arbitration, the prevailing party shall be entitled to recover any and all reasonable attorney's fees and other costs incurred in the enforcement of the terms of this agreement, or for the breach thereof. This arbitration provision shall remain in full force and effect notwithstanding the nature of any claim or defense hereunder.

Authors: If the individual manager joins a company or changes companies, this agreement goes with him. If the manager is bought out by another company, he can transfer this agreement to that company. Once again, the artist has no rights.

If this agreement is with an individual, you shall have the right to assign it to any corporation or partnership in which you are a stockholder or partner, or by which you may be employed, or to an individual by whom you may be employed. If this agreement is with a partnership, you shall have the right to assign it to a corporation in which any of the partners is a stockholder or by which any of the partners is employed, to another partnership consisting of one or more of the same partners, or to one or more of the partners. If this agreement is with a corporation, you shall have the right to assign it to an individual who is a stockholder, or to a partnership at least one of whose partners is a stockholder, or to another corporation which acquires all or substantially all of your assets.

Authors: Laws can override anything in this contract or fill in the blanks when an unusual situation comes up. The best entertainment laws are in New York and California, but if both artist and manager live in Texas, it may make sense to follow the laws of some other state. You want your lawyer to be familiar with these laws so ask the lawyer.

This agreement shall be deemed to be executed in the State of [. . .]. And shall be construed in accordance with the laws of said state. In the event any provision hereof shall for any reason be illegal or unenforceable then, and in any such event, the same shall not affect the validity of the remaining portion and provisions hereof.

Authors: The fascinating differences in legal terminology in California and New York law (the only two states with significant entertainment laws) is evident here. According to this, the people responsible for getting you work are called agencies in New York and artists' managers in California. The real point of this paragraph is to state once again that the manager is not going to try to get the artist work and is not legally allowed to do so. Here's a great reason to have a lawyer review your agreements.

You have advised me that you are not an "Artists' Manager," but active solely as a personal manager, that you are not licensed as an "Artists' Manager" under the labor code of the

State of California or as a theatrical employment agency under the general business law of the State of New York; you have at all times advised me that you are not licensed to seek or obtain employment or engagement for me and that you do not agree to do so, and you have made no representations to me, either oral or written, to the contrary.

Authors: This tells you to sign your name below (using more words than necessary, of course). It doesn't ask for a social security number or any other pertinent contact information, the lack of which will probably create a small headache later on during tax season.

If the foregoing meets with your approval please indicate your acceptance and agreement by signing in the space hereinbelow provided.

Very truly yours,

_____

Artist

I do hereby agree to the foregoing:

_____

Personal Manager

# # #

SAMPLE #2

Authors: Sample #2 has questionable wording, unrealistic recording requirements, and convoluted reasoning behind the length of the relationship, among other things. Quite a few managers use it and some clauses have certain advantages.

EXCLUSIVE ARTIST MANAGEMENT AGREEMENT DATED [DATE]

Mitch Weiss: This opening is the epitome of awkward legal language, but it does clarify that the agreement is not restricted to the United States. Unlike Sample #1, this agreement is written from the perspective of the manager to the artist (I prefer that since the manager is the one writing the agreement) and it refers to the artist with a familiar "you" that is friendly and personable. However, the manager is still a formal "manager" rather than just "me."

This agreement, when countersigned by [. . .] shall constitute the agreement between you, and [. . .] ("Manager") with respect to Manager acting on your behalf in respect of the personal management of you ("Artist") in the territory of the world (the "Territory").

Authors: Not all artists use only one manager, dividing concerts from commercials, television from recording, or sharing advice and perspective between two representatives. This agreement restricts the artist from hiring another manager. There are advantages for both artist and manager in a "sole and exclusive personal manager" but the question still remains: Is the manager sufficiently adept to advise the client in all of the topics listed here? Should the artist pay a commission to a manager who knows nothing about publicity or, even worse, may be tone deaf? This paragraph also delineates the areas in which the manager is supposed to advise the client.

1. Artist hereby engages Manager as Artist's sole and exclusive personal manager throughout the world and during the "Term" hereof (as defined herein), and Manager hereby accepts such engagement. Manager shall advise, guide, and counsel Artist in any and all aspects of the music and entertainment industry, including, without limitation, the following:
    a) Selection of musical, literary, and artistic material.
    b) Matters pertaining to publicity, public relations, and advertising.
    c) Adoption of the appropriate format for presentation of Artist's talents.
    d) Determination of the appropriate style, mood, setting, and characterization consistent with Artist's talent.
    e) Selection of artistic talents to assist, accompany, or embellish Artist's artistic presentation.
    f) Compensation for artistic values similar to those of Artist.
    g) Selection of theatrical agencies and persons, firms, and corporations which will counsel, seek, advise, and procure employment and engagement for Artist.
    h) General practices in the music and entertainment industries.

Authors: Of course, the manager can work for any number of artists even if the artist is making a lot of money and would like full-time representation.

Artist acknowledges and agrees that Manager's services hereunder shall not be exclusive to Artist, and that nothing precludes Manager from acting in a similar capacity and/ or providing similar services to other artists, or from engaging on other business activities during the Term.

Authors: This paragraph defines how long the artist and manager will work together and when the agreement officially ends. It is unnecessarily complicated and is tied into any and all deadlines for recording agreements. This means the artist may not be able to get out of working with this manager if he doesn't have a lawyer interpret when "Album Tour Cycles" begin and end. If the artist doesn't follow through with a particular recording deadline, the agreement is extended even longer. Not good for the artist; possibly good for the manager. The opening line referring to paragraph 12 can scare aware most artists until they realize that paragraph 12 only says that all changes must be sent by Certified Mail. Another example of legalese phrasing.

2. Subject to the terms and conditions of Paragraph 12 of this Agreement, the term of this Agreement (the "Term") shall commence as of the date hereof and shall continue for an initial period ending upon the later of (i) sixty (60) months, or (ii) the completion of the fifth "Album Tour Cycle," as defined below (the "Term"). Notwithstanding the foregoing, in the event that Artist has not entered into, or is not in the process of conducting substantial negotiations for, a "Recording Agreement" (as defined herein) within twelve (12) months following the later of (i) delivery by Artist to Manager of "Demos" (as defined herein) or (ii) full execution of this Agreement, then Artist shall have the right, within thirty (30) days following the end of such twelve (12) month period, to give Manager written notice of Artist's desire that this Agreement terminate, and upon Manager's receipt of such notice, this Agreement shall terminate upon Manager's receipt of such written notice. In the event that Artist fails to give Manager such notice, then this Agreement shall continue in full force and effect for the duration of the Term. For the purposes of this Agreement, a "Recording Agreement" is defined as an agreement for Artist's exclusive recording services with a third party record label or record distribution company with national distribution in the United States.

Authors: Defines how long an "Album Tour Cycle" will be (eighteen months, or until the next album begins recording or the supporting concert tour is finished) and "Demos" to mean whatever the manager (alone) considers to be good enough to shop to a label.

3. For the purposes of this Agreement, (i) an "Album Tour Cycle" shall commence upon the initial commercial release of the then-current Album in the United States, and shall expire upon the later of (a) Artist's commencement of actual recording sessions for the next succeeding Album, or (b) the completion and cessation of all touring and personal appearances in support of the then-current

Album, provided that in no event shall an Album Tour Cycle have a duration of longer than eighteen (18) months following the initial commercial release of the then-current Album in the United States; and (ii) "Demos" shall be deemed technically satisfactory demonstration recordings of Artist's musical performances, which in Manager's sole discretion are suitable to solicit offers for a Recording Agreement.

Authors: If the artist leaves the manager out of a deal—perhaps negotiating through a friend or lawyer—or tries to work without involving the manager, then this contract will be extended for the length of time that the manager was left out. In other words, if the artist wants to get rid of the manager, she can't do it by just ignoring him and using someone else, even if she pays him his commission. The purpose of this is to make sure that the manager keeps control until the artist abides by the legitimate out clause.

4. Notwithstanding the foregoing, if Artist fails for any reason to allow Manager to perform Manager's material functions as Artist's sole and exclusive personal manager under this agreement (i.e., neglect, refusal, or other failure of Artist to allow Manager to actively participate in negotiation of Artist's material agreements, or to advise Manager of Artist's current and ongoing business dealings in all aspects of Artist's entertainment career), Manager shall be entitled (by written notice specifying the nature of such alleged failure, mailed to Artist at any time) to extend the duration of the Term for a period of time equal to the duration of such failure plus the amount of time remaining under the Term immediately prior to such failure.

Authors: The manager makes 20 percent commission off of gross income from everything that is entertainment-related. Concert commission comes from net income as defined later in this section (check it carefully). There's a tricky little notation about music publishing. If the artist is a songwriter, then there is income from the songwriter share and the publishing company's share. The manager takes commission from both. Commission is also due from income that is not cash, for example, ownership in a company or a building. Everything counts for the purposes of calculating commission. When the contract ends, the manager continues to earn commission from anything that was started while he was the manager.

5. Commission.
    a) Manager shall receive, as compensation for his services, a sum equal to twenty (20) percent of Artist's "Gross Earnings" with respect to Artist's

services or the products of Artist's services which are commercially exploited in the Territory, including, but not limited to, all sales of audio and/or audio-visual recordings, all "net touring receipts" (i.e., gross tour receipts less the amounts described in subparagraph 5(b)(iv) hereof), the sale of merchandise embodying Artist's name and/or likeness, music publishing income (including the so-called "songwriter's share" thereof), and all entertainment-related income, subject to the terms and conditions of this Paragraph 5. Such percentage of Artist's "Gross Earnings" payable to Manager as consideration for Manager's services hereunder is hereinafter sometimes referred to as Manager's "Commission." Except as specifically set forth above, the term "Gross Earnings" refers to the total of all earnings which shall not be accumulated or averaged (whether in the form of salary, bonuses, royalties, or advances against royalties), interest percentages, shares of profits, merchandise, shares in ventures, products, properties, or any kind or type of income which are related to Artist's career in the entertainment industry in the Territory, directly or indirectly received by or credited to Artist or Artist's heirs, executors, administrators, or assigns or by any other person, firm, or corporation on Artist's behalf during the Term of this Agreement or subsequent to the expiration or termination hereof as a result of (i) any services performed by Artist during the Term; (ii) any contracts entered into or substantially negotiated prior to or during the Term hereof and any renewal, extension (by exercises of option or otherwise), modification, or substitution of such contract; (iii) any agreements which may be discontinued during the Term and resume within one (1) year thereafter; and (iv) any product of Artist's services or talents or of any property created by Artist in whole or in part during or prior to the Term.

Authors: These are the items on which the manager cannot take commission. If the artist's payment includes money for other people—choreographers, musicians, dancers, scenery, sound or lighting rentals, CD promotion, etc.—then the manager cannot charge commission. Also money from the artist's outside businesses, or a company owned by the manager, lawsuit awards, and refunds made by the artist plus a few more items are out of bounds. For the most part, these items come off the gross income before the manager takes his 20 percent. Basically the manager takes commission off the money that actually lands in the artist's pocket. So this manager's definition of gross income is what I call net income. And that's why accountants were born. Even if the manager is trustworthy, the artist needs someone to check his math.

b)   Notwithstanding anything to the contrary contained in subparagraph 5(a) hereof, the following items of income shall not constitute "Gross Earnings" of Artist for the purposes of this Agreement:

     (i)   Income derived by Artist from any entity in which Manager has a proprietary interest (other than publicly held companies in which Manager has less than a five [5] percent proprietary interest);

     (ii)   Sums paid to or on behalf of Artist by any production, recording and/or distribution company for bona fide third-party recording, production, manufacturing, and/or distribution costs (including, without limitation, any unaffiliated third-party producer and/or director fees, but excluding any salary or wages paid to Artist included in such sums) in connection with any audio and/or audio-visual recordings, which are paid to unaffiliated third parties (i.e., other than to the individual member(s) of Artist or any entities owned or controlled by Artist) and are actually utilized for same;

     (iii)   Sums paid to or on behalf of Artist by any production, recording and/or distribution company constituting fees, advances and/or royalties payable to unaffiliated third parties including, without limitation, producers and/or directors in connection with any audio and/or audio-visual recording;

     (iv)   Sums paid to or on behalf of Artist in connection with Artist's "live" engagements for unaffiliated third-party opening acts and/or so-called "sound-and-light" rental and all personnel directly employed by the entity providing the sound and lights; provided, however, that in the event Artist at any time provides "sound and lights" and charges concert promoters a fee in excess of the actual cost to Artist for providing for "Sound and lights," such excess paid to Artist shall be commissionable by Manager;

     (v)   Sums paid to Artist as a result of Artist's business (exclusive of the entertainment industry unless Artist makes a monetary investment in a bona fide third party entertainment industry business) which Artist invests in with monies derived from monies not commissionable hereunder or monies which have already been commissioned hereunder;

     (vi)   Sums paid to or on behalf of Artist by any third party, which are actually utilized for the purpose of so-called deficit or short-fall "tour support." The aforesaid non-commissionable deficit or short-fall "tour support" shall not include any salary or wages paid to or on behalf of Artist, the individual member(s) or Artist or any entities owned or controlled by them;

(vii)   Monies paid to Artist by any record or publishing company that are used for the purpose of independent record promotion or independent marketing;

(viii) Monies paid by or on behalf of Artist to any person, third-party firm, or corporation neither directly nor indirectly related to Artist (other than members of Artist) that co-write or co-publish with Artist or co-administer or sub-publish any of the musical compositions written by members of Artist;

(ix)   All amounts received by Artist as compensation for injury (excluding amounts received for lost income and/or lost wages);

(x)   All accounting fees, audit fees, court costs, and reasonable attorneys' fees solely from any audit and/or litigation from which income is derived; and/or

(xi)   Monies actually and properly refunded by Artist (i.e., if Artist properly refunds any money and Manager has commissioned same, Manager shall also refund its commission).

Authors: Here are a lot of words to say that the manager will earn 20 percent commission *forever* on all "products created or services rendered . . . (not defined—What doesn't fit into this category?) . . . prior to . . . (artist owes commission on products created before she worked with this manager!) . . . or during" the term of this agreement.

(c)   Notwithstanding the foregoing, solely with respect to products created or services rendered by Artist prior to or during the Term (hereinafter collectively referred to as the "Contemporaneous Products and Services"), and Artist's Gross Earnings earned or received by Artist solely from the Contemporaneous Products and Services, Manager shall be entitled to receive the full amount of Manager's Commission as set forth in subparagraph 5(a) above with respect to such Gross Earnings derived therefrom and earned or received by Artist following the expiration or termination of the Term, in perpetuity.

Authors: Just when the artist thought it was safe to leave her manager and choose a new one, here comes trouble. If the artist and manager were together for three years, then this paragraph covers the three years after the contract is over. If they were together for five years, then this paragraph covers the five years after the breakup. This manager will get half of his 20 percent commission for those things that were created after this contract is over, but are based on deals made while the manager was still around. This means that after the artist has left this manager, she may need a lawyer to determine

what is legitimately owed to the manager for things that happen after the relationship has ended. And for these years after the artist has left the manager, the Artist will pay a 20 percent commission to the new manager plus a 10 percent commission to the old one. If I were an artist, I'd call this highway robbery.

    d)   Notwithstanding the foregoing, solely with respect to products created or services rendered by Artist subsequent to the expiration or termination of the Term, all pursuant to contracts entered into or substantially negotiated prior to or during the Term, and any renewal, extension (by exercise of option or otherwise), modification, or substitution of such contract (hereinafter collectively referred to as the "Subsequent Products and Services"), Manager shall only be entitled to compensation hereunder with respect to Artist's Gross Earnings earned or received by Artist subsequent to the expiration or termination of the Term, during an additional period commencing immediately upon such expiration or termination and continuing for an additional period equal to the actual Term (the "Additional Post-Term Period"). Manager's Commission with respect to Artist's Gross Earnings earned or received by Artist during the Additional Post-Term Period solely with respect to the Subsequent Products and Services shall be reduced to (i) one-half (1/2) of Manager's otherwise applicable Commission as set forth in subparagraph 5(a) hereof with respect to such Gross Earnings earned or received by Artist during the first half of the Additional Post-Term Period; (ii) one-fourth (1/4) of Manager's otherwise applicable Commission as set forth in subparagraph 5(a) hereof with respect to such Gross Earning earned or received by Artist during the second half of the Additional Post-Term Period; and (iii) Manager shall not be entitled to any further compensation hereunder with respect to the Subsequent Products and Services following the expiration of the Additional Post-Term Period.

Authors: This says that you should use the date that a product or service is started, rather than the date of an event or a first date of sale or manufacture, to determine whether something was created while this artist and manager were working together or whether it was created after this agreement was over.

    e)   Notwithstanding anything to the contrary contained in this Agreement, for the purposes of determining whether Artist's products or services shall be deemed to be "Contemporaneous Products and Services" or "Subsequent Products and Services", such products or services shall be deemed to be "created" or "rendered" at the time such activities are commenced.

Authors: The manager is given the right to approve photos, sign contracts and booking agreements (for up to five shows and with advance artist approval), and hire and fire staff and companies on behalf of the artist. Unless the artist is not readily available or is just not interested in the details of her own career, even this rather tame list seems unnecessary.

    6.   Power of Attorney.

Artist hereby appoints Manager for the Term and any extensions thereof as Artist's true and lawful attorney-in-fact, and Manager shall have the power to sign, make, execute, and deliver any and all contracts and agreements, the material terms of which contracts and/or agreements have been approved in advance by Artist, in Artist's name, solely for the following purposes:

        a)   Approving and permitting the use of Artist's name (actual and professional), photographs, likenesses, voice, and sound effects (all as previously approved by Artist), for the purpose of advertising and promoting Artist's products and services in the music and entertainment industries;

        b)   Engagement of Artist in connection with Artist's live performance and/or personal appearances totaling not in excess of five (5) such appearances, for which Artist has pre-approved the general planning and scheduling thereof; and

        c)   Engaging, discharging and/or directing all persons, firms and corporations who may be retained to obtain employment for Artist in the music and entertainment industries.

Authors: The manager wants it to be clear that all the costs of being an artist, from travel to fees, phones, staff, and costumes, will come out of the artist's money. The only exception is that the manager pays his own overhead expenses for his own business. Since there are unscrupulous artists, this carefully points out that if the manager lays out money, the artist will pay him back quickly. But it also restricts the manager from spending more than $1,000 without the artist's advance approval.

    7.   Expenses.

        a)   Artist shall, as between Artist and Manager, be solely responsible for payment of all booking agency fees or commissions, exploitation costs, long distance telephone expenses, traveling expenses (including traveling expenses of Manager equivalent to the same travel class as Artist is using if such travel is undertaken at the request of Artist), overnight mail, wardrobe expenses, payments for the services of the "Accountant" (as hereafter defined), and all other expenses, fees, and costs incurred by Artist and/or Manager on Artist's behalf. In the event that Manager advances any of the foregoing fees, costs, or expenses on behalf of Artist, or incurs any other costs, fees, or expenses in connection with Artist's professional career or with the performance of Manager's services hereunder other than general overhead expenses of Manager, Artist shall promptly reimburse Manager as billed for such fees, costs and expenses upon presentation of receipts or other adequate supporting documentation. Notwithstanding the foregoing, Manager shall not incur any such individual expenses in excess of Five Hundred ($500.00) Dollars or aggregate expenses in excess of One Thousand ($1,000.00) Dollars per month without obtaining Artist's prior approval. Artist shall not be charged with any of Manager's overhead expenses.

Authors: The manager does not make loans nor does he advance money from concert deposits (that are not yet legally the property of the artist) or similar places. If he does, he can get it back almost anyway he wants. Unfortunately, not all artists know how to handle money and some are downright dishonest. This is why the manager must protect himself in these agreements.

b)   Manager is not required to make any loans or advances to Artist. In the event that Manager does loan and/or advance funds to Artist or on Artist's behalf, Artist hereby agrees to promptly repay all such amounts, and Artist hereby irrevocably authorizes Manager (i) to deduct, or (ii) to direct the Accountant to deduct and pay over to Manager, the full amount of any such loans and/or advances from any sums Manager (or Accountant, as applicable) may receive on Artist's behalf. At the reasonable discretion of Manager, such amounts may be repaid to Manager in installments.

Authors: This seems to require the artist to hire an accountant to do rather basic accounting procedures regarding commissions and reimbursements. While accountants are necessary consultants for taxes, most managers should be willing and able to do this basic accounting personally instead of giving an accountant more of the artist's money. It makes sense to have the accountant review the manager's math from time to time.

8.   Collection and Disbursement of Gross Earnings. All Gross Earnings shall be received together with a written accounting statement upon which such Gross

Earnings are based in the first instance by an accountant or business manager engaged by Artist and approved by Manager (the "Accountant"). All the Manager's Commission (as well as expense reimbursement) hereunder shall be due and payable to Manager (together with such written accounting statements upon which it is based) not less frequently than within ten (10) days after the end of each calendar quarter after receipt by the Accountant or by any person, firm, or corporation on the Accountant's or Artist's behalf, of the "Gross Earnings." After the payment to the Manager of his Commission hereunder (as well as applicable expense reimbursement), the Accountant shall pay over the balance of said monies to Artist. Notwithstanding the foregoing, until and unless Artist engages such Accountant, Manager is hereby authorized by Artist to collect such Gross Earnings from all third parties, to deduct and retain his compensation and expense reimbursement therefrom, and Manager shall account and pay to Artist the balance thereof promptly thereafter.

Authors: Imagine that the artist has an agreement with her cousin (who invested in her career) saying that she promises not to sign with any manager without the cousin's approval. But, the artist signs a management agreement anyway without informing the manager of her agreement with her cousin. Well, this is the section that protects the manager from a lawsuit from her cousin. It says that the artist declares that she has no reason not to sign this contract. It also says that if the cousin sues (and sometimes a manager will get sued even if it is clear that the manager is not responsible), that the artist will pay all the legal costs simply because she didn't tell the truth. This paragraph also protects the artist in case, for example, the manager is under contract with a larger company that prevents him from signing artists to a private deal.

On a whole different subject, this protects the manager only from any lawsuits caused when the artist didn't show up for a show or failed to follow through on an agreement, and additionally keeps the manager clear from any responsibilities when the artist sues someone else for not following through on an agreement. Hopefully you chose your clients carefully, but in the music industry artists are wild cards and managers can easily go down with the ship if they are not protected this way.

9. Warranties/Indemnity. Each party hereto hereby warrants and represents that such party has the right to enter into this agreement with the other party hereto and to grant such other party all of the rights with respect to such party as set forth herein. Each party warrants and represents that no act or omission by such party (the "Indemnifying Party") will violate any right or interest of any person or firm or will subject such other party (the "Indemnified Party") to any liability

or claim of liability from any person or firm. The Indemnifying Party agrees to indemnify and hold harmless the Indemnified Party against any damages, costs, expenses, or fees (including reasonable attorneys' fees) incurred by the Indemnified Party in any claim, suit, or proceeding instituted by or against the Indemnified Party in which any assertion is made which is consistent with any warranty, representation, or covenant of the Indemnifying Party under this agreement, which claim, suit or proceeding is reduced to a final non-appealable judgment or settled with the Indemnifying Party's consent. In connection wit the foregoing, Artist indemnifies and holds harmless Manager with respect to (a) any breach of contract claim, action, or proceeding brought against Artist by a third party based upon Artist's refusal, neglect, or other failure to render services; and (b) any breach of contract claim, action, or proceeding brought against a third party by Artist based upon such third party's refusal, neglect, or other failure to render services.

Authors: Even though the manager will probably make sure that the Arbitration Clause is used in all contracts to protect the artist (found in this agreement it is paragraph 14 below), this clause gives the manager the right to go to court for one reason only. It claims that the manager's rights to "advise and consult" the artist are exclusive and that this is so important that almost nothing will compensate him if the artist tries to circumvent his authority. I call this the slavery clause because it puts the manager's control of the artist above the artist's needs. The manager deserves a way to protect his income from angry or crazy artists, but it is the nature of the business that good relationships are risky and delicate. They cannot be protected by threats. No one, not even creative people, should be controlled this way.

10.   Artist acknowledges and agrees that Manager's right to represent Artist as Artist's sole and exclusive personal manager and Artist's obligations to exclusively use Manager in such capacity are unique and extraordinary rights and obligations, the loss of which cannot be adequately compensated in damages and Manager shall be entitled to injunctive relief to enforce the provisions of this agreement.

Authors: The only laws that will apply to any problems are the New York State laws.

11.   This agreement shall be construed in accordance with the laws of the State of New York governing contracts wholly executed and performed in such State. The courts of the City, County, and State of New York shall have exclusive jurisdiction in the event any action is brought in connection with the rights and obligations of the parties set forth herein.

Authors: Imagine the artist writing to the manager to terminate the agreement but sending it to the wrong address. Is the notice official if it was never received? Believe it or not, stupid things like this happen. Hence the "Notices" clause telling both manager and artist where to send official letters.

12.   Notices. All notices to the parties hereto shall be in writing and shall be sent to the party to be notified via Certified or Registered Mail, return receipt requested, postage prepaid, to such parties' address first set forth above. A copy of any such notice sent to Manager shall also be sent simultaneously in the same manner to [. . .] Esq. (Manager's attorney and address).

Authors: If the manager takes a job with a large management firm, he can take his name off the contract and put the name of the company he now works for on the contract without asking the client. If the artist forms her own corporation, she can put her company's name on the contract in place of her own without asking. Of course, the clause is written in positive terms for the manager ("He has the right . . .") and negative terms for the artist ("She has no right unless . . ."). Another example of unfriendly language.

13.   Assignment. Manager shall have the unconditional right to assign this Agreement in whole or in part to any corporation, partnership, or other entity in which Manager has an ownership interest. Artist may not assign this Agreement, except to any corporation formed by Artist to provide Artist's services in the music, recorded music, and entertainment industries.

Authors: Arbitration clause for all disputes (other than the one in paragraph ten).

14.   Any dispute or controversy between the parties relating to or arising out of this agreement or any amendment or modification hereof shall be determined by arbitration in the City, County, and State of New York, with three (3) attorney arbitrators pursuant to the rules then obtaining of the American Arbitration Association. The arbitration award shall be final and binding upon the parties and judgment may be entered thereon in any court of competent jurisdiction.

Authors: If the manager or artist fails to follow this agreement, they have thirty days after being notified that they messed up to begin fixing the problem. Otherwise, some kind of legal action can be taken. It's sort of a cooling off period before the lawyers get involved or the artist can threaten to leave the manager.

15. No breach of this Agreement by either Manager or Artist shall be deemed material unless the party alleging a breach shall have given the other party notice of such breach, and the party receiving notice of such breach shall fail to cure such breach within thirty (30) days following receipt of such notice, if such breach is reasonably capable of being fully cured within such thirty (30)-day period. If such breach is not capable of being fully cured within such thirty (30)-day period and the party accused of such breach commences to cure such breach within such thirty (30)-day period and proceeds with reasonable diligence to complete the curing of such breach, then the terms and conditions of this Paragraph 15 will be deemed to have been complied with. A waiver by either Artist or Manager of a breach of any provision of this Agreement shall not be deemed a waiver of any subsequent breach, whether of a similar or dissimilar nature.

Authors: There are no other agreements between this artist and manager hiding in someone's files and the only way to change this agreement is in writing.

16. This Agreement is the only agreement between Artist and Manager concerning the subject matter described herein and may not be modified except by an instrument in writing executed by both Artist and Manager.

Authors: This tells you to sign below—and just like the previous example it uses more words than necessary. For tax reasons, getting the social security number at the time of the contract signing will save you a lot of trouble.

If the foregoing confirms our mutual understanding of our arrangement, kindly so indicate by countersigning in the space provided below.

By: _____

Manager

ACCEPTED AND AGREED TO:

_____

Artist

_____

Social Security Number

# # #

SAMPLE #3

Authors: Sample #3 is my preference because almost every artist I've met says they can understand it on first reading. The most telling sign is the artists' ability to ask pertinent and clarifying questions as they read it. This kind of LOA (Letter of Agreement) tells the artist that you intend to be clear, straightforward, and trusting, and at the same time, both parties are covered with generous "outs" and guarantees. This sample agreement is based on the notion that good relationships last at least as long as bad ones, and when the good relationship goes bad, it's time to let it dissolve rather than force it to continue.

EXCLUSIVE ARTIST–MANAGEMENT AGREEMENT
Between [Artist's Name] and [Manager's Name] dated [Date]

Artist's Name
Artist's Address

Dear [Artist's Name]:

Authors: Artist is hiring an exclusive manager whose job it is to advise the artist. It clearly states that it's an agent's job to secure employment for the artist.

This letter confirms our agreement for me to manage you beginning on [Date]. It is clearly understood that my responsibilities primarily involve advising you in any and all aspects of your professional career and do not include securing employment for you (which is legally restricted to a licensed agent). We both agree that I will be your only manager.

Authors: Here's what the manager will do for you, but it is a team effort.

You and I will work together to create promotional materials, make artistic choices including songs, studios, and costumes, choose a team to include attorney, accountant, musicians, crew, staff, etc. as mutually agreed, and to develop and implement a career plan.

Authors: Manager will watch over all finances but will not sign anything on behalf of the artist. Artist must be available to sign her own checks and contracts. Manager will only be reimbursed up to $250 without asking the artist first.

I will be responsible for financial oversight of your professional income and taxes and will write checks and prepare documents for your signature. Under no circumstances will I sign any document or check on your behalf. You agree to be accessible and agreeable to sign all documents and checks that you approve. You also agree to reimburse me for all reasonable expenses advanced on your behalf, not to exceed $250 without your advance written approval.

Authors: Sometimes it helps to state the obvious: honesty, fairness, and hard work from both manager and artist. Also this declares that there is no legal partnership or other business entanglement between the two, only the artist-manager relationship.

We both agree to work hard, truthfully, and at all times honestly, to fulfill all contractual agreements so that no monies are forfeited because of our negligence, impropriety, or resistance of any kind and to treat each other with fairness and consideration. We have no other business relationships except as manager and client.

Authors: This agreement assumes a trial period of three months, often helpful for the artist to develop trust in the manager. I've known some managers to work for a year without a written agreement. The artist has time to review the agreement, study it, think about it, without pressure. The working relationship may require additional clauses that cannot be known before the work begins.

This agreement is being signed after three (3) months of working together on a trial basis with only a verbal understanding of these terms, that we now put in writing to solidify our professional relationship and our satisfaction to date with the direction your career is headed.

Authors: Manager earns a percentage (here it is an artist-friendly 10 percent) of net income from all entertainment industry work.

MANAGER'S COMMISSION: You agree that all monies earned by you as an Artist in the entertainment industries under the name(s) of [Artist's professional name], including merchandising, performances, recordings, royalties, film, television, etc., shall be subject to commission by me at a rate of [10 percent or other rate negotiated]. No commission will be taken on monies spent for you or your traveling entourage's reasonable hotel or travel expenses, subject to my prior approval.

Authors: This protects both manager and artist from each other. Payments are made out only in the artist's name (or corporation's name). Artist agrees to turn it all over to the manager who will do an accounting, make deposits, and deduct commissions and

expenses. The artist will get a simple statement of how the money was handled. Checks and balances.

FINANCIAL PROCEDURES. All checks paid for your services shall be made out in your name (or your corporation's name) but delivered directly to me for processing. If, for reasons beyond your control, you receive payment directly, you agree to immediately turn the payment over to me for processing. Failure to follow these instructions to the letter shall entitle me to deduct my commission from any of your earnings as I see fit, take legal action against you, and/or terminate our relationship. I will make sure you will always get a reasonably quick and clear accounting of the monies you've earned and any deductions made (never more than 90 days after money has been received).

Authors: The out clause in its simplest form. The artist can leave whenever she wants (with ninety days written notice) but the manager continues to earn commissions from work that is already in place or he has begun. If the artist has already decided to use a different manager without waiting for the full ninety days, as happens sometimes when there is distrust or anger between managers and artists, this manager earns half his commission for any new deals that the new manager puts in place before the official 90 days are up (a nice but fair protection for this manager from an artist who is jumping ship because another manager promised to get the artist a special job).

TERMINATIONS. You may terminate this agreement for any reason whatsoever with a simple written letter hand delivered to me or by fax or certified/return receipt mail at least 90 days in advance of the termination date. After the termination date, you agree to continue to pay me my full commission for all performances, recordings, etc., that have signed agreements or whose deals have been initiated before the termination date. During this 90-day period, if someone else negotiates and processes agreements on your behalf, you agree to pay me one half (1/2) of my usual commission for only these agreements even if I have not been involved.

Authors: Standard arbitration clause, but with a cooling off period of one month when both sides are supposed to try to resolve their differences themselves.

ARBITRATION. In the event we have a dispute regarding this agreement, after making a real attempt to resolve our differences for at least one month, we both agree to submit the problem to the American Arbitration Association in [insert New York City or Los Angeles]. Regardless of who loses in the Arbitrator's sole judgment, both you and I will pay our own attorney's fees and other court-related costs. [New York State or California law] shall govern this agreement and any arbitration decision.

Authors: If the manager joins a firm or the artist becomes a corporation, or even if they want their payments made out to a sick relative, it's OK as long as this manager and this artist are still the ones working with each other and as long as income is not affected.

ASSIGNMENT. You and I may each assign our payments in the name of a company or other person as we individually see fit, as long as the change doesn't affect the payment amount or schedule, and as long as the relationship remains primarily between you and me.

Authors: You agree to pay any expenses I incur for lawsuits that you caused and I had nothing to do with (other than the fact that I have a working relationship with you). Special note is made here for an artist who causes trouble on stage or destruction in hotels, etc. The manager will cover the artist's expenses when the manager is the one causing the trouble.

MUTUAL INDEMNITY. Both you and I agree that if only one of us causes a lawsuit but we are both sued, that the one who is directly the cause will indemnify (cover) the other against any damages, costs, expenses, or fees (including reasonable attorneys' fees). I make special note of any claim against you based on your refusal, neglect, or failure to perform services as required, or if you are held accountable for any destruction or expense at a concert or while traveling. You agree that you will not hold me responsible, and will indemnify me from any damages and expenses based on your lawsuit against an accountant, lawyer, or other consultant solely because I introduced you or hired him.

Authors: Use the addresses below to send official letters. If any contact information changes, the other person must be told immediately. Imagine the artist moving and not telling the manager who sends an important document and check to the old address. The artist would have trouble suing in arbitration since the contract requires notification of address changes.

OFFICIAL COMMUNICATIONS. All communications will be delivered to the addresses below and you and I will immediately tell the other of any change of address, phone, fax, email, etc.

Authors: A nice closing. It shows good will. The signatures also require all the basic business information that both manager and artist should have about each other: social security numbers and contact info.

I look forward to a long and healthy association with you for our mutual benefit and hopefully friendship.

Sincerely,

_____

Manager (with address, phone, fax, email, Federal ID or Social Security number)

AGREED:

_____

Artist (with address, phone, fax, email, Federal ID or Social Security number)

Date signed: _____

# # #

23

Sample Booking Agreement (Domestic and International Travel)

Don't just copy your forms; understand them first.

Authors: The "face" page of the contract is a summary of the key points including, Name, Date, Time, Location, Compensation, Method of Payment, Other Acts, Billing, and the official legal signing organizations (with address, phone, etc.), who are legally responsible for payments and performance.

A "rider" is the paperwork that lists additional terms and conditions not found on the face page. The face page and the rider(s) each require signatures. In-between pages should be initialed to be sure that they are not replaced at a later date. The artist's corporation is usually called the Producer—producing the act and providing the services of the artist ("f/s/o"=for services of). The promoter is called a Purchaser because that's what he's doing—purchasing the act.

In this example, we will use Helen's Booking Agency setting up a concert date for singer Jude (who works through a corporation named JCC Inc.) to perform at Macon College in Macon, Georgia on graduation day June 8, 2004. The artist will receive a guaranteed payment of $5,000 but no share of the box office income.

In order to use this agreement to develop your own version, you must carefully read every line to be sure that the unique features of Jude have been replaced with the unique features of your own artist.

Helen's Booking Agency
Address
Phone/Fax

Attached Rider(s) and Addendum(s) are hereby made part of this Contract.
Return all signed contracts to Helen's Booking Agency.

Agreement made March 1, 2004 between JCC Inc. ("Producer") f/s/o Jude ("Artist") and Macon College Student Society/Joseph Harding ("Purchaser").

The Purchaser hereby engages the Producer and the Producer hereby agrees to furnish the entertainment presentation as described below, upon all the terms and conditions herein set forth.

1. Date of Engagement: Sunday, June 8, 2004
    Number of shows: 1
    Time of show: 8:00 PM
    Length of show: 60 minutes

Authors: Ticket price scaling (below) is essential when the artist receives a percentage of the box office income. You can also get a good sense of how good a deal the artist is getting because the actual price of tickets and the number of seats being sold at each price is provided. The total is the gross income potential for the promoter, but the artist's percentage may be based on a less net amount delineated later in the contract. Of course, if the artist receives a guarantee (a flat fee), then this information is purely informational.

2. Place of Engagement: Macon College Student Affairs Hall
    4578 College Road, Macon, Georgia 56789
    Audience capacity: 1042
    Ticket Price Scaling: 600 @ $15.00
                                         350 @ $12.00
                                          92 @ $8.00
    Potential Box Office income: $13,936

3. Billing: Artist shall receive 100 percent headline billing in all forms of advertising.

Authors: The deposit (usually 50 percent of the total guaranteed fee, but sometimes less) is paid to the booking agency as a security that the purchaser won't cancel last

minute. It is assumed that the artist has locked the date away and possibly turned down other work and should therefore be entitled to some payment if the concert is cancelled. Accepted reasons for cancellation are defined in the rider. It is suggested that an artist not perform without full payment in hand. As nice or honest as most people may be, there are unscrupulous promoters and sometimes the promoter doesn't make enough money on the concert and tries to pay less than the contract says. Checks can bounce so most acts will try to get cash before they go on stage. But most promoters know there are irresponsible artists who don't perform a full show or refuse to go on for whatever reason, so they don't want to pay the artist until the show is over. The compromise is for the promoter to pay the artist just minutes prior to going on stage, usually handed to a road manager representing the artist.

"Earned performances" (below) refers to shows without a flat guaranteed payment to the artist. Perhaps the artist is taking the risk and getting only a percentage of the box office income. Perhaps in addition to the guaranteed fee, there is an additional percentage paid on ticket sales that exceed a certain level (called an "overage"). Perhaps instead of an additional percentage, the artist gets an additional flat fee "bonus" if ticket sales exceed a certain level. The phrase "verifiable signed accounting" refers to a written report (called a "statement") stating how much money was taken in at the box office, the number of tickets sold at each price, free tickets given away, and it is signed by box office and management representatives from the venue and the promoter who authorize the report as official. This is then a legally binding document from which monies owed and paid to various parties can be processed. If the artist is being paid only by a guaranteed fee, such as in this example, then this box office statement will never be seen by the artist's management since there are no percentages to be calculated. Unlike theatre, where statements are distributed after each and every performance to everyone involved, concert venues often ignore this requirement, expecting that the artist and its people will leave town the next day and not bother to ask. If there is no artist representative physically available to review the statement, then it may never be seen, and the artist will leave with the promoter's interpretation of the correct fee and percentages. Because of this, it rarely makes sense for an artist to get paid by any method other than a flat guaranteed fee. (Large megastars have staff that knows how to watch over a box office and audit statements for accuracy. They will often take a guarantee plus a percentage of sales.)

    4.   Compensation: Guarantee of five thousand dollars ($5,000), rain or shine.
All payments to be paid by Purchaser in U.S. funds as follows:
        1.   Deposit: 50 percent made out to Helen's Booking Agency by company check no later than [date to be negotiated].

2. Balance: 50 percent paid IN CASH not later than immediately prior to the first performance.

3. Earned performances, overages or bonuses, if applicable, are to be paid to Producer by Company Check with a verifiable signed accounting immediately following the last show or at a mutually agreeable time.

Authors: The following items are negotiable and may be different with every concert.

5. Purchaser agrees to provide:
   1. Sound, lights and backline equipment as required by Artist in Addendum A.
   2. Coach airfare and single hotel rooms for Artist and Artist's entourage, subject to Producer's prior approval.

Authors: You don't want to let the purchaser decide to send you at 6:00 AM with four connecting flights so you must make sure that the producer (meaning the artist's corporation through its manager) has the final say regarding air and hotels.

3. Local ground transportation between Macon airport, hotel, and venue.
4. Backstage refreshments plus one hot meal.
5. All terms and conditions contained in Artist riders and Addendums.

Agreed:

_____   _____

Full name of Purchaser including person   JCC Inc. f/s/o Jude
who will be signing on the Purchaser's   Fed.ID #12-345679
behalf. Also phone Number, Address, & Fax

(End of face page)

ADDENDUM TO BOOKING AGREEMENT: PURCHASER'S QUESTIONAIRE

TO BE COMPLETED BY PURCHASER AND RETURNED IMMEDIATELY
TO PRODUCER/ARTIST

This addendum is hereby made part of the Contract dated March 1, 2004
between JCC Inc. ("Producer") f/s/o Jude ("Artist") and
Macon College Student Society/Joseph Harding ("Purchaser").

1.　List other Artists on the bill in order of appearance:
2.　Ticket prices:
3.　Ticket sales procedures (phones, Internet, box office):
4.　Stage size (see Rider requirements):
5.　Merchandise person and contact phone:
6.　Technical person and contact phone:
7.　Is this a private engagement or corporate event without public advertising?
8.　Hotel accommodations (see Rider, paragraphs #44 and #45):
　　Name of Hotel: _____
　　Address: _____
　　Phone & Fax: _____
9.　Food Option (see Rider, paragraphs #56–58): _____

(End of addendum page)

RIDER TO BOOKING AGREEMENT

Authors: The heading to a list of the items agreed to between the artist and purchaser is called a rider. It is common for the rider to be returned by the promoter with cross-outs and changes. Phone calls between booking agent or manager to the promoter may occur to negotiate disagreements before a final agreement is reached.

**　　Written in the heading are the names and the date of the original contract face that is associated with this rider. In this rider, basic warnings are also included saying that even if there is no signature at the end of the rider, it is still considered to be in effect (sometimes sloppy promoters forget to sign all the pages, or maybe they're trying to get away with something). The third basic statement in the heading reminds the promoter that she must share this rider with all the people involved in the concert,**

including techies and the concert hall itself, so that they cannot claim to be ignorant of the items agreed upon.

While the rider doesn't say so, both purchaser and artist should initial changes to prove that both sides have given approval.

RIDER TO CONTRACT dated March 1, 2003 between JCC Inc. ("Producer") f/s/o Jude ("Artist") and Macon College Student Society/Joseph Harding ("Purchaser") is hereby made part of the contract to which it is attached by executing the face of said contract. Purchaser's failure to sign this Rider shall not release its obligations as set forth hereunder. By your signature hereunder you agree that all venues and appropriate personnel have been made aware of the provisions of this Contract and Rider and that they have agreed to all of its terms.

Authors: This says that if there's an error in this agreement and one paragraph says "yes" but another says "no", the paragraph that is better for the artist rules.

1.   In the event of any inconsistency between the provisions of this contract and the provisions of any riders, addenda, exhibits, or any other attachments hereto, the parties agree that the provision most favorable to the Producer and Artist shall control.

Authors: If the promoter doesn't do what the contract says (in all areas including fees, accommodations etc.) then artist can refuse to perform and can keep the deposit (another reason why getting a deposit is important). If the artist finds out that the promoter has a reputation for not paying up or is in financial trouble, artist can demand full payment up front or can cancel the contract.

2.   In the event the Purchaser refuses or neglects to perform any of its obligations including but not limited to payments or items to be provided, Producer shall have the right to refuse to perform this contract, shall retain any amounts theretofore paid to Producer by Purchaser, and Purchaser shall remain liable to Producer for the agreed compensation herein set forth. In addition, if Purchaser has failed, neglected or refused to perform any contract with any other performer for any other engagement, or if the financial standing or credit of Purchaser has been impaired or is in Producer's opinion unsatisfactory, Producer shall have the right to demand the payment of the guaranteed compensation forthwith. If Purchaser fails or refuses to make such payment forthwith, Producer shall have the right to cancel this engagement by notice to Purchaser to that effect, and to retain any amounts theretofore paid to Producer by Purchaser and Purchaser shall remain liable to Producer for the agreed price herein set forth.

Authors: This protects the booking agency in case the artist or the promoter does something stupid.

3. Helen's Booking Agency Inc. ("HBA") acts herein only as agent for Producer and is not responsible for any act or omission on the part of either Producer, Artist or Purchaser. It is further agreed that neither Purchaser nor Producer will name or join HBA as a party in any civil action or suit arising out of, in connection with or related to any act or omission of Purchaser, Artist, or Purchaser. In the event of any claim between the parties, HBA shall have the right to bring an interpleaded action in the event it is holding disputed monies.

Authors: Artist is an independent contractor. Artist and promoter are not entering into a business partnership. Hey, it's only one concert.

4. It is agreed that Producer signs this contract as an independent contractor and not as an employee or agent of Purchaser. This contract shall not, in any way be construed so as to create a partnership, or any kind of joint undertaking or venture between the parties hereto, nor make Producer liable in whole or in part for any obligation that may be incurred by Purchaser in Purchaser's carrying out any of the provisions of this agreement.

Authors: Should be obvious, but here we make sure the promoter will obey the stage requirements listed in this contract, will not add his own dancers or musicians to the artist's show without asking, will not put seats on the stage without asking, and will not make this concert part of a larger series without asking artist.

5. Purchaser agrees (a) to comply promptly with Producer's directions as to stage settings for the performance, (b) that no performers other than those to be furnished by producer will appear on or in connection with the engagement without Producer's prior written consent, (c) that no stage seats are to be sold or used without Producer's prior written consent, and (d) that the entertainment presentation will not be included in a subscription or other type of series without Producer's prior written consent.

Authors: Artistic control remains 100 percent in the hands of the artist. Artist can change supporting musicians, etc., without asking the promoter.

6. Producer shall have sole control over Artist's production, presentation and performance of the engagement as well as the means and methods employed in

fulfilling each obligation of Producer in all respects and in all details. Producer shall have the sole right, as Producer may see fit, to designate and change at any time the performing personnel comprising the Artist's performance, excepting Jude herself.

Authors: Promoter agrees not to do anything illegal and to abide by all relevant union rules.

7. Nothing in this agreement shall require the commission of any act contrary to law or to any rules or regulations of any union, guild or similar body having jurisdiction over the services and personnel to be furnished by Producer to Purchaser hereunder. If there is any conflict between any provision of this agreement and any law, rule or regulation, such law, rule or regulation shall prevail and this agreement shall be curtailed, modified or limited only to the extent necessary to eliminate such conflict. Purchaser agrees to comply with all regulations and requirements of any union(s) that may have jurisdiction over any of the said materials, facilities and personnel to be furnished by Purchaser.

Authors: The artist dictates payment policy. If the promoter wants to change it, he must get written permission. Here, deposits can be paid by check; otherwise it's cash.

8. Deposits may be paid by check or bank wire transfer (bank fees to be paid by Purchaser); all balances paid on the day of performance must be paid in cash unless restricted by law and with prior written approval by Producer.

Authors: If the promoter attempts to make last minute changes in the contract without advance approval in writing from the artist, the artist does not have to perform and can keep the deposit.

9. All variations, deletions or changes must be approved in advance, in writing from the Producer. If the Purchaser fails to obtain prior written approval for any alterations to this Contract and Rider, the Artist will not be required to perform and the Purchaser will forfeit its deposit to the Artist.

Authors: Sometimes a newspaper or the promoter's assistant uses an old photo from the files showing old band members; they both have many events going on at once. Unless you spell out what can and cannot be used in advertising, you are doomed to see their mistakes in print. Topics to be included are: billing, size

of print, logo, latest date that publicity must begin, interview conditions, meet 'n' greet sessions, day of show interviews, unauthorized sponsors, artist's press rep or manager to contact, right of artist to say no to anything. Regarding meet 'n' greets (paragraph #17) with contest winners, company executives, party guests, etc., be aware that people get excited being with entertainers and can keep the artist busy taking photos or signing autographs for hours. It is not fun after a while and requires limits.

BILLING/ADVERTISING

10. If Purchaser has indicated on the face of the contract that this is a private engagement, then no public advertising is required. The purchaser is nevertheless obligated to adhere to Producer's billing requirements hereunder.

11. Purchaser guarantees that Artist will receive 100 percent headline billing in any and all advertising and publicity including, but not limited to, lights, displays, and programs. No other act shall receive billing in equal size or prominence without the prior written consent of the Artist. Artist will close the performance.

12. The correct billing for Artists is as follows: 100 percent   JUDE

13. Artist's logo should be used wherever possible.

14. In cases of public concerts, Purchaser agrees to commence public advertising at least 14 days prior to the date of the performance, using materials provided by the Artist for any and all advertising.

15. Only photographs supplied by the Artist or Artist's representative may be reproduced and used for publicity.

16. Purchaser agrees that it will not commit Artist and/or any member of Artist's staff to any personal appearances, interviews, or any other type of promotion or appearances without the prior written consent of Artist.

17. Meet 'n' Greet sessions are subject to Artist's approval and availability, and will be limited to 20 people with no more than 5 group photographs. Artist's appearance at Meet 'n' Greet sessions, if approved, must take place 30 minutes prior to performance for no longer than 15 minutes.

18. There will be no signs, placards, banners, or other advertising material on or near the stage during the entire performance that implies that the performance or appearance of the Artist is sponsored by or in any manner associated with any commercial products or company, without prior written consent from the Artist.

19. Artist agrees to aid the Purchaser in publicizing the event by providing Purchaser with photographs and biographical material and, when possible, conducting

phone interviews with radio stations and newspapers, subject to Artist's sole approval. Artist does not do "morning zoo" radio shows or any "shock-jock" type show.

20. Artist does not provide live interviews on the day of performance. If the Purchaser requests, and subject to the Artist's availability and approval, Artist may be available for live interviews in advance of the show.

21. Artist will have the sole right of approval regarding all forms of advertising that contain the Artist's name, such approval not to be unreasonably withheld.

22. Interview requests should be submitted in writing to Jude c/o Mitch Weiss fax: 212-555-5555.

Authors: You don't want a video of your artist's show to be sold as a black market DVD. Even worse, imagine that, years later, when your artist has hit it big, that an early amateurish performance surfaces on a tabloid television show all over Europe provided by an employee at the venue. Ouch. There is obviously nothing you can do to prevent the audience from taping your client with their cell phones. You still need to protect your client legally by contractually restricting the promoter from such taping.

AUDIO VISUAL RECORDING

23. The Purchaser should be advised that there is to be no audio or video taping or recording made of any kind of all or any part of the Artist's show without the prior written consent from the Artist or Artist's management. Purchaser acknowledges its responsibility to make best efforts to prevent audience recordings of any kind, including clearly posted signs and announcements, as well as security efforts to detect recording devices.

Authors: If artist says that recording the show is OK, then artist gets the master copy and agrees to make sure that no copies get out to the wrong place.

24. Should the Artist consent to audio and/or visual recordings, Purchaser must ensure that Artist and/or Artist's representative receives the master copy and that Purchaser will protect the recording(s) from any unauthorized use, broadcast, or sale for profit, subject to penalties as allowed by law.

Authors: News photos are OK, but artist must be notified first.

25. Still photographs are permitted for news purposes only, subject to prior notification by the Purchaser to Artist.

Authors: It's easy to make t-shirts. Corporations want their employees to have special "premiums" (gifts) and can add the artist's name to their souvenir shirt or cap unless you tell them they can't. This is where you tell them that you own the trademarked name.

CONCESSIONS

26. Purchaser agrees that it will not sell any products identified with Jude at the place of performance or an adjacent place under its control, nor will it license third parties to do so or permit such sale by any third parties. Purchaser further agrees that Artist and/or Artist's representative shall have the sole and exclusive right to the sale of all forms and types of Artist-related souvenir items, including but not limited to booklets, buttons, t-shirts, programs, and audio and visual recordings. The Artist's name is trademarked by the Producer and may not be used without written permission.

Authors: If you want your artist to make money from merchandise, you better be sure that you're not competing with the promoter and that he won't stick your seller in a back closet away from the crowd and without security. Most venues want a percentage of the t-shirt money, but here is where you say that they get nothing unless they tell you about it in writing.

27. Should the Producer wish to sell Artist-related merchandise, Purchaser agrees to provide a visible area close to the entrance or lobby of the venue. Purchaser further agrees to make certain that sufficient security, acceptable to Artist and Artist's merchandising personnel, is provided. Unless otherwise stated in this agreement, Artist shall retain all proceeds from the sale of Artist-related merchandise.

Authors: Some venues have union agreements with concessionaires. In these cases, you must let their sellers do the selling. In that case, you need a separate agreement with the concessionaires.

28. Should the Producer wish the venue to provide sellers or should the venue require its own sellers, Purchaser and/or venue shall enter into a separate agreement for the sale of Artist-related merchandise.

Authors: Our artist Jude likes t-shirts, so we've put her personal request into the contract.

29. If Purchaser has non-Artist-related t-shirts, Artist would appreciate a souvenir medium t-shirt from your venue for her collection.

Authors: Even big name acts have ended up dressing in the kitchen. Make sure you know your artist's needs and don't assume anything, even lighting. Be sure your artist understands that the smaller venues don't provide decent spaces for dressing and you may have to live with what is realistically available. Show business is rarely glamorous.

ARTIST'S DRESSING ROOM

30. Purchaser shall provide at least one (1) comfortable, well lit, well maintained, private and secure (with either a key lock or a security guard at the door), properly heated or air-conditioned dressing room large enough to hold one (1) grown woman (Jude) and three (3) grown men (band) comfortably. This room should have access to at least one private, clean, well-maintained restroom facility that is serviced by both hot and cold running water, at least one (1) 20 amp volt AC single phase 60 cycle circuit and at least one (1) full sized mirror.

Authors: The less your artist has to pack and clean, the better. Ask for towels.

31. Artist will require a minimum of eight (8) clean, dry, large bath-sized towels in the dressing room at least one hour before the start of show.

Authors: Safety is the most important element—fire exits, etc.

32. Purchaser warrants that there are clearly marked fire-code emergency exits from venue that are easily and safely accessible from the dressing room and backstage area.

Authors: Prior to the attack on the World Trade Center on September 11, 2001, this paragraph may have been enough. You might want to be more specific than the paragraphs below about detecting weapons that might be brought into the venue by the audience or backstage by a visitor or venue employee.

SECURITY

33. It is very important and necessary that Purchaser provide an adequate number of security guards around dressing room and stage, and escorts to and from the stage. Privacy must be provided from the time Artist arrives in the dressing area and for at least one hour after the performance.

34. Security is required on stage prior to, during, and after all engagements, including private parties and festival-type venues. At no time shall any member of the audience be allowed on stage.

Authors: This is where your artist gets to act like a diva. Know the difference between what must be backstage for survival and what the artist would like to have. If you don't ask, you won't get. Some venues like State Fairs cannot legally provide beer or liquor, but they'll let you know when they change the rider. Ziplock bags are requested so that crew can take some of the food back to the hotel room.

HOSPITALITY

35. Artist requires that the Purchaser provide the following refreshments in the dressing rooms at least one hour before the scheduled engagement start time, enough for four (4) people:

a) Hot water (maintained hot throughout the show)

b) Tea, coffee, sugar, milk, lemon, and honey

c) Assortment of chilled mineral water, fruit juices, Coke, and Gatorade

d) Two large buckets of ice

e) Deli platters (turkey, cheeses, chicken, etc.) with various breads, fruit, mayo, mustard, etc. and one vegetable tray.

f) Cups, spoons, knives, forks, condiments, etc.

g) One box of ziplock lunch bags

h) 6 bottles of cold beer (not lite) delivered to the dressing room after the show.

Authors: Your artist and crew may want to thank hotel and airport people who are particularly helpful. There may be high school friends living in that town. Get enough comps, even if you don't use them.

COMPLIMENTARY TICKETS

36. Purchaser agrees that Artist will receive no less than 20 complimentary tickets per show in a preferred area. Guest lists and backstage passes are subject to Artist's approval.

Authors: As boring as this section may seem, it is perhaps the most important protection an artist can have. This is where you make the promoter assure the artist that he has a sufficient amount of insurance against property damage and audience lawsuits, enough that your artist will also be covered. Sometimes the promoter will want the artist's assurance that she has insurance too.

INSURANCE, WARRANTIES AND INDEMNIFICATION

37. Purchaser hereby acknowledges that accident and public liability insurance in the amount of no less than $1 million has been obtained and will be maintained for the duration of the term of this contract, naming Artist as an "additional insured."

Authors: This is called the indemnification clause. When people sue, they usually sue everyone connected with the event, even when only one person may be guilty. Lawyers will tell them that you never know who will end up paying, so sue them all. This paragraph says that if the artist is not the direct cause of the trouble, the promoter will not involve the artist in a lawsuit that the artist did not cause personally. In exchange, the artist promises not to involve the promoter in a lawsuit that the promoter did not cause.

38. Purchaser agrees to hold the Artist harmless for any claim whatsoever, including injury, accident, or property damage, except where such claim is a direct result of Artist's sole negligence. Artist agrees to hold the Purchaser harmless for any claim whatsoever, including injury, accident, or property damage, except where such claim is a direct result of Purchaser's sole negligence.

Authors: You want the promoter to know that you are not responsible for equipment security and that she is guaranteeing that the equipment is in good shape.

39. Purchaser warrants that the sound and lighting systems and their components are in good working condition and that it shall be the sole responsibility of the Purchaser to protect said sound and lighting systems and their components. Except as a direct result of Artist's sole negligence, Purchaser agrees to hold Artist harmless for any damage to sound and/or lighting systems and/or parts thereof for the duration of the engagement, including sound check.

Authors: These are the out clauses. There can be a thousand reasons to postpone or cancel a show. Imagine having to give up a career-making film role because you committed to a concert two months ago. Here, the artist can cancel or postpone for an important show biz job with at least a month's notice. Of course, the promoter wants protection from a crazy, irresponsible artist who doesn't show up. The artist wants to be paid if the cancellation isn't her fault.

POSTPONEMENT, CANCELLATION AND NON-PERFORMANCE

40. Artist may postpone or cancel this contract and the services to be rendered hereunder, at the group's sole discretion, by giving Purchaser 30 days prior written notice, in the event said engagement would interfere or conflict with the preparation or rehearsal of, or performance in, a television series or special, a video taping, a motion picture, a legitimate stage production, an engagement in Atlantic City, N.J. or the state of Nevada, a U.S. or international tour, or the production of a recording in which the group is involved. If postponed, said engagement shall be replayed on a mutually agreeable date within one year after the completion of the conflicting engagement.

Authors: Americans like to sue. Promoters can lose a lot of money if the artist gets sick. Here you make sure that there will be no lawsuit for illness although the artist agrees that the promoter doesn't owe any fee for the cancelled show. Believe it or not, some promoters would try to not pay the artist for previous shows (say, in a three show weekend), so this paragraph also makes sure that the artist gets paid for the performances already given.

41. Should sickness, accident to Artist, or any similar causes beyond control of Artist render performance by Artist impossible, unsafe, or not feasible per Artist's sole discretion, it is understood and agreed that there shall be no claim for damages by either party to this contract, and Artist's obligation as to such performance shall be deemed waived except Artist shall be entitled to be paid pro-rata for any performances rendered prior to any such event.

Authors: Bad weather for an outdoor concert can make a dangerous stage. Some promoters' first priority isn't the artist's safety. This says that if the artist and promoter can't agree (hopefully they will) about whether a stage is dangerous, the artist has the final say. And the artist still gets paid in full since it's not the artist's fault and she showed up ready to perform.

42. Artist's performance is "Pay Rain or Shine." Therefore, should inclement weather render performance by Artist impossible, unsafe, or not feasible as mutually agreed by Purchaser and Producer, Artist's obligation as to such performance shall be deemed canceled and in such event, Artist shall be compensated the full price guaranteed herein. If Purchaser and Producer disagree as to whether rendition of performance(s) is impossible, not feasible, or unsafe because of inclement weather, Producer's determination shall prevail. Any monies due and owing to the Artist at the time of cancellation pursuant to the terms hereof shall be paid immediately upon notice of same.

Authors: Force Majeure is a legal term referring to things that may happen that are completely out of the control of people, such as tornados, earthquakes, terrorist attacks, police actions, cancelled or delayed air flights, etc. These are sometimes referred to as "Acts of God." For example, if there is an earthquake in Los Angeles on Thursday and the promoter calls to cancel the concert on Friday, the artist agrees to return the deposit (be sure that the amount returned is *after* deducting any airfare or hotel costs that cannot be refunded). On the other hand, if the artist flies to Los Angeles on Thursday and the earthquake strikes on Friday, the promoter owes the entire fee to the artist. She was ready, willing and able to perform and deserves the payment for her time and travel. (In reality, the artist and promoter would probably reschedule or agree to a compromised fee.)

43. In the event of non-performance due to a force majeure cancellation not specifically addressed in this Rider, and if the Artist has not yet left Artist's home city, Artist shall return any deposits received less any and all bona fide expenses paid by Artist that are directly related to the performance contained herein, including but not limited to non-refundable air travel and hotel costs. The above notwithstanding, if the Artist has left Artist's home and is ready, willing and able to perform, Purchaser shall pay the full compensation hereunder.

Authors: If you don't tell the promoter what you want, you may end up in a flea-infested motel. Be clear about bed size, especially if your artist is over six feet tall. She or her entourage may not agree to share rooms but the promoter may absolutely refuse to pay for singles. If you don't ask for it, you can't get it. If your artist has medical problems or dietary restrictions, they can be affected by the quality of a hotel. There are plenty of hotels with broken vending machines and no nearby restaurants. After a show, a hungry performer will not be happy.

HOTEL ACCOMMODATIONS

44. Purchaser agrees to provide four (4) single rooms with queen size beds or larger, located close to the venue at a four (4) star hotel or better. Hotel should have a 24-hour room service availability or quality 24-hour restaurant located within the hotel or in close proximity.

45. Check-in and checkout times must be arranged in accordance with Artist's travel schedule.

Authors: The airlines can ruin your business trip with late arrivals, lost luggage carrying costumes or equipment, bad connection times, and high prices. If a promoter looks for the least expensive airfare, a trip between New York and a small Wisconsin town can take more than ten hours. If you're planning a bus tour, you still want these clauses because you never know when a bus might break down and you need to catch a flight to make a date.

DOMESTIC AIR TRAVEL

46. No airline tickets may be purchased without Artist's prior approval of flight times and seating. Failure to get Artist's prior approval shall be considered a breach of contract and may result in the cancellation of this agreement at Artist's sole discretion.

47. In all cases, seating assignments MUST be made in advance for all flights and must be printed on the tickets. Jude prefers an aisle seat. Road Manager should be seated next to Jude. Coach tickets should both be window seats.

48. Artist reserves the right to choose preferred airline. Airline carriers must be supplied with the following information in sufficient time to accommodate the following needs to Artist:

    a) Two first or business class and two coach class regular fare roundtrip airline tickets. Artist will not accept any tickets that indicate that they are free or barter tickets obtained through a sponsorship or trade deal of any kind.

    b) All flights will be nonstop, wherever available.

    c) Airline must have a minimum of 100 seats—no prop planes—unless approved by Artist.

49. Artist and entourage leave from Newark or LaGuardia airports only. If Artist must travel from a city other than New York due to work, and if Artist so requests, Purchaser agrees to fly Artist to or from that other city.

50. Should one or more of the traveling party choose to drive to the venue, Purchaser agrees to pay to Artist the full cost of the unused ticket, if logistically possible, as mileage costs.

Authors: Traveling overseas has special considerations. The first is a valid passport, work visas in the foreign country, medical conditions (prescriptions are an absolute necessity), medical emergencies, and language translators. Jet lag can take a special toll on the health of the artist and should not be taken lightly.

INTERNATIONAL TRAVEL

51. In addition to the travel conditions listed above under "Domestic Travel," Purchaser agrees to the following:

   a) For travel crossing more than six (6) time zones, at least one full day off, including two full nights' sleep before scheduling any rehearsals, sound checks, press, or additional travel. Such days off shall begin upon checking into the hotel.

   b) No return flights can be scheduled that require checking out of the hotel earlier than 10:00 A.M. on the morning following the final performance.

52. International performances in non-English speaking countries, a knowledgeable translator must be available to Artist at all times.

Authors: It makes sense for the promoter to provide roundtrip transportation between the airport, the hotel, and the venue, since the artist and entourage may not be familiar with local directions that may cause problems arriving on time. On the other hand, the artist is probably most familiar with her home airport and car services. If you can get the promoter to reimburse the ground transportation in the home city, go for it.

GROUND TRANSPORTATION

53. Ground transportation must be provided from the arriving airport to hotel and from hotel to venue, in both directions. Two town cars or limos accommodating four (4) adults plus an equipment van for nine (9) pieces of large luggage must be provided. Luggage handlers will be needed to assist Artist.

54. If ground transportation to an airport is more than one (1) hour, Artist and/or Artist's representative must be informed prior to the signing of this contract. Special vehicles may be required, at Artist's sole discretion.

55. When possible, the Artist's entourage would like to travel in shifts:

   a) One limo or town car arriving at the venue for sound check and as needed by the crew. One limo or town car arriving at the venue one hour prior to show or as needed by the Artist.

   b) One vehicle returning one half hour after the performance and one returning much later to allow remaining members to socialize with patrons and staff.

Authors: Per diems are monies paid to individuals to cover eating and other personal expenses that may arise while out of town. While everyone has to eat, there is no doubt that it is more expensive to eat out, especially at a hotel or an airport. If the negotiation is open to it, getting a little more money for your crew, musicians, and artists can't hurt. Most unions have provisions for out-of-town work.

FOOD OPTION

56. Purchaser agrees to provide a per diem of $65 per day per person for four (4) people for each day of performance plus one travel day. Per Diem will be paid in cash on the day of arrival in the performing city, but no later than prior to the first performance.
57. If purchaser requests, room service or at least two hot meals per day may be substituted for the per diem, subject to the approval of Artist.
58. Per Diem or meals must be provided in addition to dressing room catering as required in this Rider.

Authors: International travel has a number of unusual ramifications that would not be an issue in the United States. Does your artist carry a lot of scenery or props by truck? What happens if the tour is in Australia; does it all have to travel by air or sea? The cost of shipping the equipment may be astronomical. This shouldn't come out of the performance fee. The costs of attaining foreign work visas and permits should never be the responsibility of the artist. And you don't want to be stuck with any unexpected fees charged by BMI, ASCAP, or SESAC for the live performance of music in a particular venue.

MISCELLANEOUS

59. Excess baggage charges, if any, as well as the cost of visa licenses and permits, if any, will be the sole responsibility of the Purchaser.
60. Purchaser shall make arrangements for work permits, music performance rights, and any and all requirements necessary for Artist to perform. All costs related to these arrangements, plus entry and departure taxes, visas, fees, etc. shall be the sole responsibility of the Purchaser.

Authors: Hey, bad things happen to good people and badly acting people cause problems. If things go awry, you don't want to spend years in court. Arbitration is the answer. Fight for it. It will save you tens of thousands of dollars in legal fees even if you lose the case.

DISPUTES AND GRIEVANCES

61. All disputes, differences or controversies (hereafter referred to as "grievances") which may arise between the parties under the terms of this agreement, if after a reasonable attempt to settle such matter(s) has been made shall be resolved in the following manner:

   Either the Purchaser or Producer/Artist may submit the matter to arbitration before a mutually agreeable third party. In the event the Purchaser and Producer/Artist are unable to agree upon a third party, the demand for arbitration shall be submitted to the American Arbitration Association in New York City. The decision of the Arbitrator shall be final and binding upon the parties and their members, and shall not be subject to Court review except that either party may petition an appropriate Court for the enforcement of an award, if necessary. The costs of any arbitration shall be borne by the losing party in the arbitration.

Authors: Technically, the law says that a contract isn't real until an original copy has been signed and delivered. As business works faster these days, most contracts are now enforceable after they are signed and faxed.

FACSIMILE AND E-MAILED SIGNATURES

62. This agreement may be executed by copies transmitted by telecopiers (fax) and email scans, each of which shall be given the same force and effect as the original.

Authors: There is not one set of laws anywhere in the United States and certainly not throughout the world. If you go to arbitration for a dispute, someone's got to know which laws to refer to in order to settle the case. The best and most comprehensive entertainment laws are in New York and California (where most entertainment businesses are located). However, a promoter may want to base the contract on the laws in his local state so that he won't have to travel in case of a problem. You'll never know if it matters until there's a problem.

This agreement shall be deemed to have been made in New York, USA and that its validity, construction and effect shall be governed by the laws of the state of New York, United States of America.

(End of Rider)

ADDENDUM: TECHNICAL
STAGE AND TECHNICAL REQUIREMENTS—PLEASE CONTACT
ARTIST'S ROAD MANAGER IF YOU REQUIRE
ANY ADDITIONAL DETAILS.

Authors: In the early stages of a career, when the venues are small clubs, the artist is stuck with the equipment available. Your road manager along with any technical people you hire should be able to put together a detailed technical plan for your artist. Be aware that renting equipment can be expensive for the promoter and may affect how many promoters can afford to hire the artist. If the equipment makes for a special show, then make it part of the contract and be prepared to be very flexible. Outdoor stages during daytime make lighting effects worthless and some venues will not allow anything but their own in-house equipment. Here is an example of a detailed wish list.

PRODUCTION REQUIREMENTS

You want a good looking and sounding show . . . so do we. It is essential that your Sound Man contact Artist's Road Manager at least 14 days prior to the performance.

Road Manager's Name, Phone and Fax

1. Purchaser agrees to provide a solidly constructed stage that is at least 20 feet wide by 14 feet deep (from the front of the backdrop) and at least 3 feet off the floor, and heated or air conditioned appropriately. Because Artist dances during the performance, stage must not be carpeted. No exceptions. Any carpeted stage must be covered with a flat and safe-to-dance-on surface.

    a) Artist will supply a 20 by 30 foot backdrop. Purchaser agrees to provide a fly bar, metal piping for the base and stage crew to set it up. Backdrop must be set up to totally obscure any on-stage equipment from audience's view. Please contact Road Manager for details.

    b) Clear Com between stage, Front of House, lights, and monitors.

    c) All equipment set up by competent technicians and/or operators, EQ'd and functioning before sound check.

    d) Purchaser agrees to provide competent lighting operators and technicians for both sound check and show. Road Manager will determine sound check time.

Authors: Setting standards for the amount of available power (ever blow a fuse during a show?), having exclusive rights to sound channels so that your sound person can hold on to sound levels set during a sound check earlier in the day, and a generic statement

that your tech people don't want substitutions are good technical rules under any circumstance. Overall you want to address all of these categories.

SOUND REQUIREMENTS

2.   Artist requires two 117 Vac Pwr Drops of Clean Power and Ground, preferred systems: [list suggested choices here].
3.   Artist does not share House or Monitor Channels with any other acts.
4.   No substitutions without prior approval!
5.   House system 4-way active stereo capable of 118 dB undistorted at house mix with adequate coverage of venue.
6.   40 channel house console with phase reverse, phantom power, high bass filter, and 4 band EQ per channel, 8 subgroups, and VCAs.
7.   Choices: approved models for the above equipment should be listed here.
8.   Details for reverb, effects, delay, CD players, mics, Dats, mic stands, cables, etc.

MONITOR REQUIREMENTS

9.   40-channel monitor console with phase reverse, phantom power, high-pass filter, 4 band EQ per channel.
10. Choices: [approved models for the above equipment].
11. Equipment details for sidefills, floor wedges, EQs, Crossovers etc.

LIGHTING REQUIREMENTS

12. There are special lighting cues to Artist's show. If lights and sound are in separate areas, a communication system will be needed.
13. No substitutions without prior approval!
    a)   One 48 channel 2.4 Kw dimmer rack.
    b)   One F.O.H. followspot (Lycian Long Throw or equivalent).
    c)   Six way Clear Com System (1 Master, 5 Belt packs, and 6 Double Ear headsets)
    d)   Adequate power distribution system for all equipment (206v and 120v)
    e)   Adequate cables, multicore, breakouts, termination plugs, etc.
    f)   Etc.

VIDEO REQUIREMENTS

14. Artist's video presentation requires one of the following systems:
    a)   Front projection equipment with model numbers.
    b)   Back projection equipment with model numbers

Authors: Take the time to have someone draw the way the artist would like to work on stage: with mics, monitors, keyboards, cables, drums etc., and include an illustration as part of the technical addendum.

STAGE ILLUSTRATION

(End of Technical Rider)

24

Sample Form for Independent Contractors with Analysis

Don't just copy your forms; understand them first.

Authors: All workers being paid as independent contractors should sign a form declaring that they fit all the qualifications of an independent contractor. The form protects you, the employer, as long as the job is legitimately an independent contractor job. If you use this form, and then hire someone to do a job that the government defines as a job that should be a salaried job, you are still going to get in trouble because a state can claim you are trying to get away without paying payroll taxes. In this form, you are the "Company" and the worker being hired is the "Contractor."

Between
Employer/Company name and address

The Contractor's name and address

_____

_____

Employer phone and email

Contractor's phone/email/
Social Security number

_____

_____

Authors: What exactly is the worker doing for you? If it's a regular weekly desk job, then it doesn't fit the definition of a contractor. It usually involves a specific project or event.

1. Contractor will provide services (explain in detail):

Authors: The employer will not pay employment taxes and therefore the worker doesn't get unemployment, disability, or Social Security.

2. It is understood that the Contractor is an Independent Contractor and is not, nor shall be deemed to be, an employee of the Corporation, for any purpose of tax, excise, or other charge levied by the Federal, State, or Municipal law with respect to employment, wages, remuneration for employment, or any other purpose whatsoever, including any tax or contribution of the Federal Social Security Act.

Authors: The employer will not provide pension or health insurance. If the employer does offer any of these kinds of benefits, the State can say that he is not a contractor and therefore the employer will have to pay all back payroll taxes, often 17% of total income.

3. It is understood that the contractor will not be eligible to participate in any benefit programs sponsored by the company including, but not limited to, health insurance, profit sharing, and 401(k).

Authors: The employer will not provide holiday pay or vacation time, etc.

4. The contractor will not be entitled to be paid for any vacation, holiday, sick or personal days.

Authors: Here it is spelled out that the worker will not receive unemployment benefits from this gig.

5. It is understood that at the conclusion or termination of the contract between the two parties that the contractor will not be eligible to collect unemployment benefits.

Authors: Here it is spelled out that the worker will not receive worker's comp or disability should something bad happen on the job. If the worker gets hurt, he's on his own.

6.   No insurance coverage of any kind, including Worker's Compensation and Disability Insurance, is provided or implied to be provided by the Corporation on behalf of the Contractor.

Authors: If there's a contract that explains payment details, you don't have to explain it here. The rest of it says that, by law, the Employer must report any earnings over $600 to the government and send the worker a 1099 form stating what the government was told. The worker will then have to pay his own taxes on the amount declared on this 1099 form.

7.   Contractor will be paid (explain in detail):
The Corporation takes no responsibility for the manner of operation or record keeping of the Contractor's business, and assumes neither responsibility nor liability for the reporting of income or the payment of taxes to any Federal, State, or Municipal authority. The Corporation will provide a statement of income, Federal form 1099, at year's end to contractors who receive over $600.00 in an annual period from the Corporation.

Authors: Unlike employees, contractors are expected to invoice the employer for their work. This is not always necessary, but it is suggested. This just lists the information that should be included on the invoice.

8.   In order to receive payment, the contractor will submit invoices on their company's stationery which will include the following:
1.   Computation of fee
2.   Services performed
3.   Projects worked on
4.   Detail of any reimbursed expenses
5.   Federal identification number or Social Security number

Signed:
Contractor name and date   Employer name and date

_____   _____

#

Sample Record Deal Summary with a Major Record Label with Analysis

Don't just copy your forms; understand them first.

Authors: This is not the entire record contract, but it states that a formal agreement will be signed later. The number of words used by lawyers in these contracts is twice what is necessary. The over burdensome language is called legalese. It scares artists and confuses managers and other lawyers. The goal is to be clear and thorough with as few words as possible. Nevertheless, I thought it valuable to print an entire and actual Deal Summary used by a major label in the 1990s along with a one- or two-line description of the purpose of each paragraph. The author's notes are in bold. In a contract with so many details, it is important that everyone initials every single page. Otherwise it is possible, in this ugly crooked world, for someone to substitute a revised page in the middle of the agreement at a later date.

From: Label's name and address

To: Artist's company name and address

Date: Day of submitting contract

Authors: Opening paragraph states as simply as possible who is involved and what they are going to do together. In order to save space, each person or company is given a nickname to be used throughout the agreement. Remember: While technically the contractor and the artist are the same person, under the law, the contractor and artist

are not legally the same thing. The contractor is a corporation or legal organization that provides the artist's services.

When signed by and on behalf of "name of artist's company" (afterwards known as *Contractor*) and "label" (afterwards known as *Company*) in the places provided below, Contractor and Company shall be deemed to have agreed on the following basic terms and conditions of the formal Agreement yet to be made between the parties hereto (afterwards known as the *Agreement*) in respect of the recording services of the artist "name of artist" (afterward known as the *Artist*) for the purpose of recording the "Masters" (as hereinafter defined and described in more detail):

Authors: Here we learn the details of what is expected from the artist, when everything will get done and who will produce, engineer, etc. Most importantly, we learn what decisions the artist is allowed to make personally, or in conjunction with others. Remember, "Contractor" means the artist and "Company" means the recording label.

1. Artist Recording Obligation and other Services:
    a. The Artist shall perform so as to enable Company to record 7" and 12" single versions, album versions and videos of the material entitled "name of song" and of the material yet to be selected by mutual agreement for the recording hereunder of one further track. Contractor, Artist, and Company have agreed that "producer's name" shall be the producer of the Masters, provided that the video producer shall be subject to Contractor's approval, not to be unreasonably withheld. Final edit of the video shall be subject to Artist's approval not to be unreasonably withheld. Artist shall be available as Company may reasonably require, but only as mutually agreed upon by Artist and Company.
    b. In the event that this producer does not produce the second track, Contractor and Company shall mutually select another producer. For the purpose of recording the Masters, Artist shall be available in "name of city" on "dates" and at such other time(s) and/or place(s) as Company may reasonably require. Contractor warrants and shall procure that at the time of each recording session, Artist shall render services to the best of Artist's skill and ability for the purpose of completing the recording of the Masters as soon as reasonably possible and that Artist shall rehearse, repeat, and re-record the performance and follow all reasonable directions by or on

behalf of Company for the purpose of obtaining Masters satisfactory to Company for the manufacture of first class Records.

Authors: Important to state that the artist is or is not bound to this label (exclusive or non-exclusive basis) so that artist knows if she can record with others, and if so, under what circumstances.

    c.   It is expressly clarified that the Artist's recording obligation and other services hereunder shall be rendered to Company on a non-exclusive basis.

Authors: Imagine if Joe Blow of the group NoName signed a recording contract and it was later discovered that Joe Blow was no longer in the group. Imagine the label paid him in advance before finding out that he didn't have the right to speak for the group. To be safe, all companies require "Warranty" statements ("Artist warrants that . . .") that declare that the person(s) signing the contract have all the rights needed to actually make the deal happen. Also, notice how many unnecessary words are in this paragraph. When possible, a manager should rewrite contracts into simple English so as to make it "artist-friendly." What good is a business deal if the artist can't easily read it? If you do rewrite a contract, always have a lawyer double-check that nothing has been lost by the omission of a legal term.

    d.   Contractor warrants that Contractor has full right, power, and authority to enter into and perform the Agreement and that the Artist shall completely fulfill the recording obligation pursuant hereto;

    e.   Contractor warrants that Contractor and Artist have not incurred and shall not incur any liability that may diminish, impair, or otherwise affect any of Company's rights pursuant to the Agreement.

    f.   Contractor warrants that the Artist will cooperate fully with Company, its subsidiaries, affiliates, and licensees in connection with Artist's promotional and publicity efforts relating to Masters and/or Records hereunder, i.e., subject to the Artist's prior professional engagements. Contractor warrants the Artist's personal availability and/or performances hereunder for press and other media interviews, photo, and/or video recording sessions and television performances (collectively "promotional activities") subject as further specified in 1.c. hereof.

Authors: This states that label will pay the costs related to doing promotion (hotels, travel, etc.) unless someone else like a TV station is paying the costs. All that's important

is that the artist doesn't have to pay the cost of doing interviews out of his/her own pocket. The second half of this paragraph defines the artist's precise expectations for travel, hotels, food, etc. Per diem is a term for a flat daily payment to cover food and miscellaneous expenses. (Sorry about the repetitious legalese stupidity here.)

g. Artist's availability for promotional activities shall be mutually agreed from time to time and shall otherwise be free of charge to Company, its affiliates and licensees SAVE THAT (unless paid for by any other party such as any radio or TV station or network, etc.) Company, its affiliates and licensees shall be in charge of paying expenses actually incurred by way of Artist's traveling expenses and reasonable costs of accommodation if and when Artist shall be so available for promotional activities at Company's request, subject to the following: If any other party as aforesaid agrees to pay any fee(s) in connection with the Artist's promotional activities, then Company and/or any of Company's affiliates and licensees shall have the right to collect such fee(s) and deduct there from all expenses so incurred by way of Artist's traveling and accommodation costs, provided that if such fee(s) shall exceed total expenses as aforesaid, then the remaining balance shall be payable to Contractor.

Reasonable costs of accommodation with regard to hotels shall be defined as follows: at least "four star" quality hotels with late night eating facilities within or within walking distance, rooms with at least queen-size beds and per diems of $150 per day per person, full Per Diem to be paid for travel days and partial days. Seat arrangements for travel should be bulkhead or aisle only.

Authors: You may have noticed that the word "Record" is still being used even though the industry has stopped producing vinyl records. That's because the word "Record" has a special contractual meaning that doesn't necessarily match the common language use of the word. You'll notice below that "Record" also means CD and cassette and almost anything else that may be invented by the music industry in the future. Key words like this are *defined* in this section.

2. Definitions, for the purposes hereof:
    a. "Masters" means the original material object in which sounds, with or without visual images, are fixed by any method now known or later developed and from which sounds, with or without visual images, can be perceived, reproduced or otherwise communicated, either directly or with the aid of a machine, device, or process.

b. The noun "Record" means any mechanical reproduction, in any form now known or later developed, from which sounds (whether or not coupled with visual images) can be perceived, reproduced, or otherwise communicated, either directly or with the aid of a machine, device or process, including without limitation conventional-type records and tape configurations, so-called "Audiophile Records" and "Videograms."

c. "Audiophile Records" means an audio-only Record which is made for digital playback and includes without limitation compact discs ("CD"), digital audio tapes ("DAT"), digital compact cassettes ("DCC"), and a record in disc configuration utilizing technology developed by the Sony Corporation and commonly known as mini disc ("MD").

d. "Videogram" means any material object, in any form now known or later developed (including without limitation tape, cassette, film, or disc) embodying a video or a compilation, collective work or derivative work, which embodies a video together with any other video(s) and/or other audio-visual work(s), including without limitation videocassettes and the format known as compact disc video ("CDV").

Authors: This paragraph says that the label lays out the money for the recording and the video. However, don't think this is free. In this paragraph, the artist owes 50 percent of the original cost of the video back to the label. No royalties will be paid to the artist until the artist's share of video costs has been paid back. This is also where the company states that it will pay producers, remixers, etc., but that the artist is responsible for paying anyone the artist may have promised a piece of the action—like the manager. Legalese: You've got to learn to ignore phrases like "Save as herein expressly specified to the contrary," that just serve to muddle the important words and tend to scare the artist, and sometimes the manager, from reading further for fear of getting confused.

3. Recording Costs and Third Party Liabilities:

Company shall be responsible for the payment of all recording and video production costs incurred as a result of the making of the Masters (collectively "Recording Costs"). Save as herein expressly specified to the contrary, Recording Costs shall not be recoupable from royalties and/or royalty-like sums due to Contractor pursuant to the Agreement, excepting only that 50 percent (fifty per cent) of the total incurred by way of video production costs in respect of any video(s) made under the Agreement shall be recoupable from royalties and royalty-like sums (such as flat fees, if any) due to Contractor under the Agreement. Company shall enter into separate agreements in respect of the services of each of the video and other producers (including remixers) and Company shall be responsible for the payment of all monies due to any of the immediately aforesaid parties as a result of the making and/or exploitation of the Masters. The sums (including without limitation advances and royalties) due to Contractor pursuant hereto shall be deemed to include any and all monies due to Contractor and/or Artist and/or any other person(s) deriving any rights from Artist (as the case may be) in respect of the making of the Masters and/or exploitation of the Masters and Records subject to the Agreement.

Authors: The label owns the copyrights to the Masters and recordings (not the songs themselves) and can do almost anything its wants with them including using them in movies, etc. If the company wants to sell them to another company or let related companies use them, they can. Label can also use artist's name, bio, and photos. And this is all "in perpetuity," meaning forever. [Question: So you are saying that the label can do whatever it wants with the masters and these particular recordings of the song, and the artist won't see another penny, either as the performer or as the composer, even if the recording is used as the sound track of a blockbuster movie? The answer is YES.]

4.   Ownership of Masters:

The Masters and all duplicates and derivatives thereof (including the copyright in such Masters for the full term of copyright and any renewal and/or extension of such copyright), together with the performances embodied therein, shall, from the inception of recording, be exclusively and perpetually Company's property, free of any claim whatsoever by Contractor, Artist and/or any person(s) deriving any rights from Artist. Without limiting the generality of the foregoing, Company and/or its subsidiaries, affiliates, licensees, and assigns shall have the sole, exclusive, and unlimited right in perpetuity throughout the world and the universe ("Territory") to exercise all or any of its rights in and to the Masters, to use any Master(s) in whole or in part (whether or not together with any other recording(s) and/or other material) for synchronization in motion picture, television or any other audiovisual soundtracks as background music or for any other purposes, to manufacture Records by any methods now or hereafter known embodying any portions or all of the Masters (whether or not together with any other recording(s) and/or material), to transmit, perform publicly and broadcast such Records, to release, market, distribute, advertise, publicize, promote, deal in, exploit for promotional, commercial, and/or any other purposes (including without limitation by sale, lease, license, and rental), to re-package, re-release or otherwise use, transfer or dispose of any part or all of the Masters and/or Records hereunder in any manner or media (including but not limited to "free," "pay," "public," "cable," and "subscription" television, theatrical and non-theatrical distribution), through any trademarks, trade names, or labels as shall be determined or approved by Company in its sole and exclusive discretion, or notwithstanding any provisions hereof, Company, its affiliates, subsidiaries, licensees, sub-licensees and/or assigns may at their election delay, refrain or resume any part or all of the foregoing at any time. Contractor warrants and agrees that Company, its affiliates, subsidiaries, licensees, sub-licensees, and/or assigns shall have the non-exclusive perpetual right throughout the Territory to use and to authorize other persons to use the Artist's name, biographical material, and likenesses in connection with the exploitation of the Masters and/or Records hereunder.

Authors: Finally a simple statement . . . Artist cannot release a re-recording of the same material for five years from the date the masters are delivered to the company.

5. Duration of Artist's Re-Recording Restriction in respect of any Material contained in the Masters:
Five (5) years from and after the delivery of the completed Masters to Company.

Authors: The artist gets paid, how much and when (in this example $10,000; $5,000 when this contract is signed and $5,000 when the finished masters are delivered to label). More importantly, since it's an "advance", the artist will not be paid a penny more until the artist's royalties equal more than the $10,000 already paid up front. That's the meaning of "advance." This is not a fee for work done; this money says that you are promised no less than $10,000 in royalties and the label agrees to pay the guaranteed amount at the start whether or not your record does well. There's an excellent chance that the artist will never see another dime unless the record is a big hit. For this reason, negotiating a big advance is always advantageous.

6. Payments, due to Contractor in full and final consideration of Contractor's and the Artist's services and the rights granted to Company under the Agreement:
   a. An advance of U.S. Dollars 10,000 (ten thousand), payable by two equal installments, the first of which shall be due upon the execution of the Agreement and the second of which shall be due upon the later of the date of the execution of the Agreement or the delivery to Company of all the Masters to be recorded in accordance with the provisions hereof. The advance shall be fully recoupable from any and all royalties and royalty-like sums (such as flat fees, if any) due to Contractor pursuant to the Agreement and shall otherwise be non-returnable provided that Contractor and Artist shall have complied with their warranties and obligations under the Agreement.

**Authors: How do you know if and when the label owes the artist more than the ad-
vanced amount (in this example $10,000)? Royalties must be calculated based on some
mathematical computation. This paragraph defines the complex and almost unverifi-
able maze of percentages (often called "points" in the music industry). The standard
ceiling for artists is up to 14 percent, usually reserved for famous artists. It's all based
on the RBSP (the wholesale price of a CD or a cassette, etc.) on which different percentages are paid to the artist. And the percentages change subject to different sales prices
in different markets (music clubs versus stores, foreign versus domestic). There ought
to be clear definitions, but there rarely are. Every one of these percentages is negotiable. It's hard to ask for more unless you understand each category and why you deserve
more. That's why an experienced manager is better than an inexperienced one and
a good experienced lawyer is worth his fee. My advice to both managers and artists:
Don't get upset. It is impossible to understand it all. Someday you'll pay an accounting
firm to audit your royalties and they will tell you if the rules have been followed.**

b.   Subject to applicable recoupment provision and all relevant provisions
relating to the computation of royalties under the Agreement, Company
shall pay the following royalties for all "net sales" (as defined) of Records
embodying any of the Masters:

(i)   Subject always to the provisions of sub-paragraph (iii) of this
sub-clause b., in respect of audio-only Records sold

(aa) through regular trade channels in full price category: 11
percent of the applicable Royalty Base Selling Price ("RBSP").
However, if the aggregate net sales in the Territory through
regular trade channels of any particular audio-only Record consisting solely of Masters recording under the Agreement shall
have exceeded 500,000 full-priced units, then the royalty due
to Contractor with respect to further net sales effected through
regular trade channels in full price category of such same particular Record which are over and above said 500,000 units shall
be 12 percent of the applicable RBSP.

(bb) through regular trade channels in medium price category:
8.25 percent of the applicable RBSP;

(cc) through regular trade channels in low or budget price category: 5.5 percent of the applicable RBSP.

(dd) in any price category by any method and/or through any
trade channels other than regular trade channels (including
without limitation audio-only Records sold through or to clubs,

mail order, direct mail, or to any governmental body, educational institutions or libraries, by way of premiums, to any commercial purchaser for re-sale through army sales channels or for use or re-sale as premiums), as the case my be: 5.5 percent of the applicable RBSP.

Authors: Videograms is a legal term for a video, DVD or any other visual version of the song. The same complexities of royalties for records apply to video sales.

(ii)   Subject always to the provisions of sub-paragraph (iii) of this sub-clause b, in respect of Videograms sold

(aa) through regular trade channels in full price category: 5.5 percent of the applicable RBSP.

(bb) through regular trade channels in medium price category: 4 percent of the applicable RBSP.

(cc) through regular trade channels in low or budget price category: 2.75 percent of the applicable RBSP.

(dd) in any price category by any method and/or through any trade channels other than regular trade channels (including without limitation Videograms sold through or to clubs, mail order, direct mail, or to any governmental body, educational institutions or libraries, by way of premiums, to any commercial purchaser for re-sale through army sales channels or for use or re-sale as premiums), as the case may be: 2.75 percent of the applicable RBSP.

Authors: This says the artist is paying out of her royalties, at least partially, for any major advertising campaign. The definition of a "major" campaign is not spelled out. The label will reduce all of the above percentages by 25 percent if the label lays out the bucks to advertise. It might be better for the artist to do her own publicity campaign.

(iii)   Notwithstanding anything to the contrary, if Records or Videograms are promoted by any major TV- or radio- or magazine- or cinema-advertising campaign(s), a reduced royalty shall apply which shall equal 75 percent of the royalty otherwise applicable pursuant to the provisions set forth in sub-paragraph b.(i) or b.(ii) (as the case may be) of this Clause 6.

Authors: The above paragraph mentions clause 6. Don't get lazy when reading "subparagraph" and "clause" references. A good manager will check the reference and be sure that all items affected by one paragraph are understood. Basically this reference says that the reduction in royalties affects every single percentage listed in those subparagraphs.

Authors: Compilation albums using songs from various artists, usually created after a song has been around for years, pay royalties to more than one song and artist. This says that royalties for these albums will be divided equally among all the songs on the album.

    c.   Further provisions relating to royalty computation under the Agreement:

        (i)   If any audio-only Record or Videogram (as the case may be, including without limitation any multiple album or multiple videogram) embodies any Master(s) together with any other recording(s) which are not subject to the Agreement, then the applicable royalty due to Contractor under the Agreement shall be computed on a pro rata numeric basis.

Authors: This definition of "net sales" affects the next few paragraphs. As described before, "Net" means after deductions. In this case, the deductions are any returns or credits. So if the label sells $50,000, but $2,000 in CD sales have been returned, then the royalties will be based on "Net sales" or $48,000.

        (ii)   "Net sales" or "sales" or "sold" shall mean 100 percent of all sales of Records (whether audio-only Records or Videograms) containing any of the Master(s), less returns and credits for any reason and subject to the following:

Authors: Freebies don't count as records sold. Discounted records result in discounted royalties (logical).

        (aa) If Records hereunder are sold subject to a discount or merchandising plan, the number of Records deemed to have been sold hereunder shall be determined by reducing the number of Records so sold by the percentage of discount granted. If a discount is granted in the form of free goods, such free goods shall not be deemed included in the number of Records sold under the Agreement. (N.B. Records subject to the Agreement shall be subject to the same sales, discount, free goods, returns, deletion, and sell-off policies normally applied from time to time by Company and/or its respective affiliate, subsidiary, licensee, or assign (as the case may be) in relation to comparable Records sold to or through the respective trade channels in comparable price categories).

(bb) Notwithstanding anything to the contrary contained hereunder, Contractor shall not be entitled to receive any royalty or other payment in respect of any of the following:

1) Exhibition copies (including without limitation promotional giveaways);
2) So-called "bonus" or "dividend" Records or free club records;
3) Records sold as "scrap," "overstock," or "surplus," which terms shall mean excess inventory of a particular Record which is listed in the respective catalogue(s) and sold at one third (1/3) or less of the otherwise applicable selling price;
4) Records deleted from the respective catalogue(s) and sold off as discontinued merchandise at so-called "cut-out prices";
5) Records destroyed for any reason.

Authors: Because the quantity of refunds isn't immediately known, labels hide some money away to cover these expected refunds or exchanges. The amount put aside in "reserves" should be clearly defined and can be negotiated. In this version, they can put aside up to 30 percent of all records shipped for up to two years! Ouch! The smaller you can get them to make this reserve the better for your client, usually around 15–20 percent, but in one case, the figure went down to 5 percent.

(cc) In computing the quantities of Records sold hereunder, Company, its affiliates, subsidiaries, licensees, and assigns shall have the right in each accounting period to establish and maintain reasonable reserves for returns and exchanges, provided that such reserves shall be in accordance with their normal reserves policy (but in any event not in excess of 30 percent of the records shipped) and shall be liquidated in succeeding accounting periods (over a maximum of two years) based on actual returns and exchanges and on accepted royalty accounting practices.

Authors: The definition of "RBSP" requires other definitions that require additional clarifications that make all of this a mess. I've counted at least fifty words of legalese that have no applicable significance to anyone. An important reference hiding in the

first paragraph is made to a "container allowance." Containers, which are not defined anywhere in this agreement but should be, are the CD jewel case or the vinyl album cover or the plastic cassette case plus any printed material that goes with it. The words "container allowance" isn't mentioned again until paragraph (cc) below. The importance of the definition of RBSP and "Net Selling Price" cannot be overstated. It can mean a fortune if a CD goes platinum. How many items can be deducted from the price of a CD, and at what rate, before calculating the artist's royalty is what is at stake.

> (iii) The "RBSP" or "Royalty Base Selling Price" shall mean the applicable "Net Selling Price" (as defined) less the applicable "container allowance" permitted pursuant hereto. For the purpose of the immediately aforesaid,
>
> (aa) "Net Selling Price" shall mean the applicable "Selling Price" (as defined and subject as hereinafter specified) exclusive of all of the following:
>
> > 1. Any taxes (if any) actually included in the applicable Selling Price;
> > 2. Any donations (if any) actually included in the applicable Selling Price which shall be payable to any charity or welfare or other relief organization(s);
> > 3. Any packing and/or shipping expenses (if any) actually included in the applicable Selling Price.
>
> (bb) "Selling Price" in respect of audio-only Records or Videograms (as the case may be) sold hereunder shall mean the "PPD" save as expressly otherwise provided for hereunder, PROVIDED THAT
>
> > 1. "PPD" shall mean the applicable published price to dealers in respect of the respective Record configuration in the respective price category as so published from time to time by the respective distributor in the country of sale;

Authors: More definitions that can be negotiated are included here. Premiums, though not defined, can mean free gifts from a company to its employees and purchased at a discounted group rate, or just promotional copies of the CD given out by the label. The label also wants to make sure that they don't have to pay the artist a royalty based on the store rate when and if the label isn't charging libraries, record clubs or the military the store price.

2. Notwithstanding anything to the contrary contained in the foregoing, in respect of Records sold in the form of finished product to any government or educational institutions or libraries or to any commercial purchaser for use as "premiums" or for resale through army sales channels or to any club or direct mail or mail order or similar type operations (as the case may be), the "Selling Price" shall mean the per unit purchase price payable by the respective purchaser;

3. Notwithstanding anything to the contrary contained in the foregoing, where any Master(s) hereunder have been licensed (as opposed to any sale in the form of finished product)

    a. To any club operation for use on and/or for sale in the form of Records to be sold through club channels, the "Selling Price" shall mean 80 percent of the club's selling price to club members in the country of sale to the ultimate consumer;

    b. To any direct mail or mail order or similar type operation for use on and/or for sale in the form of Records through mail order, direct mail or similar type distribution channels, the "Selling Price" shall mean 80 percent of the selling price to the ultimate consumer;

    c. To any party for use on and/or for sale as "premiums", the Selling Price" shall mean the fictitious price approved by Company from time to time in connection with the computation of royalties due to Company in respect of such premiums.

Authors: Finally the "container allowance" is mentioned again. The following example shows why it is so important: The music video sells for $20. The label builds the

cost of packing and shipping into the price at a rate of $1 per video. The container allowance as stated in this agreement is 25 percent, equaling $5 per video. So an artist's ten-point (percent) royalty based on $20 would be $2 per video. But in this example, the artist's ten-point royalty will be based on $14 equaling $1.40 per video. If 100,000 videos are sold, the Artist has just lost $60,000. Ouch! Some of these deductions may be standard, but if the lawyer or manager doesn't ask for something better, the possibility is lost.

> (cc) In respect of audio-only Records, the permitted "container allowance" shall mean a deduction equal to 10 percent of the applicable Selling Price SAVE THAT in respect of so-called "Audiophile Records" the permitted container allowance shall equal 15 percent of the applicable Selling Price. In respect of Videograms, the permitted container allowance shall mean a deduction equal to 25 percent of the applicable Selling Price.

Authors: The label has to tell you how it calculated the artist's royalties. This is called the "royalty accounting" and in this agreement the label must do an accounting every six months. Some agreements require an accounting only once a year. Since it takes some time to do an accounting, this gives the label ninety days to do the math. Then a check must be cut and by the time you see a royalty check, almost a year will have passed. An artist should be told not to expect money for a year.

What happens if the label makes a mistake in its math, or worse, it tries to cheat the artist? So much money is spent on and received for worldwide music sales, that it is extremely easy to understand why industry people would try to cheat. This long paragraph explains what to do if you want to challenge an accounting and what the label can do if it wants to argue with your argument, and so on and so on.

You have only two years to analyze the royalty payment and accounting before you lose your right to challenge it. Many artists wait too long and, because they don't want to antagonize their label, probably lose a lot of money.

7. Miscellaneous:
   a. Royalty accounting on a semi-annual basis within ninety (90) days from the end of June and December of each year during which Records have been sold hereunder. Each royalty statement or other account shall become binding upon Contractor and Artist unless Contractor shall advise Company in writing of the specific basis of objection and/or claim within two (2) years from the date of such statement or account, and if Company denies the validity of objection and/or claim unless suit is instituted

within six (6) months from the date of Contractor's receipt of Company's notice denying the validity of the respective objection and/or claim, subject always to the following: If Contractor and/or Artist commences suit on any controversy or claim concerning statements or other accounts rendered by or on behalf of Company; the scope of the proceeding will be limited to the determination of the amount of royalties and/or other sums for the periods concerned, and the court will have no authority to consider any other issues or award any relief except recovery of any royalties and/or other sums found owing (plus interest thereon at the rate of interest specified in the Agreement). Recovery of royalties and/or other sums plus interest as aforesaid will be the sole remedy available to Contractor and/or Artist by reason of any objection and/or claim related to statements and/or other accounts or resulting from any audits hereunder, i.e., without limiting the generality of the preceding, Contractor and/or Artist shall not have the right to seek termination of Company's exploitation rights and/or rights or ownership in and to the Masters as a result of any such objection and/or claim.

Authors: If you think the label miscalculated royalties, there has to be a way for the artist to prove it. In this paragraph, you can hire an accountant to go into the label's private financial records to find the truth. The artist's cost for this audit is high, unless it is discovered that the royalty payment was off by more than ten percent when the label is required to reimburse the artist and to pay interest on the money owed.

b.   Contractor may, not more than once during any calendar year (but only once with respect to any statement or account rendered hereunder) audit Company's books and records insofar as same relate to sales of Records hereunder and provided that Contractor shall have notified Company in writing not later than thirty (30) days prior to the commencement date of any such audit. All audits shall be made by an independent Certified Public Accountant during Company's regular business hours of regular business days and at Company's regular business place of business or where Company's books and records are maintained, and each audit shall be at Contractor's own expense, provided that if it is found that Contractor has been underpaid by 10 percent or more for the period under review, then Company shall reimburse Contractor for an amount equal to the reasonable costs actually incurred in respect of such particular audit which resulted in such finding. In the event that any audit reveals underpayment, Company shall pay to Contractor the amount shown properly to be still due, together with interest thereon (at the rate of two [2] percentage points above the applicable official minimum lending rate of the [name of bank] Bank from time to time) on such amount from the date on which payment thereof should have been made until the date of actual payment.

Authors: The above was not the actual recording contract. This was a "short summary" of the major points of the deal. By the time the really long version of this major label's agreement is ready, managers will have had an opportunity to adjust definitions and details in favor of the artist. It may be too late to change facts already included in this summary, but the manager who reads the fine print on the final version can make the deal sweeter for the artist with nuances and clever additional points. Check with your attorney to find favorable details in some other agreements.

8.   All further particulars subject to formal Agreement.

Sincerely,
On behalf of [. . .] Record Label   AGREED:
                                                      On behalf of Contractor

_____

                                                      _____

# # #

The Authors

MITCH WEISS

Mitch Weiss's twenty-five years of management experience include successful and well-known recording, sports and theatrical artists, Disney Theatricals International, New York Shakespeare Festival, Big Apple Circus, and over three dozen Broadway and off-Broadway shows including Tony Award–winners *A Chorus Line* and *The Grapes of Wrath*.

He has served on the board of the Association of Theatrical Press Agents and Managers and has been a certified ATPAM manager since 1985. He currently teaches arts management at New York University's School of Continuing and Professional Studies. He has also been a guest speaker and taught courses on theatre management and directing.

Weiss graduated from Oberlin College and acts as director, composer/lyricist, and producer for a wide variety of shows and events through his New York-based production and management company, MW Entertainment Group.

PERRI GAFFNEY

Actress/writer Perri Gaffney's in-depth interviews and articles covering art and cultural events have been published in *ROUTES* and *Black Masks* magazines. She has also been commissioned to create theme poems for several organizations, including the 2007 *National Black Theatre Festival* and *Girl Friends*. Perri has penned two books: a novel, *The Resurrection of Alice*; and *The Substitute*, a short story collection recalling her years as a substitute teacher.

As an actress, Ms. Gaffney was *Nurse Bentley* on *As The World Turns*, and still receives residuals from *Law & Order* and *Law & Order: SVU*. She received a Helen Hayes Award nomination for Best Supporting Actress in a Musical for her portrait of Dicey Long in Zora Neale Hurston's *Polk County*. Perri also received several AUDELCO Viv nominations including Best Solo Performer for *The Resurrection of Alice*, a one-woman show she adapted from her novel.

She developed this book's fictional vehicle, which presents the educational information in an entertaining format. Her arts background combined with her bachelor's degree in business administration from Kent State University contributed a knowledgeable artist's perspective to the text.

Credits

Whole Circle graph produced by Rachel West.

The authors wish to express their gratitude to these actors and models for portraying the fictional characters in photographs throughout the book:

Max X.	Chapter 1	Jay Poindexter
Robert O.	Chapter 2	Steven LeLuca
Phat J & Kathy	Chapter 3	Carl Cofield, Sherri Linton
George	Chapter 6	Lenny Varnedoe
The Redd Family	Chapter 7	L–R: Andre Montgomery (front), S. Robert Morgan, Gabrielle Goyette (front), Bus Howard, Daryl Davis, Phil Wiggins, Keith N. Johnson (front), John Cephas
Suzanne & Security	Chapter 8	Amy K. Bennett, Andre M. Mauly
PMS	Chapter 8	L–R: Amber Dickerson, Karin Graybash, Christie Kelly
Lonnie	Chapter 9	Harrison Lee
Indiana	Chapter 14	Jennie Miller
Jeremy & promoter	Chapter 16	L–R: Rudy Roberson, Daniel Rosenberry
Don Juan	Chapter 18	Alec Timerman
Dana Goode	Chapter 19	Harriett D. Foy
Pollyanne Heart	Chapter 19	Denise Nostrom
BoyBand	Chapter 21	Damien Vallejo, Jared Hopkins, Sylvester P. Lukasiewicz, Nilton Colon, Boris Vmiroshnikov
Fanny	Chapter 21	Liz Jones

Index

Books from Allworth Press

Allworth Press is an imprint of Skyhorse Publishing, Inc. Selected titles are listed below.

Making and Marketing Music: The Musician's Guide to Financing, Distributing, and Promoting Albums
by Jodi Summers (paperback, 6 x 9, 240 pages, $18.95)

Making It in the Music Business: The Business and Legal Guide for Songwriters and Performers, Revised Edition
by Lee Wilson (paperback, 6 x 9, 288 pages, $18.95)

Rock Star 101: A Rock Star's Guide to Survival and Success in the Music Business
by Marc Ferrari (paperback, 5 1/2 x 8 1/2, 176 pages, $14.95)

How to Grow as a Musician: What All Musicians Must Know to Succeed
by Sheila Anderson (paperback, 6 x 9, 256 pages, $22.95)

Gigging: A Practical Guide for Musicians
by Patricia Shih (paperback, 6 x 9, 256 pages, $19.95)

Booking and Tour Management for the Performing Arts, Revised Edition
by Rena Shagan (paperback, 6 x 9, 288 pages, $19.95)

The Diva Next Door: How to Be a Singing Star Wherever You Are
by Jill Switzer (paperback, 5 ½ x 8 ½, 208 pages, $19.95)

The Songwriter's and Musician's Guide to Nashville, Revised Edition
by Sherry Bond (paperback, 6 x 9, 256 pages, $18.95)

Career Solutions for Creative People
by Dr. Ronda Ormont (paperback, 320 pages, 6 x 9, $19.95)

The Quotable Musician: From Bach to Tupac
by Sheila E. Anderson (hardcover, 7½ x 7½, 224 pages, $19.95)

Creative Careers in Music
by Josquin des Pres and Mark Landsman (paperback, 6 x 9, 224 pages, $18.95)

The Art of Writing Great Lyrics
by Pamela Philips Oland (paperback, 6 x 9, 272 pages, $18.95)

How to Pitch and Promote Your Songs, Third Edition,
by Fred Koller (paperback, 6 x 9, 208 pages, $19.95)

The Secrets of Songwriting: Leading Songwriters Reveal How to Find Inspiration and Success
by Susan Tucker (paperback, 6 x 9, 256 pages, $19.95)

To see our complete catalog or to order online, please visit www.allworth.com.